FOREWORD

Dear Reader -- I am presenting to you for your study, this explanation of the Book of Daniel. I have prepared it in response to the requests of our radio listeners. I give it to you praying that as you study its message your life will be enriched, and if you have not as yet given the Blessed Holy Spirit, who lives in your body, complete control of your life, I sincerely hope that studying this book will lead you to do so for it is the only way you can reach the maximum possibility of your life.

To interpret the prophecies of Daniel is not an easy task. I found that most Bible teachers were agreed on the interpretation of the prophecies though many differed considerably in the explanation of the details given. I found the eleventh chapter the most difficult to interpret for I found most Bible teachers and commentaries differed on many details. I have given you what I believe actually took place. I hope you take plenty of time in the study of this chapter for it is history written in advance.

I have written this book for those who love to study God's Holy Word. I have used words and language I trust any boy and girl can understand for I want this book to be as helpful as possible. Try to answer every question given; look up every reference, and use your Bible as you read.

If you receive as much blessing in the reading and study of this book as I received in its preparation I will consider the time well spent. When you have finished studying the book, loan it to a friend; keep it in circulation until it is worn out.

Yours for Souls,
John Zoller

INTRODUCTION

We are now to begin our study of one of the most outstanding prophetic books in all God's Holy Word. I not know whether you have given much time to the study of this Book of Daniel, I do know that most Christians give but little time to the study of Bible Prophecy. Some will read the book through once or twice, perhaps once in the King James Version and once in modern speech and let it go at that. Many of our teenagers just pass up the reading of the book saying that it is too hard to understand.

Prophecy is history written in advance. Hundreds of religious books have been written but no author of note would dare to make any predictions concerning the future for the passing of time would reveal the ignorance of the writer. God's Holy Word is the only book that tells us of God's plan for the ages. You ask, "How could the men who wrote the Bible know what was to take place in the centureis to come? Did they possess a wisdom unknown to us in this space age in which we are now living? If not, how could they know what events were to take place in the years to come?

God's Holy Word gives us the answer to our question. Consider what is told us,-

.... *"For the prophecy came not in old time by the will of man, but holy men of God spake as they were moved by the Holy Ghost."*

II Peter 1:21

I want you to know this truth, dear reader, every prophecy given in God's Holy Word has been fulfilled, IN ITS TIME, without a single exception in a period covering thousands of years. With this thought in mind I want you to greatly enjoy your study of this Book of Daniel for it tells us of many prophecies which have already been fulfilled, and of prophecies which are now being fulfilled in this space age in which we are living, and of the events which are to take place in the years to come. I hope I can get you who read these lines TO KNOW AND BELIEVE that God's Holy Word is true, and that a faithful and systematic study of this Book of Daniel will reveal to you that Our Heavenly Father does indeed have a plan for this world in which we live and that He is carrying out this plan to its glorious completion.

CONTENTS

Part I
The Historical Division
The beginning of the "Times of the Gentiles", the story of the early life of the prophet Daniel in the court of King Nebuchadnezzar in Babylon and his life under the kings that followed.

Chapter I
The Conquest of Jerusalem

Chapter II
The Forgotten Dream of Nebuchadnezzar

Chapter III
King Nebuchadnezzar's Great Image

Chapter IV
The Humbling of King Nebuchadnezzar

Chapter V
Belshazzar's Impious Feast

Chapter VI
Daniel in the Lion's Den

Part II
The Prophetic Division
Chapters 7-12

Chapter VII
Daniel's Vision of the Four Great Beasts

THE TIME BETWEEN THE REIGN OF ANTIOCHUS EPIPHANES AND THE COMING OF CHRIST

THE BOOK

The Book of Daniel is a book which tells us of Kings and Kingdoms, of thrones and dominions. Of all the sixty-six books which compose God's Holy Word there is no book that has been attacked by so many enemies as has this Book of Daniel. These enemies tell us,-

1. That the prophet Daniel never existed, there was no such person, that the book was written by a holy and pious Jew who lived after the time of King Antiochus Epiphanes who ruled 165 years before Christ was born. They tell us that the events recorded never happened, that the Book of Daniel is pure fiction, just an interesting story.

2. That the Book of Daniel was not written on the date given, B.C. 533 but was written B.C. 168 at a time when the Jews were so severely persecuted, that it was written to comfort and encourage them, in their terrible time of trouble.

3. That this Book of Daniel was written during the time of the Maccabees, long after the date mentioned, long after some of the events prophecied had been fulfilled. This man was an enemy of Christianity who lived in the third century, his name was Porphyry.

I could say much more regarding the attack made upon this Book, it was the devil working thru men who tried his best to destroy it but to no avail. It is a part of God's Holy Word and will endure forever.

THE AUTHOR

The author of the book was the Prophet Daniel. While it is true that we know more about him than we do about any other prophet yet the facts concerning hirth and lineage are not given to us. We know that he was born in Jerusalem, was a member of the tribe of Judah, he was no doubt of the royal line of the House of David. The first mention of him is given in the first chapter of the book which bears his name; he is seen here to be one of the captives King Nebuchadnezzar brought from Jerusalem at the commencement of the seventy years captivity.

Daniel was held in the highest esteem by his three companions Shadrach, Mesach, and Abed-nego, the prophet Ezekiel tells us of the spirit-filled life Daniel led in this pagan land of Babylon. Note that the prophet Ezekiel compares him with Noah and the prophet Job,-

"If I send a pestilence into that land, and pour out my fury upon it in blood, to cut off from it man and beast; though NOAH, DANIEL and JOB were in it, as I live, saith the Lord God, they shall deliver neither son nor daughter; they shall but deliver their own souls by their righteousness."

Ezekiel 14:19-20.

The prophet Ezekiel lived at the same time as the Prophet Daniel, he knew that Daniel was noted for his wisdom. Speaking of the wisdom of Daniel the Prophet Ezekiel was led of the Holy Spirit to say regarding the King of Tyrus,-

"Behold thou art wiser than Daniel; there is no secret that they can hide from thee."

Ezekiel 28:3.

While the critics deny the authenticity of the Book of Daniel our highest authority is our Blessed Lord Jesus who said in his prophetic message,-

"When ye therefore shall see the abomination of desolation, spoken of my Daniel the prophet, stand in the holy place, (whoso readeth, led him understand).

Matthew 24:15

Therefore those who deny the authorship and inspiration of this Book of Daniel must also deny the Deity of our Lord Jesus making Him a lair for He plainly tells us that there was such a man as Daniel, and that there would come one whom would one day stand in the holy place in the Temple, he is known in God's Holy Word as "The Abomination of Desolation".

The writer of the Book of Hebrews also bears testimony to the spirit-filled life that Daniel lived. His name is not mentioned in the faith chapter (Hebrews 11) but his deeds are,-

"Who through faith subdued kingdoms, wrought righteousness, obtained promises, STOPPED THE MOUTHS OF LIONS."

Hebrews 11:33

One thing we do know, the Prophet Daniel was a great man of prayer, this is made clear to us as we read the book. He prayed three times a day, I do believe he lived in an atmosphere of prayer, no threats against his life could get him to change his daily habit of praying. Is it any wonder that God could use him in such a wonderful way? Just consider this, he was given the privilege of talking face to face with the angel Gabriel.

Dear reader, may I tell you how wonderful it is to live a spirit-filled life! How I pray that you are a person of prayer! God is not a respecter of persons (Acts 10:34), you may think that Daniel was a different person than what we are but this is not true. He faced temptation just as we do, he could have neglected

3

the reading of God's Word he could have neglected prayer, yes, he could have given the flesh nature with which he was born complete control but had he done so he would never have been given the revelations which are recorded.

Yes, the Prophet Daniel actually lived, he did write the book which bears his name. Do you know why the enemies of the book have tried so hard to destroy it? The reason is not hard to find. The devil is behind the effort, he knows that every prophecy given in the book up to this very hour of this space age has been fulfilled to the very letter. He knows as well that all the prophecies that have not been fulfilled as yet WILL BE FULFILLED and he does not want you to believe this. He knows that if he can destroy the Book of Daniel, if he can get you to believe the word of the critics, then he has accomplished his purpose in destroying your faith in God's Holy Word.

So do not let the attack of these enemies against this Book of Daniel upset you, and cause you to doubt the inspiration of God's Holy word. Let the enemies of the Word do everything they can, they cannot destroy it for the promise of God's Holy Word is,-

"Heaven and earth shall pass away but my words shall never pass away."

Matthew 24:35

"The word of the Lord endureth forever."

I Peter 1:25.

Dear reader, do not be misled by the type of men who have attacked the accuracy of God's Holy Word. It matters not whether they be men working in a shop or factory, or whether teaching in some school or unviersity, or some modernist standing behind a pulpit. Just because they may be men in some exalted position, holding a place of influence and authority, does not mean that what they teach, preach or write against the Bible is true. Do not be deceived by those who tell us that this book of Daniel was never written by the Prophet Daniel, that it was written by some holy, pious Jew several hundred years later, do some constructive study and thinking for yourself.

THE TIME.

The time this book of Daniel was written was around 606 years before the Lord Jesus was born. The Prophet Jeremiah and the Prophet Habakkuk were sounding out God's warnings at this time. It was at the beginning of the seventy years captivity of the Jews, the time when King Nebuchadnezzar brought the captives from Jerusalem. The Prophet Ezekiel began his message soon after, he, too, was one of the captives who was brought from Jerusalem.

4

THE PLACE

The Book of Daniel was written in Babylon. The
Babylon was founded by Nimrod who was the great gra
Noah who lived over 2000 years before the Lord Jesus w.. porn.
Now read the record given in God's Holy Word,-
*"And Cush begat Nimrod: he began to be a mighty one in the
earth.*

*He was a mighty hunter before the Lord: wherefore it is
said, Even as Nimrod the mighty hunter before the Lord.*

*And the beginning of his kingdom was Babel (Babylon) and
Erech and Accad, and Caineh, in the land of Shinar."*

Genesis 10:8-11.

Babylon at the time of Daniel was a world empire. According
to Daniel all the countries of the then known world were under its
control.

The city of Babylon was the capital of the empire. It was the
home of King Nebuchadnezzar, its ruler. The city was laid out in
a square sixty miles in circumference, fifteen miles on each side.
The city was surrounded by a wall 350 feet high and 87 feet wide
at the top. Running around the outside of the wall was a deep
ditch nearly a hundred feet wide. There were 150 gates of solid
brass in this wall which surrounded the city.

The city of Babylon was one of the wonders of the world. The
Temple of BEL, its leading God, was three miles in circumference. King Nebuchadnezzar had two royal palaces, the
largest was eight miles around it, the smaller three and a half
miles. The palaces were connected by a subterranean tunnel
which ran under the river Euphrates which divided the city. It
was in this city of Babylon where Daniel lived and where he wrote
the book which bears his name.

THE MESSAGE

This Book of Daniel is composed of two parts and is written in
two languages. The first chapter and the first three verses of
chapter two are written in Hebrew; chapters eight to twelve are
written in Hebrew as well. From the fourth verse of chapter two
to the end of chapter seven the language used is Aramaic which is
the ancient language of Syria. The Prophet Daniel was fluent in
the use of both languages; the prophecies concerning the Gentile
empires is written in Aramaic while the prophecies relating to
the Jews is written in Hebrew.

The Book of Daniel traces the entire course of what God's
Holy Word calls "The Times of the Gentiles" from its beginning

5

to its tragic close. Its prophecies tell of the movements of the nations, the revival of the Roman Empire, the coming of the Anti-Christ, the great tribulation, the battle of Armageddon, the return of Christ to earth and the wonderful millennium reign of our Blessed Lord.

As you begin this study of the Book of Daniel do so with an open mind, receptive to the leading of the Holy Spirit. Remember that the Spirit of God is there where you are, if you are a born again believer He is living in your body for God's Holy Word says,-

"If the Spirit of him that raised up Jesus from the dead dwell in you, he that raised up Christ from the dead shall also quicken your mortal bodies by his Spirit that dwelleth in you."

Romans 8:11.

Ask that spiritual discernment be given you, remember that we are studying the most remarkable prophecy contained in all God's Holy Word. it is the first prophecy which gives us a complete picture of the world events which were to take place from the beginning of "THE TIMES OF THE GENTILES" to the end of time. Remember that the Holy Spirit is the author of this Book of Daniel, the Prophet is but the channel God used.

"We have also a more sure word of prophecy; whereunto ye do well that ye take heed, as unto a light that shineth in a dark place, until the day dawn, and the daystar arise in your hearts:

Knowing this first, that no prophecy of the scripture is of any private interpretation.

For the prophecy came not in old time by the will of man: but holy men of God spake AS THEY WERE MOVED BY THE HOLY GHOST."

II Peter 1:19-21.

I have one more word to give you before you begin your study of the book and its a wonderful word, this Blessed Holy Spirit who is living in your body will be your teacher. Now read the promise,-

"Howbeit when He, the Spirit of truth, is come, He will guide you into all truth: for He shall not speak of Himself; but whatsoever He shall hear, that shall He speak; and He will shew you things to come. He shall glorify me; for He shall receive of mine, and shall shew it unto you."

John 16:13-14

The Prophet Daniel was "beloved of God" (Daniel 9:23) and so will you, dear reader, if you study God's Holy Word with a desire to know the truth and make known its message contained in its pages. So let us now open this wonderful book of Daniel and study it verse by verse.

PART I

Chapters 1 - 6

The Historical Division,

The Beginning of "The Times of the Gentiles". The story of the early life of the Prophet Daniel in the court of King Nebuchadnezzar in Babylon, and his life under the Kings that followed.

CHAPTER 1
THE BEGINNING OF "THE TIMES OF THE GENTILES"
THE CONQUEST OF JERUSALEM
Verse 1

"In the third year of the reign of Jehoiakim king of Judah came Nebuchadnezzar king of Babylon and beseiged it."

What five historical facts does the Prophet Daniel state in verse one? Now read what God's Holy Word tells us about King Jehoikim, -

"In his days Nebuchadnezzar king of Babylon came up, and Jehoikim became his servant three years; then he turned and rebelled against him.

And the Lord sent against him bands of the Chaldees, and bands of the Syrians, and bands of the Moabites, and bands of the children of Ammon, and sent them against Judah to destroy it, according to the word of the Lord, which he spake by his servants the prophets.

Surely at the commandment of the Lord came this upon Judah, to remove them out of his sight, for the sins of Manasseh, according to all that he did,;

And also for the innocent blood that he shed: for he filled Jerusalem with innocent blood; which the Lord would not pardon."

II Kings 24:1 - 4.

"Jehoiakim was twenty and five years old when he began to reign, and he reigned eleven years in Jerusalem; and he did that which was evil in the sight of the Lord.

Against him came up Nebuchadnezzar king of Babylon and bound him in fetters, to carry him to Babylon.

Nebuchadnezzar also carried of the vessels of the house of the Lord to Babylon, and put them in his temple in Babylon."

II Chronicles 36:5 - 7.

7

Now read the story of the conquest of Jerusalem and the sacking of the temple in Jeremiah 52:12-30. In what year of the reign of King Jehoikim did these events take place? The Prophet Jeremiah tells us that this conquest of Jerusalem took place in the fourth year of the reign of King Jehoiakim, the Prophet Daniel says it was in the third. There is no contradictions here, both are right for the conquest of Jerusalem began near the close of the third year of the King's reign, this is the time that Daniel states, while the completion of the conquest of Jerusalem did not take place until the close of the fourth year, so the Prophet Jeremiah is also right in what he says.

Verse 2

"And the Lord gave Jehoiakim king of Judah into his hand, with part of the vessels of the house of God: which he carried into the land of Shinar to the house of his god; and he brought the vessels into the treasure house of his god."

Notice that God gave Jehoikim into the hand of King Nebchadnezzar, He allowed him to be defeated. Why did God allow this to happen? *"Whatso ever a man soweth, that shall he also reap"* No man living is wise enough and shrewd enough to sin and get away with it, even a king. King Jehoikim was taken, he was bound with fetters and the temple of God was ransacked and many of the golden vessels used in the worship of God were taken to Babylon. These sacred vessels were taken from the temple three different times,-

1. The occasion here mentioned.
2. When King Jeconiah was defeated some time later.
3. Eleven years later under the reign of Zedekiah when Jerusalem and the temple were completely destroyed. See II Kings 25:8-15. Note the words, *"the treasure house of his god"*. King Nebuchadnezzar was an idolater, he worshipped the idol god *"BEL"* and had a temple erected to him. King Belshazzar used these same vessels of gold at the feast on the night that he was slain.

"Belshazzar the king made a great feast to a thousand of his lords, and drank wine before the thousand.

Belshazzar, whiles he tasted the wine, commanded to bring the golden and silver vessels which his father Nebuchadnezzar had taken out of the temple which was in Jerusalem; that the king, and his princes his wives and his comcubines, drank in them."

Daniel 5:1-3.

God had warned the Jews through His holy prophets telling them what would happen if they persisted in following their evil,

8

sinful ways. And now the sentence is carried out. God used King Nebuchadnezzar to execute His judgment. Three times his armies marched against Jerusalem. These verses tell of his first visit which was in 606 B.C. This is the time when Daniel and his companions were among the hundreds carried captive to Babylon. In the year 598 B.C. King Nebuchadnezzar came the second time, more people were taken captive and carried into slavery, the prophet Ezekiel was one of those taken at this time. And in the year 587 B.C. King Nebuchadnezzar completed the downfall of Jerusalem, the city was burned and leveled to the ground. God's judgment was complete. Jerusalem was now given over to the Gentiles, and what is now known in God's Holy Word as "The Times of the Gentiles" began. It has continued throughout the centuries, we, living in this space age are living in the closing days of this "Times of the Gentiles", it will end when our Lord Jesus returns to earth, and I believe this will be very soon.

Verse 3.-4.

"And the king spake unto Ashpenas the master of the eunuchs, that he should bring certain of the children of Israel, and of the king's seed, and of the princes;

Children in whom was no blemish, but well favoured, and skillful in all wisdom, and cunning in knowledge, and understanding science, and such as had ability in them to stand in the king's palace, and whom they might teach the learning and the tongue of the Chaldeans."

A eunuch is a desexed man. The words "children of Israel" means the young men who were brought into captivity from Jerusalem. I want you now to read the words of a prophecy which was made over a hundred years before by the Prophet Isaiah and which was now literally fulfilled,- *"Hear the word of the Lord of Hosts: behold, the days come, that all that is in thine house, and that which thy fathers have laid up in store until this day, SHALL BE CARRIED TO BABYLON; nothing shall be left, saith the Lord. And of thy sons that shall issue from thee, which thou shalt beget, shall they take away: and they shall be EUNUCHS in the palace of the King of Babylon."*

Isaiah 39:5-7.

We see from this prophecy that Daniel and his three companions, Hananiah, Mishael and Azariah were descendants of King Hezekiah who was a God fearing King, so they were all four of royal blood. Remember this fact, all the prophecies in God's Holy Word were literally fulfilled or will be literally fulfilled, IN GOD'S OWN TIME! It is very important that you recognize this fact. God always keeps His word.

9

Why was Daniel and his three companions chosen instead of native Babylonians? What was the physical condition of Daniel and his three friends? What was their mental condition? What objective did King Nebuchadnezzar have in view? The Chaldeans exceeded the Egyptians in knowledge and wisdom in the arts and sciences, this is why the King wanted them taught the learning and language of the Chaldeans.

Verse 5.

"And the king appointed them a daily provision of the king's meat, and of the wine which he drank: so nourishing them three years, that at the end thereof they might stand before the king."
How were Daniel and his companions treated? What food and drink were given to them? Why was this done? How long was this diet to be continued? Remember that this was to be a period of training, it was a school period during which they were to learn the language and to become well versed in the science of the Chaldeans.

Put yourself in the place of Daniel and his companions, what would you have done? Would you have rejoiced that you were placed in such a favorable position, to be given the privilege of getting the best possible education, and to be able to enjoy the same food that was eaten by the king and to enjoy all the many pleasures of Babylon? What would you have done, I ask this question again?

Verses 6 - 7.

"Now among these were of the children of Judah, Daniel, Hananiah, Mishael and Azariah:
Unto whom the prince of the eunuchs gave names; for he gave unto Daniel the name of Belteshazzar; and to Hananiah, of Shadrach; and to Azariah, of Abed-nego."
There were four Jewish young men chosen, Daniel is the first to be mentioned. It is believed that they were about twenty years of age when they were chosen. The first thing that Aspenaz who had charge of all the eunuchs did was to change their names. This was done, no doubt, to get them to adopt the religion of the Babylonians and to live like those who lived about them and to forget entirely the past life they lived in the city of Jurusalem. Aspenaz knew that all Jewish names had a meaning, this may be the reason why the change in names was made.

The name Daniel meant - "God is my Judge".
The name Hananiah meant - "Beloved of the Lord."
The name Mishael meant - "Who is as God".
The name Azariah meant - "The Lord is my help".
The name given to Daniel was BELTESHAZZAR which means, "Whom Bel favors". The name given to Hananiah was

Shadrach which means "Illumined by the Sun-God". The name given to Mishael was MESHACH which means "Who is like Venus" The name given to Azariah was ABED-NEGO which means "The servant of Nego".

Is it any wonder that Aspenaz who was master of the eunuchs changed their names? The names they had honored and glorified the true and living God therefore they were not allowed to continue, they were given terrible names that honored their heathen gods.

Verse 8.

"But Daniel purposed in his heart that he would not defile himself with the portion of the kings meat, nor with the wine which he drank: therefore he requested of the prince of the eunuchs that he might not defile himself."

Why did Daniel refuse to use the King's food and drink? Do you think that the reason was only physical? Note that Daniel's decision not to partake of the king's meat and drink was a heart decision. Daniel would not dishonor the Living God for he knew that the Babylonians did eat pork and the meat of other unclean beasts as well as the meat of strangled beasts, meat which God forbade the Jews to eat. The Babylonians even offered these beasts to their idols before they were killed and used for food, wine was also poured out before their idols. The Apostle Paul faced this same decision hundreds of years later when he was asked to eat the meat of beasts whose blood had been offered to idols. Note his words,-

"Wherefore, if meat make my brother to offend, I will eat no flesh while the world standeth, lest I make my brother to offend."

I Corinthians 8:13.

Here is a rule every born again believer should follow, never do anything which would cause a weaker brother to stumble. In case of doubt give the Lord the benefit of the doubt. Daniel purposed IN HIS HEART that he would not defile himself with eating the king's meat and drinking the king's wine, and the Lord greatly blessed him for not doing so.

Verse 9.

"Now God had brought Daniel into favour and tender love with the prince of the eunuchs."

God favored Daniel, God always honors those who go all the way with Him. Try it, dear reader, take your hands off of your life, give the Holy Spirit who is living in your body (Romans 8:11) complete control and you will find this to be true.

Little Johnny fell out of bed. His mother asked him, *"Johnny, how did you come to fall out of bed?"* Johnny answered, *"I guess it was because I lay too close to the place where I get in!"*

11

Think of the thousands of professed christians who have no power with God and little or no peace or victory in life because they live too close to the world level in life. What about you? You are a professed Christian, you have been baptized, you are a member of the church, do you have power with God? Suppose YOU had been in Daniel's shoes, what would you have done? Would you have said, "When in Rome do as the Romans do!" and eat the king's meat and drank his wine? Ask yourself this question! Do you think that Daniel would have had power with God had he lived as those about him?

Daniel took a definite, positive stand, he purposed in HIS HEART that he WOULD NOT defile himself with that which the law of God said was unclean. Then he definitely declared himself, he made his desire known to Aspenaz, and doing so he soon realized that God was giving him the guidance he needed, he was given the favor and love of the prince of the eunuchs.

Verse 10

"And the prince of the enunchs said unto Daniel, I fear my lord the king, who hath appointed your meat and your drink: for why should he see your faces worse liking than the children which are of your sort? then shall ye make me endanger my head to the king."

When Daniel presented his request to the prince of the eunuchs what answer was given to Daniel? I want you to note that this prince was thinking of himself, human nature always looks first to self preservation. Aspenaz knew that King Nebuchadnezzar had made the arrangements for their food and drink. The prince of the eunuchs feared that if he granted the request of Daniel a change of diet would bring about a decided change in their physical appearance, and as result he, Aspenaz, would lose his head.

Verses 11-13

"Then said Daniel to Melzar, whom the prince of the enunuchs had set over Daniel, Hananiah, Mishael, and Azariah,

Prove thy servants, I beseech thee, ten days; and let them give us pulse to eat, and water to drink.

Then let our countenances be looked upon before thee, and the countenance of the children that eat of the king's food: and as thou seest, deal with thy servants.

What does Daniel do? To whom does he go? Consider this fact, Daniel and his companions were to be under instruction for three years, so during this time and for all time to come these young men would not touch the king's meat or drink.

Daniel did not flaunt his past teaching or take an holier than thou attitude. He did not condemn the Chaldeans and others for

12

their workship of idols, in a simple, humble manner he asked Melzar, the steward, to let him make a test. This test was suggested,-
1. It was to be for ten days. (Ten in Sripture is the number of testing and trial.)
2. They would live on a vegatable diet.
3. At the end of this ten days test they would know if this diet would keep them in a good physical condition.

Verse 14
"So he consented to them in this matter and tested them ten days."
Melzar, the steward, granted their request. So Daniel and his three companions began their vegetable diet, they eat pulse and grain and drank nothing but water. Pulse is a small vine-like plant which lies or grows flat upon the ground. I have it growing in my garden, it has a wax type leaf and is delicious when prepared with spices and a little vinegar.

This vegetable diet was not as severe as you might at first imagine. There are an abundance of vegetables and grains which, no doubt were available to them, theirs was a simple but wholesome diet. Many people to-day will not eat meat of any kind, my wife's mother lived most of her life on a vegetable diet, and she lived to be nearly ninety years of age before she died. It is the diet prescribed for athletes while they are in training and is a good diet for all of us to follow. I am not a vegetarian. I eat meat, I have always done so and always will.

Verses 15-16
"And, at the end of ten days, their countenances appeared fairer and fatter in flesh than all the youths who did eat the portion of the king's food.
Thus Melzar took away the portion of their food, and the wine that they should drink, and gave them vegetables."
Vegetables plus God Win! Let me say here that Daniel had no objection to thee eating of meat, He knew that God allowed this, that God had given instruction as to the kinds of meat they could eat which were designated as clean such as beef, lamb, mutton and certain kinds of fish and fowl. The reason why Daniel refused the meat of Babylon was because he knew that they served pork which was declared unclean by God, also meat from which the blood had not been drained and meat which had been offered to idols, and to eat such meat would be disobeying the law of God which was given for the best health of the people.

I think it would be helpful if I gave you God's Holy Word concerning what they could eat and what was forbidden to them,-
"Whatsoever parteth the hoof, and is cloven-footed, and

cheweth the cud among the beasts, that shall ye eat.

Nevertheless these shall ye not eat of them that chew the cud, or of them that divide the hoof: the camel, because he cheweth the cud, but divideth not the hoof; he is unclean unto you.

....And the swine, though he divide the hoof, and be cloven-footed, yet he cheweth the cud; he is unclean to you.

Of their flesh shall ye not eat, and their carcass shall ye not touch; they are unclean to you.

These shall ye eat that are in the waters: whatsoever hath fins and scales in the waters, in the seas, and in the rivers, them shall ye eat..

And all that have not fins and scales in the seas, and in the rivers, of all that move in the waters, and of any living thing which is in the waters, they shall be an abomination unto you.

Leviticus 11:3-4,7-10.

I would like to have you stop now and read the 17th chapter of Leviticus before you read further.

I want you to note here what the New Testament has to say regarding the eating of meat offered to idols,-

"As concerning, therefore, the eating of those things that are offered in sacrifice unto idols, we know that an idol is nothing in the world, and that there is no other God but one.

However, there is not in every man that knowledge; for some with conscience of the idol unto this hour eat it as a thing offered unto an idol, and their conscience, being weak, is defiled.

But meat commendeth us not to God; for neither, if we eat, are we the better; neither, if we eat not, are we the worse."

I Corithians 8:4,7-8.

Daniel was just a young man but he had come face to face with the realization that he had to make a decision as to whether he would follow God's commands and give the Holy Spirit complete control of his life. This had to be more than a head decision, it had to be a decision of the heart. He did not know what the outcome would be, he deliberately made the decision, there was a definite time and place where this decision was made. I am sure you realize this. You, too, face this same decision. God has not changed, He is the same, yesterday, to-day and forever. (Heb 13:8) You are living in this space age, you are given the same opportunity to be used of the Lord IF YOU WILL MAKE THIS SAME DECISION! Have you made it? If not, will you make it NOW?

Daniel knew that if he and his companions eat of the king's food and drank the king's wine they would defile themselves in God's sight. Daniel did not know what this refusal to eat the king's food would cost him, he did know that it might very easily cost all

14

four of them their lives. Here they were, four young men who were captives living in the court of a heathen king, who, in cold blood, would not hesitate to kill another king's sons before his eyes and then put out those eyes, now read the record given in God's Holy Word,-

"But the Chaldeans' army pursued after them, and overtook Zedekiah in the plains of Jericho: and they brought him up to Nebuchadnezzar king of Babylon to Riblah in the land of Hamath, where he gave judgment upon him.

The King of Babylon slew the sons of Zedekiah in Riblah before his eyes: also the King of Babylon slew all the nobles of Judah.

Moreover he put out Zedekiah's eyes, and bound him with chains, to carry him to Babylon."

Jeremiah 39:5-7.

Daniel knew that this same King Nebuhadnezzar would not hesitate to roast them alive in the fire if he was displeased with them, for he did this to others of his prisoners and captives, read the record, -

"Thus saith the Lord of hosts, the God of Israel, of Ahab the son of Koliah, and of Zedekiah, the son of Maaseiah, which prophecy a lie unto you in my name; Behold, I will deliver them into the hand of Nebuchadnezzar, King of Babylon; and he shall slay them before your eyes;

And of them shall be taken up a curse by all the captivity of Judah which are in Babylon, saying, The Lord make thee like Zedekiah and like Ahab, whom the King of Babylon roasted in the fire."

Jeremiah 29:21-22.

So you see what Daniel and his three companions faced when they determined that they would not eat the king's meat or drink his wine. Suppose you were there and you faced the same decision, would you have decided as Daniel did? Suppose Daniel HAD NOT made this decision, suppose he and his companions had decided to eat at the King's table and drank his wine, do you think God could have used him as He did? I know what your answer is even before you give it.

God is looking for men to-day who will unreservedly give the Blessed Holy Spirit complete control of their lives. You, dear reader, are needed to give a live, vital spiritual testimony through your life there where you live and where you work. God is looking for those through whom He can release His power. God will release power to the degree that He can trust you with it. Little trust, little power; more trust, more power: much trust, unlimited power. God is ready and waiting to use YOU, will you let Him?

The temptations you face are no greater than the temptations Daniel and his companions faced in the wicked and immoral court of the King of Babylon. whether you question this or not it is true. Do you know that the starting point for the world's immorality was at Babylon? See Revelation 17: 5. Do you think that Daniel and his companions would have been able to conquer the trials and temptations of the Court at Babylon if they had NOT surrendered their lives fully to the Lord?

Verse 17

"As for these four children, God gave them knowledge and skill in all learning and wisdom: and Daniel had understanding in all visions and dreams."

We are told that these young men were given knowledge and skill in all learning and wisdom, who gave them this? Dear reader, God is in the blessing business, how God loves to bless and use those He can trust. God is not a respecter of persons (Acts 10:34). You, too, are precious in His sight, He will release His power through you to the degree that He can trust you with it.

Daniel and his companions were given the unusual privilege to be trained by the best teachers in the then known world. I know of nothing recorded in God's Holy Word which forbids us or even discourages us in getting the best possible education in the arts and sciences, in fact we are encouraged to do so. It was said of the Apostle Paul who was a well educated man, "Much learning doth make thee mad!" (Acts 26:24.)

I want to add this word to you who are teen-agers, get all the education you can, it will put windows into your life. If you plan to attend some college or university do not give up the idea even though you may find it difficult to meet the expense involved. If you plan to enter full time Christian service you will need the best possible education you can get because you will be meeting and dealing with many college trained men.

However I must warn you if you choose one of our modern colleges or universities you will have to sit under the instruction of some teachers who are atheists and unbelievers who will do their utmost to destroy your faith in God and in His plan for our lives. Therefore I urge you to attend a Christian college or University, whose teachers believe and teach God's Holy Word.

Because Daniel and his three companions were determined to obey God's commands and to live for Him God not only blessed them physically, He gave them much more spiritually, they were given knowledge and skill in all learning and wisdom. God has promised us that *"He will give us more than we ask or think."* (Ephesians 3:20.) What other man was given wisdom and knowledge in answer to his request? (For the answer see I Chronicles 1:10-12.) Our Lord Jesus also gave this wonderful promise to His disciples,-

"I will give you a mouth and wisdom which all your adversaries shall not be able to gainsay or resist."

Luke 21:15

You ask, "May I, a born again believer, be given this same wonderful gift? Yes, indeed, if you will, like Daniel, give the Holy Spirit complete control of your life and will ask for it, for the promise is,-

"If any of you lack wisdom, let him ask of God that giveth to all men liberally, and upbraideth not: and it shall be given him."

James 1:5.

Daniel was given the ability to interpet dreams and visions. Do you believe that dreams and visions have a meaning?

Verses 18-20

"Now at the end of the days that the King had said he should bring them in, then the prince of the eunuchs brought them in before Nebuchadnezzar.

And the King communed with them; and among them all was found none like Daniel, Hananiah, Mishael, and Azariah: therefore stood they before the King.

And in all matters of wisdom and understanding, that the King inquired of them, he found them ten times better than all the magicians and astrologers that were in his realm."

Three years have now passed by since Daniel asked Melzar the steward to allow them to live on a vegetable diet. Three years they had studied under the best teachers of Babylon, now they were ready to be examined. Now King Nebuchadnezzar gives the order to the Prince of the Eunuchs asking him to bring these young men before him, for he wanted to know for himself just how much they had learned. I want you to note that King Nebuchadnezzar was well qualified to examine these men for he was well versed in the knowledge and arts of the sciences of the Chaldeans. And you may believe that they were indeed given a thorough examination. What did King Nebuchadnezzar discover as a result of his examination.

Think of it, Daniel and his companions were not only the best of all the young men who had been under instruction for the past three years, the King discovered that they were TEN TIMES BETTER in matters of wisdom and understanding than all the magicians and astrologers in his vast Empire.

What is the great outstanding lesson we learn from the study of this first chapter? If I give you the answer in one word I would say, "Separation". Daniel and his three companions lived a separated life, this is why God could bless them as He did. They knew they had no hope of returning to Jerusalem, their native land. They could have accepted the habits and customs of Babylon and lived as the Babylonians lived but they chose to live lives separated unto the Lord regardless of the cost.

I cannot close our study of this first chapter without an appeal to you, dear reader, I am so anxious that you understand and know and experience the separated life, will you give serious consideration to this? If there is any one truth that God's Holy Word emphasizes, which is definitely commanded and is constantly urged, it is that we live separated lives. Why? Because living a separated life brings God's wonderful guidance, God's unlimited blessing and God's soul-satisfying peace.

God has a plan for every life. Dear reader, God has a plan for your life, you have been assigned a time to be born, a span of life to live and a definite time to die. You were born for a purpose, God has a definite work for you to do just as He had a definite work for Daniel and his three companions to accomplish. You occupy an important place in God's plan. He has given you talent and ability to use it that you might do your work efficiently.

But He has also given you a will and this gives you the power of choice. You can give the Holy Spirit the privilege of living in your body and giving you guidance and direction as Daniel did or -- you can let this flesh nature with which you were born take over, just as many do. This flesh nature is a sin nature, it hates God and does not want the Holy Spirit to be allowed to enter your body and take control.

"For they that are after the flesh do mind the things of the flesh; but they that are after the Spirit the things of the Spirit.

For to be carnally minded is death; but to be spiritually minded is life and peace.

Because the carnal mind is emnity against God: for it is not subject to the law of God, neither indeed can be.

So then they that are in the flesh cannot please God,"
Romans 8:5-8.

Different names for this sin nature are given in God's Holy Word, Romans 6:6 it is called "The old man", in Romans 6:12-14 it is called "sin", in Romans 7:5 it is called "flesh", and in Romans 7:14 it is called "carnal". This same term "carnal nature" or "flesh nature" is given in Romans 8:7.

Each and every one of us living in this world, no matter what color of skin we may have, are born with this flesh nature. You, dear reader, were born with it, this flesh or sin nature is living in your body even now as you read thse lines. Daniel and his three companions were born with it, but they gave the Blessed Holy Spirit control of their lives, this is why God could bless them as

He did.

I am so anxious that you understand what you must do if you would live a separated life. Since the secret of living a separated life and of overcoming the pull of this flesh nature lies in giving the Holy Spirit complete control of your life the question some of you ask is, "How does the Holy Spirit get entrance into my body?" Let me take the time, here and now, before we continue the study of this first chapter to make clear to you how the Holy Spirit enters your body and what you must do if you, like Daniel, would live a separated life.

There is only one way the Blessed Holy Spirit can enter your body, YOU MUST INVITE HIM TO COME IN. As I have already told you, God has given you a will, you can admit the Holy Spirit or not, the choice is yours. The Holy Spirit will not, in fact He cannot, enter your body until you, by a definite decision at a definite time and at a definite place open the door of your heart and invite Him to come in. The Holy Spirit knocks at the door of your heart asking entrance but He will never force His way in YOU MUST LET HIM TO COME IN.

"Behold, I stand at the door and knock: if any man hear my voice, and open the door, I will come in to him, and will sup with him, and he with me."

Revelations 3:20.

WHAT HAPPENS WHEN THE HOLY SPIRIT ENTERS

When the Holy Spirit enters your body the first thing He will do is to apply the Holy Blood of our Lord Jesus to your wicked, sinful heart. When this sacred Blood is applied to your sinful heart every sin you have committed from the day you were born to this present day is cleansed, you are now in God's sight as though you had never sinned.

"The Blood of Jesus Christ God's Son cleanseth us from all sin."

I John 1:7.

Do you know what God does with your sin? God's Holy word tells us that four things take place, now consider them,-

1. Your sins are removed from you as far as the east is from the west.

. . . . *"As far as the east is from the west, so far hath He removed our transgressions from us."*

Psalm 103:12.

Tell me, dear reader, how far is east from west? Suppose you took an aeroplane flying with the speed of light and left this earth on a tangent flying east, on and on .... tell me, would you ever get to the end of east? Now repeat this experience flying west, flying on and on .... would you ever reach the end of west? Now consider

19

what God's Holy Word tells us,- *"So far hath He removed our transgressions from us."*

2. Your sins are blotted out as a thick cloud.

"I have blotted out, as a thick cloud, thy transgressions, and as a cloud, thy sins."

Isaiah 44:22.

Do you remember when you were young how you would lie on vour back on the grass and watch the clouds in the sky above you ҫ ow larger and thicker and blacker until they completely blotted out the sun? This is what takes place when the Holy Spirit applies the Blood of Christ to your sinful heart, all your sins are blotted out, they will never be seen again.

3. Your sins are cast into the depths of the sea.

"Thou wilt cast all our sins into the depths of the sea."

Micah 7:19.

The story is told of a pastor who had a church member who was continually praising the Lord, much to the consternation of the pastor. One day while calling at the home of the pastor he was taken into the pastor's study where he sat awaiting the pastor who had stepped out for a few moments.

Imagine the surprise of the pastor who when he returned found his caller standing in the study, a book of science in his hand, praising the Lord. The pastor asked him, "Charles, what have you found in that book of science that leads you to praise the Lord? Charles smiling said, "Pastor, I was just reading in this book of science that there is a place off the coast of Japan where the ocean is over nine miles deep. The Bible tells us that there is a place in the depths of the sea where God casts our sins and if my sins are put down over nine miles, praise the Lord they will never bother me again!

4. *"Your sins and your ininquities will I remember no more."*

Hebrews 8:12.

Now you know what the Blessed Holy Spirit will do with your sins when you give Him entrance into your body. Your sins are covered with the Holy Blood of our Lord Jesus, which He shed for you upon Calvary's cross. But this is not all, it is but the beginning of what the Holy Spirit will do for you. When your sins have been covered by the Precious Blood of our Lord Jesus then the most important event you will ever experience in all the days of your life here on earth will take place, it is the miracle of the new birth. THE BLESSED HOLY SPIRIT WILL UNITE WITH YOUR SPIRIT. The very moment this takes place you are spiritually born, this is what I mean when I use the term "born again believer". Your name is now written in God's Book of Life (Revelation 20:15). The Blessed Holy Spirit is now living in your

20

body, He is the one who will give you victory in your battle with this flesh nature.

I have taken the time to explain to you what is involved in living the separated life. You, too, face the same testings that Daniel and his three companions faced. The testings that we face in this space age are just as real though they may be presented in a different form but the flesh nature with which we are born has never changed, no matter in what age you live. It is also true that the Holy Spirit has not changed. He is the same yesterday, to-day and forever.

I pray that you, like Daniel, will live a separated life!

Verse 21.
"And Daniel continued even unto the first year of King Cyrus".

Note the words, "even unto". Daniel lived even unto the first year of the rule of King Cyrus. This does not mean that Daniel died during the reign of King Cyrus, for we are told that he lived a number of years after. He was possibly in the late eighties at this time, for the first year of the reign of King Cyrus was the year that the seventy year captivity ended and the Jews were allowed to return to Jerusalem.

Dear reader, you have now completed the reading and the study of the first chapter of this wonderful prophetic book of Daniel. You will note that I have asked you many questions, I will continue to do this as we study this book of Daniel verse by verse. I hope you will take the time to look up all the references I have given, and that you do not continue your study until you have answered the question I have asked.

I wan to add an additional word. You will get out of the study of this book JUST WHAT YOU PUT INTO IT. I want you to enjoy every hour of your study, so do not hurry in your reading, take plenty of time ask the Holy Spirit to direct you and to help you to retain in your mind that which you have learned.

We now consider Chapter II.

CHAPTER II.
THE FORGOTTEN DREAM OF NEBUCHADNEZZAR
In this chapter we see the result of living a life fully surrendered to the guidance of the Holy Spirit. Daniel put God first and foremost in his life, the decision was made not in his head but IN HIS HEART. Much is said in God's Holy Word regarding your heart. Now read a few passages which I will give you,-

"Out of the heart proceed evil thoughts, murders, adulteries, fornications, thefts, false witness, blasphemies,

These are the things which defile a man."
                                                    Matthew 15:19-20.
"A good man out of the good treasure of his heart bringeth forth that which is good; and an evil man out of the evil treasure of his heart bringeth forth that which is evil; for of the abundance of the heart his mouth speaketh."
                                                         Luke 6:45.
"As a man thinketh in his heart, SO IS HE."
                                                      Proverbs 23:7.
"Keep thy heart with all diligence; for out of it are the issues of life."
                                                      Proverbs 4:23.

Do you see now that the power you have with God and with man is determined by the thoughts of your heart? Can God trust you with His power? Would you use this power of God to glorify our Lord Jesus or would you use it to glorify yourself? Are you willing, even NOW, to allow the Blessed Holy Spirit to reveal to you your inmost heart life? I mean NOW, to-day, EVEN NOW, as you are reading these lines. Remember, GOD WILL ONLY RELEASE HIS POWER IN A LIFE TO THE DEGREE THAT HE CAN TRUST YOU WITH IT!

But there is still more that I want you to know. God has two books in which the records of man are kept, THE BOOK OF WORKS and THE BOOK OF LIFE. The name of every born again believer no matter what color of skin or station in life is recorded in God's BOOK OF LIFE. If your name is not recorded in God's BOOK OF LIFE even tho you are a baptized member of the church, then you are cast into the lake of fire.

"And whosoever was not found written in the book of life was cast into the lake of fire."
                                                    Revelation 20:15.

God has a complete record of your life, yes, He has the record of every one of us whether you are a born again believer or not. Do you know that God has a record of every thought of your heart from your early childhood even to this very hour?

Daniel was given knowledge and wisdom because his thought life and his heart life were right in God's sight. God could trust him fully and completely, this is why He could reveal to him the entire span of the "TIMES OF THE GENTILES" from its beginning to its tragic close. Knowing from the record given in God's Holy Word that these things are true we are now ready to begin our study of Chapter II.

Verse 1.

And in the second year of the reign of Nebuchadnezzar, Nebuchadnezzar dreamed dreams, wherewith his spirit was troubled, and his sleep brake from him."

King Nebuchadnezzar had a very vivid dream which aroused him from his sleep, it stirred him to the very depths of his being. It was really like a vision, he was so troubled that he could no longer sleep. What year of his reign did this take place? Make note of this. We know from the record given that Daniel and his three companions were among the great number of Jews that were carried into captivity from Jerusalem the first year of the reign of the King. We have already seen that Daniel and his three companions were in training for three years so how could Daniel explain the meaning of the dream to the King in his second year? The answer is that King Nebuchadnezzar reigned conjointly with his father Nebopollassar for two years then his father died and King Nebuchadnezzar reigned alone, he was now the supreme monarch of the empire. This was the second year of his reign alone when he had this striking dream. It was the year 603 B.C. according to the Chaldean records, the fourth year according to the Jewish calendar. Daniel and his companions had completed their course of training, they had been carefully examined by King Nebuchadnezzar himself personally, he had found them TEN TIMES BETTER in wisdom and knowledge than all his magicians and astrologers. (chapter 1:20). Think of it, they were TEN TIMES BETTER in knowledge and wisdom. Do you agree that it pays to obey God's commands?

At this point in our study I want you to note three very interesting facts,-

1. All men, no matter whether they be presidents, kings, or the lowest servant, all men at times find that they cannot sleep. I am sure you would be surprised if you knew how many of the leaders of our land, men who occupy positions of authority, take tranquillizers and sleeping pills of one kind or another in an effort to obtain restful sleep.

2. God's revelations are given to whomsoever He wills, even at times to unsaved and wicked men. Why was King Nebuchadnezzar given this dream, why didn't God give it to Daniel? I believe the answer is that God had chosen King Nebuchadnezzar to rule the world at this time. This answer is given to us by the Prophet Jeremiah who said,-

"Thus saith the Lord of hosts, the God of Israel; Thus shall ye say unto your masters;

I have made the earth, the man and the beast that are upon the ground, by my great power and by my outstretched arm, and have given it unto whom it seemed meet unto me.

And now I have given all these lands into the hand of Nebuchadnezzar the King of Babylon, my servant; and the

23

beasts of the field have I given him also to serve him.

And all nations shall serve him, and his son, and his son's son, until the very time of his land come: and then many nations and great kings shall serve themselves of him.

And it shall come to pass, that the nation and kingdom which will not serve the same Nebuchadnezzar the King of Babylon, and that will not put their neck under the yoke of the King of Babylon, that nation will I punish, saith the Lord, with the sword, and with the famine, and with the pestilence, until I have consumed them by his hand."

Jeremiah 27:4-8.

3. God promised to reveal His will to old men through dreams and young men through visions. This was given to us by the prophet Joel and was emphasized by the Apostle Peter on the Day of Pentecost. Now read the record,-

"And it shall come to pass afterward, that I will pour out my spirit upon all flesh; and your sons and your daughters shall prophesy, your old men shall dream dreams, your young men shall see visions:

And also upon the servants and upon the handmaids in those days will I pour out my spirit."

Joel 2:28-29.

Now we turn to the New Testament where we read of the fulfillment of this wonderful prophecy,-

"But Peter, standing up with the eleven, lifted up his voice and said unto them, Ye men of Judea, and all ye that dwell at Jerusalem, be this known unto you, and hearken to my words:

For these are not drunken, as ye suppose, seeing it is but the third hour of the day.

But this is that which was spoken by the prophet Joel;

And it shall come to pass in the last days, saith God, I will pour out of my Spirit upon all flesh: and your sons and your daughters shall prophesy, and your young men shall see visions, and your old men shall dream dreams:

And on my servants and on my handmaidens I will pour out in those days of my Spirit; and they shall prophecy."

Acts 2:14-18.

Verse 2.

"Then the King commanded to call the magicians, and the astrologers, and the sorcerers, and the Chaldeans, for to shew the King his dreams. So they came and stood before the King.

Troubled in soul and spirit because of this most unusual dream King Nebuchadnezzar had brought before him four different groups of men, they were known as "his wise men". As they stood before him he asked them to tell him what this unusual dream was and what it meant. Let me try to explain to you who these men were and what they claimed to be able to do,-

1. The MAGICIANS practiced and superstitions and sacred rites and ceremonies of the fortune tellers. They professed to be able to reveal hidden things; to foretell future events; to make known mysteries entirely beyond human foresight and to do this by the help of supernatural persons.

2. The ASTROLOGERS were men who claimed to be able to tell the future by means of the stars. Many of our daily newspapers print the signs of the Zodiac giving advice to the reader for the day, a different message for each month of the year depending upon which month you were born. Radio stations, that is some of them, do the same thing. Astrology is not new, it is as old as man.

It may be that you are one of those who go to the newsstands and buy the booklets and magazines which are on sale there. Have you any idea how many there are? I recall that some time ago with a friend we went into a shoe shine parlor to have our shoes shined. The owner operated a newsstand also and while my friend was having his shoes shined I looked over the magazines. I was attrached by the number of magazines which he carried, I decided to count them and when I finished I found that he was carrying seventeen different kinds of magazines which dealt with astrology giving horoscopes and advice, this will give you an idea of how many people there are who rely on astrology to goverr the actions of their lives.

No true born again believer will rely on the predictions given by these astrologers. True born again believers trust the Lord to supply their needs, they place their lives fully in His hands, they let the Holy Spirit be their instructor and their guide. Read God's wonderful promise,-

"I will instruct thee and teach thee in the way which thou shalt go: I will guide thee with mine eye."

Psalm 32:8

3. The SORCERERS were men who claimed that they were able to communicate with the dead. Sorcery is always used in God's Holy Word in this connection. Modern spiritualism is nothing more than a revival of Old Testament sorcery which is definitely forbidded by God.

"Regard not them that have familiar spirits, neither seek after wizards, to be defiled by them: I am the Lord your God."

Leviticus 19:31.

"The soul that turneth after such as have familiar spirits, and after wizards, to go a whoring after them, I will even set my face against that soul, and will cut him off from among his

people."

"When thou art come into the land which the Lord thy God giveth thee, thou shalt not learn to do after the abomintions of those nations.

There shall not be found among you any one that maketh his son or his daughter to pass through the fire, or that useth divination, or an observer of times, or an enchanter, or a witch,

Or a charmer, or a consulter with familiar spirits, or a wizard, or a necromancer.

For all that do these things are an abomination untio the Lord: and because of these abominations the Lord thy God doth drive them out from before thee.

Thou shalt be perfect (mature) with the Lord thy God."
Deuteronomy 18:9-13.

There are many more passages I could give you which make clear to us the hatred of God against all who will have anything to do with familiar spirits or demons. It may be that you have been given an invitation to attend a spiritualistic seance, you are thinking of attending, I urge you not to go, have nothing to do with things which are definitely forbidden by God. I want you to know that while most of these mediums are frauds and imposters yet there are those who are demon possessed. These demons or familiar spirits as the Bible calls them are about us all the time, there are literally millions of them in the world. A legion (12,000) can live in your body. The demon possessed man of Gadara had a legion of demons living in him, this is why he was so strong that no chains could bind him.

"And Jesus with his disciples came over unto the other side of the sea, into the country of the Gadarenes.

And when he was come out of the ship, immediately there met him out of the tombs a man with an unclean spirit (a demon),

Who had his dwelling among the tombs; and no man could bind him, no, not with chains;

Because that he had been often bound with fetters and chains, and the chains had been plucked asunder by him, and the fetters broken in pieces: neither could any man tame him.

And always, night and day, he was in the mountains, and in the tombs, crying, and cutting himself with stones.

But when he saw Jesus afar off, he ran and worshipped him,

And cried with a loud voice, and said, What have I to do with thee, Jesus, thou Son of the most high God? I adjure thee by God, that thou torment me not.

For he said unto him, Come out of the man, thou unclean spirit (demon).

And he asked him, What is thy name? and he answered, saying, My name is Legion: for we are many."

Mark 5:1-9.

Let me give you two more instances of demon possession and how they work out of the many given in God's Holy Word. I want you to read the story of a demon possessed girl who was used by her masters for telling fortunes.

"And it came to pass, as we went to prayer, a certain damsel possessed with a spirit of divination met us, which brought her masters much gain by soothsaying:

The same followed Paul and us, and cried, saying, These men are the servants of the most high God, which shew unto us the way of salvation.

And this did she many days. But Paul, being grieved, turned and said to the spirit (demon), I command thee in the name of Jesus Christ to come out of her. And he came out the same hour.

Acts 16:16-18.

It was this demon who was living in the girl who gave her the power to tell fortunes. When the demon was driven out of her body she had no more power so her masters had Paul and Silas brought before the rulers (officers), men of authority.

The last instance I want to give you took place while the Apostle Paul was in the city of Ephesus. The Chief of the Priests was a man by the name of Sceva. He had seven sons who watched the Apostle Paul healing the sick and driving out demons by using the name of the Lord Jesus.

"Then certain of the vagabond Jews, exorcists, took upon them to call over them which had evil spirits (demons) the name of the Lord Jesus, saying, We adjure you by Jesus whom Paul preacheth.

And there were seven sons of one Sceva, a Jew, and chief of the priests, which did so.

And the evil spirit (demon) answered and said, Jesus I know, and Paul I know; but who are ye?

And the man in whom the evil spirit (demon) was leaped on them, and overcame them, and prevailed against them, so that they fled out of that house naked and wounded.

And this was known to all the Jews and Greeks also dwelling at Ephesus; and fear fell on them all, and the name of the Lord Jesus was magnified."

Acts 19:13-17.

Because of this experience the news spread until the entire city knew of the power that these demons have for these seven sons were known throughout Ephesus., since their father was chief of the priests. A mighty revival broke out, I suggest you read this chapter before you continue farhter with this study. I want you to know that demons are real, that they are about us even now as you read, that they would like to live in YOUR body, and bring wreck and ruin to your life. YES, SORCERERS consorted with demons, they carried on practices which were forbidden by God.

4. The CHALDEANS were philosophers, the most ancient in the world. They made science their special study. They would kill animals and birds and pretend to tell the future by examining the entrails of each. This is how the auguries of ancient Rome were conducted.

King Nebuchadnezzar used all four of these groups. They all claimed to be able to reveal the future, to interpret dreams and visions each group in his own way. This dream of King Nebuchadnezzar was so important to him that he called for all four of these groups of wise men to be brought before him. But they were powerless to help him, they were all frauds and imposters, they could not reveal the future any more than you can. Try and visualize these four groups as they stand before the king.

Verse 3.

"And the King said unto them, I have dreamed a dream, and my spirit was troubled to know the dream."

The King has now stated his problem. Every man in these four groups now realize the magnitude of the struggle they face.

Verse 4.

"Then spake the Chaldeans to the King in Syriack, O King, live forever: tell thy servants the dream, and we will shew the interpretation."

The Chaldeans were the spokesmen for the group. What request did they ask of the King? Do you think that King Nebuchadnezzar was unreasonable and unjust in his demand? They professed to be able to reveal dreams and their interpretation therefore he had a right to expect that they were able to do what they claimed. He provided for them, he fed and clothed them and their families, now let them provide him with the dream and its interpretation.

These Chaldeans tried in every way to get the King to tell them what he had dreamed. They lived by their wits. If the King had been able to tell them what he had dreamed they would have agreed among themselves what to tell him, they would give him an interpretation that would not endanger their lives. They now realized that it was a case of hang together or to hang separately.

Verses 5-6.

"The King answered and said to the Chaldeans, The thing is gone from me: if ye will not make known unto me the dream, *with the interpretation thereof, ye shall be cut in pieces, and your houses shall be made a dunghill.*

But if ye shew the dream, and the interpretation thereof, ye shall receive of me gifts and rewards and great honor: therefore shew me the dream and the interpretation thereof."

What answer did King Neubchadnezzar give to them? He put before them a clear cut issue, either reveal to him the dream and its true interpretation and receive honor, wealth and exalted social position or else suffer a terrible death and have all their possessions confiscated and destroyed as well. It was one or the other. They claimed to be able to interpret dreams, let them now reveal to him this dream together with its interpretation ..... or die.

Verses 7-11.

"They answered again and said, Let the King tell his servants the dream, and we will shew the interpretation of it.

The King answered and said, I know of a certainty that ye would gain the time, because ye see the thing is gone from me.

But if ye will not make known unto me the dream, there is but one decree for you: for ye have prepared lying and corrupt words to speak before me, till the time be changed: therefore tell me the dream, and I will know that ye can shew me the interpretation thereof.

The Chaldeans answered before the King, and said, There is not a man upon the earth that can shew the King's matter: therefore there is no king, lord, or ruler, that asked such things at any magician, or astrologer, or Chaldean.

And it is a rare thing that the King requireth, and there is none other that can shew it before the King, except the gods, whose dwelling is not with flesh."

Imagine that you were placed in the same position these wise men now found themselves. They knew that their lives were hanging in the balance, they tried desperately to get the king to tell them the dream, something that the King could not do. He tells them that they are asking him to tell them a dream that he has forgotten. What do the Chaldeans now tell him? At their answer what does the King assume?

There is no question in my mind but that these Chaldeans were very sincere in their answer. They believed that it was absolutely impossible for any living man to reveal the forgotten dream to the King together with its interpretation.

While it is possible that these sorcerers were able to use the knowledge given to them by demons, if so, why didn't the demons re. al to them the dream? Do you know why? Demons are wise, yes, the. are much wiser than you or I but the reason why they

29

could not give this dream to the sorcerers is BECAUSE THIS DREAM WAS GIVEN TO KING NEBUCHADNEZZAR BY GOD FOR A DEFINITE PURPOSE, the demons did not know what it was.

Verses 12-13.

"For this cause the King was very angry and very furious, and commanded to destroy all the wise men of Babylon.

And the decree went forth that the wise men should be slain; and they sought Daniel and his fellows to be slain."

The King has now issued the death decree, these wise men are all now staring death in the face. What do you suppose they did in their desperation? Where do you suppose Daniel and his companions were during this time? The King knew that Daniel and his companions were TEN TIMES BETTER IN KNOWLEDGE AND WISDOM THAN ALL HIS WISE MEN (Chapter 1:20; why didn't the King call for Daniel and his companions at once instead of his wise men? Note that Daniel and his companions were included in this death decree.

May I give you what I think is the answer? I believe God had a definite reason in this, there is a definite reason behind all of God's actions. God had a plan, because He had a man He could trust, a man who was determined to serve Him body, soul and spirit, no matter what the circumstances or the opposition. He needed a man to whom He could reveal His plan for the ages, His plan as I see it was to reveal this plan through a dream which He would give to a heathen King, a dream which would be revealed and explained by Daniel, this man He could trust. We shall see, as we continue our study, how step by step this plan was revealed.

Verses 14-15.

"Then Daniel answered with counsel and wisdom to Arioc the captain of the King's guard, which was gone forth to slay the wise men of Babylon:

He answered and said to Arioc the King's captain, Why is the decree so hasty from the King? Then Arioc made the thing known to Daniel."

Arioc, the captain of the King's guard, was the man the King had chosen to do the killing, (see verse 24). The guiding hand of God is seen all through this testing experience. No doubt you have been asking yourself this question, "Why was the knowledge of the dream God gave to King Nebuchadnezzar withheld from him?

There is only one answer to this question, our Heavenly Father wanted it to be known through all the succeeding generations of man that all the magicians, astrologers and spiritualists, all such are but frauds and imposters, that only God can reveal the future for He is the only one who knows what it is. I want you to note that the knowledge, wisdom and counsel that God gave to Daniel at once won the confidence and respect of Arioc, the Captain of the King's guard. There is a profitable lesson in this for us, if you would win the favor, the respect and confidence of those you know, those with whom you work, you must FIRST win the favor, respect and confidence of God. This can only be secured by giving the Holy Spirit complete control of your life.

What question did Daniel ask Arioc? What was the Captain's answer?

Verse 16.

"*Then Daniel went in, and desired of the King that he would give him time, and that he would shew the King the interpretation.*"

I want you to notice the boldness of Daniel who now, without any delay, meets King Nebuchadnezzar face to face. He really risked his life to do this for to do so often brought death to the seeker depending upon the will of the King. Queen Esther realized this, read the reference,-

"*All the King's servants, and the people of the King's provinces, do know, that whosoever, whether man or woman, shall come unto the King into the inner court, who is not called, there is one law of his to put him to death, except such to whom the King shall hold out the golden sceptre that he may live.*"

What request did Daniel ask of the King and what promise did Daniel give to the King if his request were granted?

Daniel had absolute confidence in God, there was no doubt whatever in his mind, Daniel had a steadfast and unshakable faith that God would reveal to him the King's dream and give him the interpretation as well. Here is where faith goes into action. I ask you, how much faith do you have? God has not changed, He is the same yesterday, and to-day and forever." (Hebrews 13:8). It is the measure and the degree of your faith which enables the Blessed Holy Spirit to release God's power to meet the need you have even as you read.

Daniel's request for time to consider the matter of the dream is granted by the King.

Verses 17-18.

"*Then Daniel went to his house, and made the thing known to Hananiah, Mishael, and Azariah, his companions:*

That they would desire mercies of the God of heaven concerning this secret; that Daniel and his fellows should not perish with the rest of the wise men of Babylon."

31

DANIEL'S PRAYER FOR WISDOM

When Daniel returned home after his visit with the King, what was the first thing he did? It is possible that Daniel's three companions did not know of the King's decree, did not know that their lives were hanging in the balance, that they faced death if Daniel was not able to reveal the dream and its interpretation. Be that as it is, they knew now after it was revealed by Daniel that death stared them in the face. They knew that only the true and living God that they worshipped was able to save them.

I want you to try to visualize these four young men down on their knees crying out to God in this, their hour of extreme need. They have a definite request to ask of God, they are now expecting a definite answer without any delay. It is true that Daniel could have prayed alone but Daniel knew the power of united prayer so he asked his companions to pray with him. I am sure that they prayed all night for they knew that if God did not answer and if Daniel was not able to keep his promise to the King they would all be killed. So in united prayer they asked God to reveal to them the dream with its interpretation.

Have you ever prayed ALL NIGHT? Do you realize the power of united prayer? Our Lord Jesus gave us this wonderful promise,-

"If two of you shall agree on earth, as touching anything that they shall ask, IT SHALL BE DONE FOR THEM of my Father which is in heaven."

Matthew 18:19.

None of us know how long these four prayed however I am sure that they continued to pray until one or the other had received the assurance that their prayer would be answered and they would not die.

Verse 19.

"Then was the secret revealed to Daniel in a night vision. Then Daniel blessed the God of heaven."

THE DREAM REVEALED TO DANIEL.

God honored the faith of Daniel by revealing to him the dream in its entirety together with its interpretation. How this was done is not stated, we are told that it was revealed in a "night vision". Could it be that after they ended their praying and retired for the night that God gave Daniel the exact vision that He gave to King Nebuchadnezzar, with the added information as to the meaning of the dream. Perhaps it happened in this way,-

"And I heard a man's voice between the banks of Ulai, which called, and said, "Gabriel, make this man to understand the vision.

So he came near where I stood: and when he came, I was afraid, and fell upon my face: but he said unto me, Understand, O son of man: for at the time of the end shall be the vision.

Now as he was speaking with me, I was in a deep sleep on my face toward the ground: but he touched me, and set me upright.

And he said, Behold, I will make thee known what shall be in the last end of the indignation: for at the time appointed the end shall be."

Daniel 8:16-19.

Dear reader, God does answer prayer when we ask in faith believing, never doubting. Note that Daniel does not forget to thank God for the answer given, he is deeply grateful and praises God for honoring him with the answer. So often in our need we cry out to God but we forget to thank God for the answer given and the blessing received. When our Lord Jesus cleansed the ten lepers ONLY ONE returned to thank Him for healing them.

"And one of them, when he saw that he was healed, turned back, and with a loud voice he glorified God,

And fell down on his face at his feet, giving thanks: and he was a Samaritan.

And Jesus answering said, Were there not ten cleansed? but where are the nine?

There are not found that returned to give glory to God, save this stranger."

Luke 17:15-18

Dear reader, God is pleased when we thank Him for the answers to prayer He gives us.

Verse 20.

"Daniel answered and said, Blessed be the name of God forever and ever: for wisdom and might are his."

The prayer Daniel offered is not given to us, no doubt it was a most impassioned cry that came from the depths of his heart, however his prayer of thanksgiving is recorded word for word. God is in the blessing business, He knows how to bless YOU. Daniel knows this for he blesses God and thanks Him for the wisdom and might given to him.

Dear reader, God loves to answer prayer for you, really He does, when we ask in faith believing and according to His Holy Will. THERE IS NO LIMIT TO THE RESOURCES AVAILABLE TO US, no matter whether your need be physical, material or spiritual, GOD IS ABLE TO SUPPLY IT!

Verse 21.

"And he changeth the times and the seasons: he removeth kings, and setteth up Kings: he giveth wisdom to the wise, and knowledge to them that know understanddng."

33

Note the all inclusiveness of Daniel's prayer of thanksgiving there are four things which Daniel realizes,-

1. He changeth the times and the seasons.

We all know that this is true. Our Heavenly Father not only controls the weather and brings on the seasons each in his own time and way, He also regulates them by definitely established laws.

2. He removeth Kings and setteth up Kings.

This is true whether we believe it or not. God's Holy Word definitely states that this is true. Let me give you several examples taken from God's Holy Word which illustrate this truth,-

"They shall drive thee from men, (King Nebuchadnezzar), and thy dwelling shall be with the beasts of the field, and they shall make thee to eat grass as oxen, and they shall wet thee with the dew of heaven, and seven times shall pass over thee, till thou know that the most High ruleth in the Kingdom of men, and giveth it to whomsoever he will."

Daniel 4:25.

"Let every soul be subject unto the higher powers. For there is no power but of God; the powers that be ARE ORDAINED OF GOD."

Romans 13:1.

"Submit yourselves to every ordinance of man for the Lord's sake: whether it be to the King, as supreme;

Or unto governors, as unto them that are sent by him for the punishment of evildoers, and for the praise of them that do well. FOR SO IS THE WILL OF GOD."

I Peter 2:13-15.

Do you believe that even now, in this space age, that God takes a hand in the appointments and in the removing of national leaders? I am sure that you do for God's Holy Word definitely states that He does as we have just seen.

3. He giveth wisdom unto the wise.

There is a big difference between those who are considered wise as far as this world is concerned, and those who actually are wise in God's sight. There are many in this world who hold University degrees and have won high honors because of their accomplishments yet these are absolutely ignorant as far as true knowledge is concerned. Worldly wisdom is needed as far as getting on in this world is concerned but there is a very decided difference between man's wisdom and the wisdom given by the Holy Spirit to born again believers. Now read what God's Holy Word says about this,-

"I will destroy the wisdom of the wise, and will bring to

nothing the understanding of the preudent.
Where is the wise? Where is the scribe? Where is the disputer
of this world? hath not God made foolish the wisdom of this
world?
For after that in the wisdom of God the world by wisdom
knew not God, it pleased God by the foolishness of preaching to
save them that believes.
For ye see your calling, brethren, how that not many wise
men after the flesh, not many mighty, not many noble, are
called;
But God hath chosen the foolish things of the world to con-
found the wise; and God hath chosen the weak things of the world
to confound the things which are mighty;
And the base things of the world, and things which are
despised, hath God chosen, yea, and things which are not, to
bring to nought things that are:
That no flesh should glory in his presence."

I Corinthians 1:19-21; 26-29.

Do you see now the difference between man's wisdom and
God's wisdom? Daniel's wisdom was the wisdom given him by
God, he experienced the wisdom received not only from men but
from God as well.

4. He giveth Knowledge to them that know understanding.
God needs men that He can trust, there is no limit to what
God can do through such men. As you study your Bible you will
note that from the very beginning of God's Holy Word the men
who were greatly used of the Lord in their time were the men God
could trust. You are living in this space age, an age when God
needs every man and woman to live for him, I ask, can God trust
YOU? Do YOU have an understanding of God's plan for this age,
if so and if God can trust you, then He will give you the knowledge
needed to be used in the most fficient manner to glorify His holy
name.

Verse 22.

"He revealeth the deep and secret things: he knoweth what is
in the darkness, and the light dwelleth with him."
Our God is omnicient, I mean by this that there is nothing
that He does not know. He has infinite knowledge, nothing you do
or say can be hidden from Him. He has a book of works for every
one of us in which all the thoughts and actions of our hearts are
recorded. Do you question this? If so, read what God's Holy Word
says,-
"And I saw the dead, small and great, stand before God; and
the books were opened: and another book was opened, which is
the book of life: and the dead were judged out of those things

which were written in the books,according to their works."
God's Holy Word tells us that this book of works will be opened on the day that we stand alone before God. I do believe that God has an individual book of works prepared for us which contains the complete record of our lives. It is possible that you may tremble as you read these words for you know that the life you are now living does not please God. But let me give you a wonderful promise,-

"If we walk in the light, as he is in the light, we have fellowship one with another, and the blood of Jesus Christ his Son cleanseth us from all sin.

If we say we have no sin, we deceive ourselves, and the truth is not in us.

But if we confess our sins, he is faithful and just to forgive us our sins, and to cleanse us from all unrighteousness."
I John 1:7-9.

Yes, there is coming a day when the deep and secret things will be revealed. God does indeed know what is in the darkness for He is light. King Nebuchadnezzar was in darkness, he was a heathen king who could not remember the dream which had been given to him. Daniel, too, was in darkness as far as this dream was concerned, he knew that only God could reveal this dream and its interpretation to him and he thanks God and praises His Holy Name because this information was given to him.

Verse 23.

"I thank thee, and praise thee, O thou God of my fathers who has given me wisdom and might, and hast made known unto me now what we desired of thee: for thou hast now made known unto us the king's matter."

I want you to note that Daniel does not take the credit for the answer that God gave to him in revealing to him the dream and its interpretation, he honors his three companions who shared the burden they carried and who prayed with him. Note the "we" and the "us" that he used in this verse. Daniel was a very humble man, there was not a bit of pride in him, this is why God could use him and bless him as he did.

Verse 24.

"Therefore Daniel went in unto Arioc, whom the King had ordained to destroy the wise men of Babylon: he went and said thus unto him; Destroy not the wise men of Babylon: bring me in before the King, and I will shew unto the King the interpretation."

Daniel's first thought is for these wise men of Babylon. He knew the terror they and their loved ones were experiencing with death staring them in the face. He makes a plea for their lives, he asks that he be brought before the King so he could reveal to him the forgotten dream and its interpretation. Daniel knew that these wise men, so called, were but frauds and imposters, he knew they deserved to die, yet he could not bear the thought of them all being killed together with all their innocent loved ones and their possessions confiscated and destroyed. He knew that he was the only man who could save their lives.

Illustration after illustration is given in God's Holy Word showing us how the wicked were helped and even their lives were saved all through the presence and prayers of a faithful man of God. If only ten righteous persons could have been found living in Sodom then all the wicked people living there would have been spared. See Genesis 18:23-33.

See also Acta 16: 26, here we see that all the prisoners in the jail were loosed of their bonds because of Paul and Silas, men of God. Let me mention just one more illustration which is recorded in Acts 27: 24, here we see that the lives of all who were on this ship caught in a terrible storm were saved because of the Apostle Paul.

Tell me, dear reader, why has God spared this wicked world from a terrible nuclear war as long as he has? Is it not for the sake of the righteous who are living here?

Dear reader, God has no pleasure in the death of the wicked. Note what God's Holy Word tells us in this regard,-

"God is not willing that any should perish, but that all should come to repentance."

II Peter 3:9.

But God cannot take a sinner into Heaven, to do so Heaven would be turned into a Hell. I do believe that wicked as this world is in this space age, it is saved because of the born again believers who are in it. But may God have mercy upon those who are left behind when our Lord Jesus returns'. We are told that unless the time were shortened there would no life be left upon this earth. See Matthew 24: 22.

Verse 25.

"The Arioc brought in Daniel before the King in haste, and said thus unto him, I have found a man of the captives of Judah, that will make known unto the King the interpretation."

What does Captain Arioc do? What does he tell the King? Note the words "in haste", you may be sure that as soon as Daniel told him that he could make known to the King the dream and its interpretation he at once hurried to the King with the good news. What were the first words Arioc said to the King? Do you think that Arioc hoped to get a reward for finding Daniel? But as

37

soon as the King saw Daniel he knew that he was the man who had appeared before him previously asking for time and he would tell the King the dream with its interpretation. But there is more to be considered here. Arioc actually believed that Daniel could reveal the dream to the King else he would not have hurriedly gone to the King with the word. Had Daniel been unable to reveal the dream Arioc as well as Daniel and his companions and all the wise men and their families would have been killed for we are told that the King was furious, indeed very much so, (see verse 16) he certainly would have destroyed them all.

Verses 26-27.

"The King answered and said to Daniel, whose name was Belteshazzar, Art thou able to make known unto me the dream which I have seen, and the interpretation thereof?

Daniel answered in the presence of the King, and said, The secret which the King hath demanded cannot the wise men, the astrologers, the magicians, the soothsayers, shew unto the king:"

Note the question the King asked Daniel and the answer Daniel gave to him. Daniel wanted this King to know that these astrologers, magicians, sorcerers and Chaldeans were all a group of frauds and imposters, men who were absolutely unable to reveal the dream and its interpretation, he wanted the King to realize this. He wanted the King to know that it was impossible for his wise men to shew him the dream, they did not have the knowledge or the ability to do so. Daniel's desire was to show the King that he was looking to the wrong source for the answer to his problem, I do believe that this is the time when King Nebuchadnezzar was given his first knowledge that there was a true God, a living God who alone could reveal the dream He gave him and its interpretation. King Nebuchadnezzar could never get away from this knowledge, it remained with him to the end of his days.

Verses 28-30.

"But there is a God in heaven that revealeth secrets, and maketh known to the King Nebuchadnezzar what shall be in the latter days. Thy dream, and the visions of thy head upon thy bed are these;

As for thee, O King, thy thoughts came into thy mind upon thy bed, what should come to pass, hereafter: and he that revealeth secrets maketh known to thee what shall come to pass.

But as for me, this secret is not revealed to me for any wisdom that I have more than any living, but for their sakes that shall make known the interpretation to the King, and that thou mightest know the thoughts of thy heart."

God alone is given the credit for revealing the dream to Daniel together with its interpretation which is as it should be! What a wonderful opportunity is given to Daniel to testify to the existence of a true and living God, a God of unlimited power and wisdom! Note that Daniel does not take one bit of credit to himself for revealing the forgotten dream and its interpretation. Daniel admits to the King his own limitations. Now we face a great question. Why did God give his dream to a wicked, idol worshipping King? Why? There is a reason for this-

I believe God gave this dream to King Nebuchadnezzar that he might know that there was a true and living God. I want to continue to emphasize this truth. God gave the dream to King Nebuchadnezzar but the interpretation had to be given through one of God's true, loyal and faithful servants.

Daniel was a humble man who wanted the King to know that this dream was given, not just for King Nebuchadnezzar but for God's born again believers who would live throughout the many coming generations. Daniel wanted the King to know the folley of trusting in the so called revelations of his false and fraudulent wise men. Daniel wanted the King to know that although the dream had been given to him, it was not just for him that the interpretation was given but it was for the born again believers who would follow in the centuries to come.

God accomplished much through revealing the King's dream to Daniel. There were five things I should like to mention here:

1. He revealed to the King what he wanted to know.

2. He saved Daniel and his three companions from being killed.

3. He revealed to the King as well as the nation that He was the only true and living God.

4. He revealed the falsity and inability of the King's wise men.

5. He honored His own name and exalted his servants in the eyes of the King and the nation.

Verses 31-36.

"Thou, O King, sawest, and behold a great image. This great image, whose brightness was excellent, stood before thee; and the form thereof was terrible.

This image's head was of fine gold, his breast and his arms of silver, his belly and his thighs of brass,

His legs of iron, his feet part of iron and part of clay.

Thou sawest till that a stone was cut out without hands, which smote the image upon its feet that were of iron and clay, and brake them to pieces.

Then was the iron, the clay, the brass, the silver and the gold, broken to pieces together, and became like the chaff of the summer threshing floors; and the wind carried them away, that no place was found for them: and the stone that smote the image became a great mountain, and filled the whole earth."

THE GREAT IMAGE DESCRIBED.

May I suggest that you read these five verses over and over slowly at least seven times until you can clearly visualize in your mind this great image. This image has an important meaning, it represents a number of earthly Kingdoms, these Kingdoms cover the entire period of time during which the Gentile nations were to dominate and control the earth. IT IS VERY IMPORTANT THAT YOU RECOGNIZE THIS TRUTH!

Let me state this once again, this great image which represented great world empires covers the entire period of years from the beginning of "THE TIMES OF THE GENTILES" which began when Jerusalem was captured in 606 BC until the close of the period which ends with the overthrow and destruction of the Anti-Christ and the False Prophet and the setting up of the Millennial Kingdom of our Lord Jesus Christ. No prophecy is as all inclusive, no prophecy in all of God's Holy Word covers a greater span of time.

Imagine how stirred King Nebuchadnezzar must have been when he heard Daniel's words, "Thou, King, sawest and behold a great image". At once, when he heard these words, HE REMEMBERED, thus he knew that what Daniel said was true, Daniel knew all the details of his dream and could give him the interpretation. Whether the wise men were there or not, God's Holy Word does not say, if they were there you can image how surprised they were to hear Daniel reveal the dream which they were unable to do. I want you to visualize Daniel standing before the King boldly describing this great image. He had no fear for he knew he was God's chosen representative to reveal to King Nebuchadnezzar the utter emptiness and worthlessness of earthly pomp and glory. To do this in a way that this King could easily understand God used the figure of a great image. The head of this image was composed of fine gold, he most precious of metals, as we consider the rest of the image we see it composed of baser metals, finally we have the coarsest and crudest of metals, iron mingled with miry clay- then the entire image is dashed to pieces and made like empty chaff, worthless, so light that it was completely blown away; after which the stone that destroyed the image grows larger and larger until it fills the entire earth. This was God's way to show King Nebuchadnezzar that all earthly Kingdoms would eventually pass away, but God's

Kingdom would increase until it filled the earth, and it would endure forever.

Verses 36-38.

"This is the dream: and we will tell the interpretation thereof before the King.

Thou, O King, art a king of kings: for the God of Heaven hath given thee a kingdom, power, and strength, and glory.

And wheresoever the children of men dwell, the beasts of the field and the fowls of the heaven hath he given into thine hand, and hath made three ruler over them all. Thou art this head of gold." **THE INTERPRETATION OF THE DREAM.**

THE FIRST WORLD EMPIRE: BABYLON UNDER KING NEBUCHADNEZZAR.

We now come to the meaning of this great image. Note that it had a head of gold. Daniel tells the King that even though he was the ruler of the entire known world of his day yet it was God, the true and the Living God who gave him his kingdom, his power and his glory. Yes, he was indeed this head of gold.

Verse 39.

"After three shall arise another kingdom inferior to thee, and another third kingdom of brass, which shall bear rule over all the earth." **THE SECOND WORLD EMPIRE: MEDIA PERSIA.**

Daniel now makes a statement that must have jolted King Nebuchadnezzar, he told him that while he was now the ruler of a world emqire, enjoying absolute power, yet his world empire was not to endure forever. You can image how surprised King Nebuchadnezzar must have been to hear this! What was the name of the Kingdom that was inferior to Babylon and that followed after him? **THE THIRD WORLD EMPIRE - GREECE.**

Daniel now told King Nebuchadnezzar that a third Kingdom which is represented by the belly and thighs of this great image would be the next world empire to follow, and that this empire would rule all the earth. I have already told you that this third great world empire is Greece. I suggest that you now read the Beast vision which God gave to Daniel which is recorded in Chapter seven. I know that you will find the study of this chapter helpful at this time.

Verses 40-43.

"And the fourth Kingdom shall be strong as iron; forasmuch as iron breaketh in pieces and subdueth all things: and as iron that breaketh all these, shall it break in pieces and bruise,

And whereas thou sawest the feet and toes, part of potter's clay, and part of iron, the kingdom shall be divided; but there

*shall be in it of the strength of the iron, forasmuch as thou sawest
the iron mixed with miry clay.*

*And as the toes of the feet were part of iron, and part of clay,
so the Kingdom shall be partly strong and partly broken.*

*And whereas thou sawest iron mixed with miry clay, they
shall mingle themselves with the seed of men: but they shall not
cleave one to another, even as iron is not mixed with clay.*

THE FOURTH WORLD EMPIRE - ROME.

King Nebuchadnezzar now knows that three great world
empires are to follow him in the centurees to come. Try and
visualize this scene, King Nebuchadnezzar sitting on his throne,
Daniel the young man standing before him, boldly picturing a
great image and explaining the meaning of this image and the
world empires represented. Daniel stood before the king absolutely fearless for he had a message to deliver and he knew it.
He tells the King that four great world empires are to come, this
present empire of Babylon is the first; Medo-Persia is the
second; the Grecian world empire is the third and now Daniel
mentions a fourth world empire. Consider carefully what Daniel
tells us about this fourth great world empire. It is represented by
the legs of this great image and since the image has two legs this
world empire is to be divided. Of what materials were the legs of
this great image composed?

We see as we continue our study that this fourth world
kingdom is the Roman empire. It is not so named in this book of
Daniel but it is clearly pointed out. It is to be strong for as iron
breaketh in pieces and subdueth all things, so shall this fourth
world empire conquer all its enemies. Here indeed is history
written in advance.

But now I want you to note several important things, that we
are told are to take place in this fourth world empire. I told you
that it is represented by the legs of this great image, the legs take
up nearly half of the height of the image. So we now know that
this fourth world empire is to continue much longer in time than
any of the other world empires.

Then we note that this image has two legs, I have already told
you that this fourth world empire is to be divided. This did indeed
happen, the Roman empire WAS divided into two divisions; the
eastern division had the city of Constantinople as its capital, and
the western division which had the city of Rome as its capital.
This took place in A.D. 364.

You will also note that the feet of the image had ten toes. This
will be the empire in its final form. These ten toes of iron and clay
represent the final form of the Times of the Gentiles. They are
typical of ten kings for Daniel tells us in verse 44 that it is ''in the

days of these kings that the God of Heaven shall set up a kingdom". In Chapter 7 Daniel is given another vision which relates to this final form of "The Times of the Gentiles." The fourth beast that he saw had ten horns, these ten horns are ten kings. There is still one more reference given in God's Holy Word, it is found in the Book of the Revelation,

"And the ten horns which thou sawest are ten kings, which have not received no kingdom as yet: but receive power as kings one hour with the beast."

Revelation 17:12.

God's Holy Word is a unity, a marvelous and a complete whole, believe this, do not doubt! God's plan is clear, He wants us to know that He has a plan for this world and He is carrying it out to glorious completion. The Roman empire is to be revived and there will be ten nations, they will be unified under one head and that head will be the Anti-Christ.

While the legs of the image are of iron and the toes are of iron and of potter's clay verse 43 makes it clear to us that there is no union of the iron and the clay. Clay is a definite earthly substance, it is not a metal. Each metal spoken of in the image represents a monarchy, but now something is brought in that is not a metal, what does this mean?

I believe that the clay stands for democratic rule, the rule of the people. As we study the history of these nations we see that these nations, one after another, became increasingly unstable. The empire of Babylon was an absolute monarchy. This could not be said of the Medo-Persian empire for the King was bound by "The laws of the Medes and the Persians" King Darius who issued the edict condemning Daniel to the lion's den could not recall his edict, the command had been given, it had to be carried out. The empire of Greece was a monarchy really governed by the military. And now we come to Rome. Its emporers were chosen by the people, but the people, had no voice in the government, these Roman emperors were bold, determined men, cruel, well symbolized by iron. Rome was noted for her iron rule.

This mixture of iron with clay shows that these nations will try to strengthen themselves by forming alliances with each other, no doubt through the intermarriage of their rulers, but this will not be successful for you cannot mix iron with clay. This is the meaning of the words given in verse 42, "they shall mingle themselves with the seed of men," but they shall not adhere "one to another."

There is yet more that I want to add at this point. You have seen that in the beginning of the "Times of the Gentiles" that it was possible for one nation, through its strength and power to

43

conquer the other nations, to attach them and consolidate them all into one huge, vast empire, while one man, sitting upon the throne, could send forth his will as law to all the nations of the earth. This was true of the Babylonian Empire of which King Nebuchadnezzar was the head. But when Babylon was taken by Darius of the Medes and Persians such possibilities forever passed away. For the iron was mixed with the clay when Rome fell,the possibility of forming one great world empire ended. Time and again men tried to do this. Charlemagne tried to do it and failed. Charles V tried to do it and failed. Louis XIV tried to do it and failed. Napoleon tried to do it and failed. Hitler tried to do it and failed. Before this can happen the Roman empire has to be revived and the ten kingdoms come into existence. This is gradually taking form at the present time, so we know that prophecy is being fulfilled, we are fast nearing the close of "The times of the Gentiles."

Verses 44-45.

"And in the days of these kings shall the God of heaven set up a kingdom, which shall never be destroyed; and the kingdom shall not be left to other people, but it shall break in pieces and consume all these kingdoms, and it shall stand forever.

Forasmuch as thou sawest that the stone was cut out of the mountain without hands, and that it broke in pieces the iron, the bronze, the clay, the silver, and the gold, the great God hath made it known to the king what shall come to pass hereafter; and the dream is certain, and the interpretation of it sure."

Here we reach the climax of this tremendous prophecy, it is at this time that God is going to set up a Kingdom that will never be destroyed, a Kingdom that no individual or nation can conquer, a Kingdom that will stand FOREVER. In his dream King Nebuchadnezzar saw a stone fall out of Heaven, this stone struck this image, not in the head, or in the body or the legs but it struck the image upon the ten toes, this caused the image to fall breaking it in pieces. Suddenly before his eyes King Nebuchadnezzar saw the brozen pieces of the image turn into dust, then a mighty wind carried away the dust, and as the King watched this happen he saw that nothing remained of the image but the smiting stone kept growing larger and larger until it filled the entire earth.

Image the King witnessing this destruction of the image by the smiting stone! I imagine his knees shook and he trembled with terror as he watched, wondering what this experience could mean.

THE SMITING STONE IS OUR LORD JESUS

Why do I say this? What proof can be given? God's Holy Word

44

makes this clear. In Isaiah 28:16 we read,

"Behold, I lay in Zion for a foundation stone, a tested stone, a precious corner stone, a sure foundation".

"The stone which the builders rejected, the same is become the head of the corner, this is the Lord's doing, and it is marvelous in our eyes.

And whosoever shall fall on this stone shall be broken, but on whomsoever it shall fall, it will rind him to powder."

Matthew 21:42.44.

Do you think that Jesus had the dream of King Nebuchadnezzar in mind when he spake these words? There is no question but that the falling stone Jesus speaks of and the smiting stone in the dream refer to Himself. I know that some of you are now wondering when this stone is going to strike and when it will grow until it becomes a mountain that fills the entire earth? In answer let me say that this event is still to take place in the future. Before the stone can smite there must be the formation of the revived Roman Empire (the ten toes).

One thing I do believe, the Lord will return before the smitting stone brings an end to the Times of the Gentiles. There are several things that must come to pass before our Lord Jesus returns,-

"Jesus answered and said unto them, Take heed that no man deceive you.

For many shall come in my name, saying, I am Christ: and shall deceive many.

And ye shall hear of wars and rumors of wars; see that ye be not troubled; for all these things must come to pass, but the end is not yet.

For nation shall rise against nation, and kingdom against kingdom; and there shall be famines, and pesteilences, and earthquakes, in various places."

Matthew 24:4-7.

Let me show you that these things are now taking place in this age in which we live. Do not blind your eyes to these facts, observe them and know that the coming of our Lord Jesus to this earth is near, that it could happen at any time. Are you ready to meet Him when He comes? I know that there are those who scoff at this Bible truth, even men who are pastors of churches, but God's Holy Word tells us that there will be those who scoff, read it,-

"Knowing this first, that there shall come in the last days scoffers, walking after their own lusts,

And saying, Where is the promise of his coming? For since the fathers fell asleep, all things continue as they were from the

beginning of the creation."
II Peter 3:3-4.

Now let me list some of the very things that we are told would take place just before our Lord Jesus returns,-

1.   There is a tremendous increase in knowledge, it was revealed to Daniel that this would take place. Consider how many new inventions that have been given to us in the last twenty-five years. Think of the scientific achievements that have been accomplished, this is indeed the age of computers; consider the inventions that improve travel, and industry; the printing of books upon almost every subject known to man, the productions in music and art. We have put men on the moon; we have through the satellites sent to the planet Mars the makeup of its surface, the chemical compositon of its atmosphere, and etc. Yes, there is indeed in this space age, a very definite increase of knowledge.

"But thou, Daniel, shut up the words, and seal the book, even to the time of the end; many shall run to and fro, and knowledge shall be increased."
Daniel 12:4.

2.   Pestilences are taking the lives of countless thousands of people every year. While much is being done to eliminate disease yet cancer and heart disease and other ills continue to spread. You know that this is true.

3.   We have famine in India and in Africa and in other nations in which hundreds die daily because of the lack of food. Even in our own land there are hundreds who suffer from lack of food.

4.   Earthquakes are becoming increasingly prevalent. Do you know that in this century alone over one million people have died in earthquakes, and the floods which followed as well as the fires which were caused and the famine. Modern prophets tell us that the west coast faces the danger of a tremendous earthquake that could destroy the entire west coast of California and kill thousands.

5.   False Christs have appeared and are appearing. You know of the late Father Devine who claimed to be Christ, and a man by the name of Johnson who lived in Detroit, and there have been several on the west coast. Their coming fulfills the word of Jesus who said they would come at the end time.

6.   There is one thing more that I would mention in this connection, it is the movement towards the formation of a world church. In 1962 four of the large denominations united, this has increased until now ten of the great denominations are united, meetings have been held with the Catholics with the thought of forming a great world church. This is the church that will even-

46

tually be taken over by the Anti-Christ.

Yes, the Lord Jesus is the smiting stone which shall smite the great image seen by King Nebuchadnezzar upon the feet and brake it to pieces. When will this take place? I believe it will take place when our Lord returns to this earth bringing all the redeemed with Him, this is the time when he will bring an end to the rule of the Anti-Christ and the False Prophet, the time when they will be thrown into the lake of Fire.

After our Lord Jesus has brought an end to the Battle of Armageddon and has thrown the Anti-Christ and the False Prophet into the Lake of Fire then He will begin the Thousand years of peace, the time when the entire world will be enjoying His wonderful rule. This is the meaning of the smiting stone growing until it fills the entire earth.

"And the Beast (the Anti-Christ) was taken, and with him the False Prophet that wrought miracles before him, with which he deceived them that had received the mark of the Beast, and them that worshipped his image. These both were cast alive into a lake of fire burning with brimstone."

Revelation 19:20.

"The Lord of hosts shall reign in Zion, and in Jerusalem."

Isaiah 24:23.

The curse which is now upon the earth will be lifted in that wonderful day when our Lord Jesus is ruling this entire world from Jerusalem. There will be no destructive hurricanes and tornadoes or very cold or very hot weather, but weather which is conducive to a long life will prevail. The sunlight will be seven times more powerful with ultra violet health giving rays.

"The light of the moon shall be as the light of the sun, and the light of the sun shall be sevenfold as the light of seven days, in the day that Jehovah bindeth up the hurt of His people and healeth the stroke of their wound."

Isaiah 30:26.

The curse upon the animal kingdom will be removed. All flesh eating animals will have changed appetites.

"The wolf shall dwell with the lamb, and the leopard shall lie down with the kid, and the calf and the young lion and the fatling together, and a little child shall lead them.

And the cow and the bear shall feed; their young ones shall lie down together. And the lion shall eat straw like the ox.

And the nursing child shall play on the hole of the asp, and the weaned child shall put his hand on the adder's den.

They shall not hurt nor destroy in all my holy mountain; for the earth shall be full of the knowledge of the Lord, as the waters cover the sea.

What a wonderful day this will be! Can you image what it will be like? The curse upon the body will be removed.

"Then shall the eyes of the blind be opened, and the ears of the deaf be unstopped. Then shall the lame man leap as the hart, and the tongue of the dumb shall sing."

Isaiah 35:5-6.

"There shall be no more thence an infant of days, nor an old man that hath not filled his days; but the child shall die a hundred years old, but the sinner being a hundred years old shall be accursed."

Isaiah 65:20.

Think of it- a thousand years of glorious peace when all these blessings will be enjoyed! And all this time the devil will be chained and thrown into the bottomless pit unable to bring any harm to anyone. But at the end of the thousand years reign of our Blessed Lord the devil will be released, he will at once deceive the nations, getting as many as he can to join him. A large army formed in battle array, then God sends down fire from Heaven which destroys the devil's army. The Devil is then thrown into the Lake of Fire where he will spend eternity.

"And when the thousand years are expired Satan shall be loosed out of his prison,

And shall go out to deceive the nations which are in the four quarters of the earth, Gog and Magog, to gather them together to battle; the number of whom is as the sand of the sea.

And they went up on the breadth of the earth, and compassed the camp of the saints about, and the beloved city; and fire came down from God out of heaven, and devoured them.

And the devil that deceived them was cast into the lake of fire and brimstone, where the beast and the false prophet are, and shall be tormented day and night forever and ever.

Revelation 20:7-10.

KING NEBUCHADNEZZARS RESPONSE TO THE DREAM
Verse 46.

"Then the King Nebuchadnezzar fell on his face, and worshipped Daniel, and commanded that they should offer an oblation and sweet odours unto him."

When Daniel completed giving the King the interpretation of the dream, what did the King do? No doubt the King's wise men, his magicians, astrologers, sorcerers and Chaldeans were with him and heard the revelation of the dream and its interpretation. I imagine they heaved a sigh of relief for they now knew that they and their families would not be killed. Note that the King fell on the floor on his face before Daniel, he at once commanded his men to honor Daniel. Can you visulaize this all powerful World Monarch on his face before Daniel? Do you think that Daniel hesitated to tell the King that his great World Empire was going to be taken from him? I know it took courage on the part of Daniel to tell the King what was going to happen, Daniel did not know but what the King would order him killed for even saying such a thing. But the opposite effect gripped the King, do you think that God softened his heart? I do, for the King knew in his heart that what Daniel told him was the truth, so he fell on his face and wanted to worship Daniel. Daniel at once took the King by the hand and asked him to get on his feet, He wanted the King to know that worship was only given to the Living God whom he served.

I cannot get these wise men out of my mind. I am wondering what effect Daniel's revelation of the dream and his interpretation of it had upon them? What do you think? There is one thing they did know, they knew that Daniel was possessed of wisdom they did not have, that he served a God unknown to them, that they owed their lives to Daniel's superior wisdom.

Verse 47.

.... "The King answered unto Daniel, and said, Of a truth it is, that your God is a God of gods, and a Lord of Kings, and a revealer of secrets, seeing that thou couldest reveal this secret."

Now that the King is standing on his feet, what did he say to Daniel? Do you believe that he meant what he said? Consider the words that he used, "your God is a God of gods, and the Lord of kings" this is a tremendous admission from an idol worshipping King. The King knows that only a Living God could reveal this forgotten dream, and having done so give him its interpretation by Daniel. He was absolutely convinced of this fact. And this is indeed true for God's Holy Word says that it is the Spirit of God who gives God's faithful and trusted servants a revelation of the deep things of God.

"But God hath revealed them unto us by His Spirit: for the Spirit searcheth all things, yea, the deep things of God.

For what man knoweth the things of a man, save the spirit of man which is in him? even so, the things of God knoweth no man, but the Spirit of God. ."

I Corinthians 2:10-11.

"But the anointing which ye have received of Him abideth in you, and ye need not that any man teach you: but as the same anointing teacheth you of all things, and is truth, and is no lie, and even as it hath taught you, ye shall abide in Him."

49

"Howbeit when He, the Spirit of truth, is come, He will guide you into all truth, for He shall not speak of Himself, but whatsoever He shall hear, that shall He speak: and He will shew you things to come."

Verse 48.   **John 16:13.**

"Then the King made Daniel a great man, and he gave him many great gifts, and made him ruler over the whole province of Babylon, and chief of the governors over all the wise men of Babylon."

What reward did the King give to Daniel? We are told that he made Daniel "a great man", that he gave him many great gifts, one thing we know he was made ruler of the province of Babylon and made chief over all the king's wise men. How do you suppose these wise men regarded this promotion given o Daniel?

You can be sure of this, all the gifts and honors given to Daniel did not change him one particle, he did not get "the big head" as many men would have done. Daniel was still God's humble servant who was determined to live for God, no matter what the cost. God loves to reward those He can trust, can He trust you? Are you living the kind of life that will merit a reward? I hope that you are.

Verse 49.

"Then Daniel requested of the King, and he set Shadrach, Meshach and Abed-nego over the affairs of the province of Babylon: but Daniel sat in the gate of the King."

Note the request Daniel made of the King. Daniel did not forget his companions who had prayed all night with him, who had stood with him when he had refused to eat the King's meat and drink the King's wine. Now he wanted them to share the reward with him, he wanted them to help him in the work the King asked him to do. Do you know what the words, "Daniel sat in the gate of the King" mean? You say that you don't, very well, I'll tell you, they mean that Daniel acted as judge in the King's Court.

Before we go on to the study of chapter III, I suggest that you review again this second chapter because it gives us a prophetic outline of what is to take place in the years ahead, the coming of our Lord Jesus to this earth, the end of the period of time known God's Holy Word as "THE TIMES OF THE GENTILES", and the setting up of the Millennial kingdom in which our Lord Jesus is to reign for 1000 years.

If you want to get the most out of your study of Bible Prophecy then do not hurry in your study, take plenty of time. Read the Bible verses of each chapter over and over, before you read the explanation I have given, try to discover the meaning of the verse yourself. Look up all the scripture references I give you, pray much, ask the Holy Spirit to give you the spiritual discernment you need. If you have faith to believe, it will be given to you. We now begin the study of chapter III.

CHAPTER III
KING NEBUCHADNEZZAR'S GREAT IMAGE
Verse 1.

"Nebuchadnezzar' the King made an image of gold, whose height was threescore cubits, and the breadth therof six cubits: he set it up in the plain of Dura, in the province of Babylon."

Do you think that the dream God gave to King Nebuchadnezzar which we considered in chapter II had any influence upon him causing him to erect this image? Some Bible teachers think so, however twenty-three years had passed since he experienced this dream image, so most likely it was only a memory. Whether this image was of his god Bel or Baal whom he worshipped, or whether it was an image of himself that he had made to perpetuate his memory and his glorious reign, is not known. All God's Holy Word tells us is that he made a great image. We know that it was the custom of the Egyptian kings to have statues of themselves made, they were carved out of solid rock, many of these statues exist to-day, I saw some of them when in Cairo, Egypt some time ago while visiting Egypt.

Suppose we try to put down the reasons we can assume why King Nebuchadnezzar erected this image,-

1. The King was an idol worshipper, it may be he wanted to honor his idol Bel or Baal. Idolatry and the deification of man are the first moral characteristics mentioned which are to prevail during the "TIMES OF THE GENTILES". In chapter II King Nebuchadnezzar honored God by saying that he was "THE GOD OF GODS" AND LORD OF KINGS" (chapter II verse 47) note the reference the King gives to the Trinity in the words "GOD OF GODS". But now he ignores all this, he sets up an image or idol demanding that it be worshipped by everyone under the penalty of death. The King honored God with his lips but denied him by his actions. Our Lord Jesus said, concerning this,-

"Those things which proceed out of the mouth come forth out of the heart; and they defile the man.

For out of the heart proceed evil thoughts, murders, adulteries, fornications, thefts, false witness, blasphemies;

These are the things which defile a man."

Matthew 15:18-20.

51

King Nebuchadnezzar had a form of religion but "denied the power thereof." Oh how common this is in this space age! God's Holy Word tells us that this formal kind of religion will prevail in the closing days of this space age, now read the record,-
"This know also, that in the last days perilous days shall come.
For men shall be lovers of their own selves, covetous, boasters, proud, blasphemers, disobedient to parents, unthankful, unholy,
Without natural affection, trucebreakers, false accusers, incontinent, fierce, despisers of those who are good,
Traitors, heady, highminded, lovers of pleasures more than lovers of God,
Having a form of godliness, but denying the power thereof: from such turn away."
II Timothy 3:1-5.
This is the curse of the church to-day! Think of the many baptized church members who have but a head belief! They have never had a born again experience, they do not even know what it is! Their joy is in form and ceremony, they have a form of religion but that is all it is, just a form. Dear reader, I hope and pray you are a true born again believer, not in word only but in your daily life!

2. Then it may be that King Nebuchadnezzar erected this great image as a monument to himself. Some years before the King had conquered Egypt, he saw the many images the kings of Egypt had made of themselves and he decided he would do the same. There was no rock in the area Babylon was located so he decided to build an image that would surpass anything any former king anywhere had made.

3. There is yet a third reason I want you to consider why he made this great image. The King knew that his great Empire was composed of people from many nations, there people had different religious beliefs, so to keep his great Empire unified he would erect this great image and have all the people in the Empire worship the image., death was the penalty for those who disobeyed the command. So this third reason may be the true reason why this image was erected.

THE SIZE OF THE IMAGE.

It is important that you consider carefully the size of this image. We are told that it was sixty cubits high, a cubit is 18 inches or one and a half feet, so sixty cubits would make this image ninety feet high. It was six cubits or nine feet wide. We are told that this image was made of gold. I don't think that it was made of solid gold, God's Holy Word does not say that it was, so most likely it was made of other materials, possibly of wood, and covered with gold leaf. Could it be that King Nebuchadnezzar was not satisfied to know that he was to be succeeded by another king, so he made the entire image, not jus the head, of gold. Do you know how much gold it would take to make an image, 90 feet high and 9 feet wide of solid gold? An interested person took the time to find out. He found that the image would contain 5725½ cubic feet, and as there are 19000 avoirdupois ounces in a cubic foot of gold, the weight of this image would be 8,262,806 pound and ten ounces of gold. Do you know how much an image would cost if it were made of solid gold? I'll tell you - since there are 19000 ounces in one cubic foot of gold and since gold is worth $54.00 an ounce one cubic foot of gold would be worth $1,028,090.00 we multiply this by 5725½ (the number of cubic feet in the image) and we find this image would be worth $5,885,929,295.00 or nearly six billion dollars.

I want you to note the number six that is used in connection with the image 60 cubits high and 6 cubits wide. Have you ever studied the numerology of the Bible? Seven is God's number, its the number of completeness. Twelve is the number of the earth, six is the number of man, it is the number of the anti-christ.

"As the darkest hour immediately precedes the dawn, even so the darkest years are those just before the Millennial reign of our Blessed Lord, so the number preceding the complete seven is the worst of all. The sixth body in the solar system is the shattered one. The sixth epistle to the churches tells of an hour of universal sufferings and trials. The sixth seal brings destruction and death. The sixth trumpet destroys a third part of men. The sixth vial introduces the unclean spirits who gather the kings of the earth and the whole world to the war of the great day of God Almighty. The number of the Anti-Christ is three sixes, six units, six tens, six hundreds -- 666 the completion of everything evil,"

Hodges.

I am sure of one thing that is that King Nebuchadnezzar did not know, when he built this great image, that he was foreshadowing the image that the False Prophet will erect for the Anti-Christ in the closing days of "The Times of the Gentiles". This image will speak, all who will worship this image will also be killed, not by being thrown into a fiery furnace but by being beheaded. I suggest you stop now and read Revelation 13:13-18. also Revelation 20:4.

THE LOCATION OF THE IMAGE

We are told that the image was set up in the plain of Dura of the province of Babylon. There several reasons why King Nebuchadnezzar did not set it up in the city of Babylon. He wanted it to be located on a plain where there was plenty of room for everyone to see it. He was ruler over many provinces, his plan was to have the people attend from all of these provinces, they would then have to worship the image or be killed. Then, too, he didn't want any of the large fine buildings and statues of the city of Babylon to detract from this golden image. It was most probably placed on a pedestal, high enough so it could be seen for a long distance.

Verse 2.

"Then Nebuchadnezzar the king sent to gather together the princes, the governors, and the captains, the judges, the treasurers, the counsellors, the sheriffs, and all the rulers of the provinces, to come to the dedication of the image which Nebuchadnezzar the king had set up."

When the image was completed and set up on the large flat Plain of Dura, then the invitation was sent to the eight different groups of leaders, each group is designated, because the King wanted to be sure that they would all be there, that none would be overlooked. Every person of importance was asked to come to the dedication of the image. It was really an order, none dared to disobey the invitation of the King, fact is, none wanted to miss this great event. And they came, none stayed away, for it was a great outstanding occasion, everyone who could possibly get there, attended. A great throng of loyal subjects were present, all nationalities were represented, all languages were spoken. All the leaders of the Empire were there, all dressed in their regalia, they were present not only to give pomp and dignity to the great event but to maintain order as well and to see that the commands of the King were obeyed.

I want you to try to visualize this great occasion. The city of Babylon was decorated for this event, banners were flying from every pinnacle. The city was crowded with people, they were there from everywhere. Then the day for the dedication arrived. It was a clear sunny day, the great image stood majestic, its golden form reflecting the sunlight. A great crowd, extending as far as eye could see, stood before the image. Bands were playing, I imagine that all these leaders were told that this image was built to honor the King, I am sure they did not know that this dedication would be a worship service.

Was Shadrach, Meshach, and Abed-Nego there? Yes, indeed they were there. Did they know that this was to be a religious service? I do not think that they did, but they, no doubt, knew that the King had a definite reason for erecting the image, they may have surmised that everyone would be commanded to worship the image and they knew that if the command were given they would not obey, they would not bow to an idol to worship no matter what the cost!

Verse 3.

"Then the princes, the governors, the captains, the judges, the treasurers, the counsellors, the sheriffs, and all the rulers of the provinces, were gathered together unto the dedication of the image that Nebuchadnezzar had set up: and they stood before the image that Nebuchadnezzar had set up."

What a tremendous scene this was! From every area of the Empire they had come, we see this huge crowd facing this golden image. You have, no doubt, seen the statue of a mammoth man, fifteen to twenty feet high, standing before a filling station or some other place of business. But now imagine seeing a golden statue 90 feet high and 9 feet across, an ordinary man would seem like a pigmy. I imagine that a platform was erected before the statue upon which King Nebuchadnezzar, was seated upon his throne. About him were his men, and his musicians.

Verses 4-6.

"Then an herald cried aloud, To you it is commanded, O people, nations and languages,

That at what time ye hear the sound of the cornet, flute, harp, sackbut, psaltery, dulcimer, and all kinds of music, ye fall down and worship the golden image that Nebuchadnezzar hath set up:

And whoso falleth not down and worshippeth shall the same hour be cast into the midst of a burning fiery furnace."

The time has now arrived for the opening of the dedicatory program. King Nebuchadnezzar stands before his throne, he raises his arm and in a few moments all is still. Then the herald, a man who has a strong powerful voice, comes forward to the front of the platform and facing the crows he begins to speak. There were no public address systems in that day so he had to speak loudly to make himself heard. As he spoke his message was repeated by other men chosen for the purpose until those on the outskirts of the crowd could hear what was being said.

Everyone wondered what the herald would say, note the command that he give,- *"O people, you of many nations and languages, the King commands that when the music begins everyone here present is to fall down on his face and worship this great golden image, all who refuse to worship the image will be thrown alive into yonder hot burning furnace of fire!"* I hope you see that music had a vital part in the worship of this image. Six kinds of instruments are mentioned, the cornet, the flute, the harp, the sackbut (this is a wind instrument something like a trombone), the dulcimer (this is an instrument of two pipes which are attached to a leather sac, it is an instrument something like a bagpipe), the psaltery (a stringed instrument).

Here we see, once again, the number six, the number of the Anti-Christ, used in connection with worship. In years to come we are told that the False Prophet will see that an image is made of the Anti-Christ and that all who will not worship the image will be beheaded. All people must accept his name or his number which is 666 or be killed. I have already mentioned this, I want you to keep it in your mind. Note that this is the first time in God's Holy Word that a division of time into hours is given. This was possibly an invention of the Chaldeans.

Verse 7.

"Therefore at that time, when all the people heard the sound of the cornet, flute, harp, sackbut, psaltery, and all kinds of music, all the people, the nations, and the languages, fell down and worshipped the golden image that King Nebuchadnezzar had set up."

The music began, this great throng, led by King Nebuchadnezzar, and followed by his leaders and the representatives of the nations, all fell on their faces and worshipped the image. Everyone knew that the command of the King was law, it was either bow or burn. No one wanted to burn so they all fell on their faces and worshipped the image.

Do you think that there was much conviction on the part of the people as regards worshipping this golden image? I don't think that there was, they were all idol worshippers, some nations worshipped one idol and others another, so I suppose it didn't make a great deal of difference to them which idol they worshipped.

Verse 8.

"Wherefore at that time certain Chaldeans came near, and accused the Jews."

The scene changes, while the great throng of people were lying flat on their faces worshipping the image it was naturally easy to see anyone who was standing, who would not worship the golden image. Shadrach, Meshach and Abed-Nego Daniel's three companions who were compelled to be there, attended the dedication of the great image at the command of the King, but they would not bow down and worship an idol. Daniel was not present, he was mostlikely away on business for the King.

I am wondering whether King Nebuchadnezzar told his leaders that this dedication of the golden image was to be a religious service. I am sure that he did not. These leaders, and no doubt most if not all the crowd expected this dedication to be a formal affair, a time for music and speeches. It is plain to be seen that King Nebuchadnezzar had a definite plan in his mind, He knew and believed what Daniel had told him years before, that he was going to lose his Empire, and since he governed many different nations whose people spoke different languages and worshipped different gods, he decided that he would have but one religion for the Empire, he would have all the people worship the Golden Image. To make sure that this plan would be a success he made it known to all that those who refused to worship the image would be thrown into the fiery furnace. So to make sure that there would be no rebellion he had a furnace built near to the great image, it was hot and burning when the dedicatory service began. I suppose that the people wondered why this great furnace was there, but they soon found out.

King Nebuchadnezzar did not know it but he was paving the way for the organization of the coming World Church which God's Holy Word tells us will be organized centuries later. The prophecies in God's Holy Word tell us that in the closing days of "The Times of the Gentiles" there will be a union of all the religions of the world under one head this head will be the Anti-Christ. The movement leading up to this is now well under way. The denominations are merging, representatives of the World Council of Churches and the Catholic church have had several meetings in Rome, the day is not too far off when the plans will be completed and there will be just one world church, one world religion.

This will be a bloodless religion that will exalt man and all his works. Many of these Modernist pastors preach this bloodless religion to-day, they preach sermons on ethics, sociology, economics, politics, human betterment, book reviews, etc. No one is ever saved, people join the church much the same as you would join a club or a lodge. When our Lord Jesus returns and all who are true born again believers are caught up to be with our Lord, then this world church will carry on. All the religions of the world will be merged into this world church, the Anti-Christ will be its head. At the end of three and a half years the Anti-Christ will enter the Temple, and demand that he be worshipped as God. Dear reader, have nothing to do with these liberal, modernisitic churches, locate a church where the true Gospel is faithfully preached, where souls are saved, where believers know our Lord and who look for His return.

Verses 9-12.

"They spake and said to the King, "O King, live forever."

Thou, O King, hast made a decree that every man that shall hear the sound of the cornet, flute, harp, sackbut, psaltery, and dulcimer, and all kinds of music, shall fall down and worship the image:

And whoso falleth not down and worshippeth, that he should

57

be cast into midst of a burning fiery furnace."

There are certain Jews whom thou hast set over the affairs of the province of Babylon, Shadrach, Meshach and Abed-Nego; these men, O king, have not regarded Thee, they serve not thy gods, nor worship the golden image which thou has set up." These Chaldeans go directly to the King. Note the three charges they made against these three men,-

1. They have not regarded thee.
2. They will not worship thy gods.
3. They will not worship this golden image.

Verse 13.-15.

"Then Nebuchadnezzar in his rage and fury commanded to bring Shadrach, Meshach and Abed-Nego. Then they brought these men before the King."

Nebuchadnezzar spake and siad unto them, Is it true, O Shadrach, Meshach and Abed-Nego, do not ye serve my gods, nor worship the golden image which I have set up?

Now if ye be ready that at what time ye hear the sound of the cornet, flute, harp, sackbut, psaltery, and dulcimer, and all kinds of music, ye fall down and worship the image which I have made; well: but if ye worship not, ye shall be cast the same hour into the midst of a burning fiery furnace; and who is that God that shall deliver you out of my hands?

The music stops, everything becomes as still as death. All eyes are fixed upon these three young men who are standing, straight as an arrow, shoulders erect, clear of eye, resolute of purpose, before the king. What was the reaction of the King to these three charges? I want you to note the words "rage and fury". The King was beside himself with anger, he never for a moment thought that there would be anyone who would oppose his command. What question did the King ask them? We must give King Nebuchadnezzar credit for two things, first he did not condemn them to death in the furnace without questioning them, he had them brought before him, and second, he wanted to question them for a direct answer, he would not accept the word of Chaldeans. Why do you think King Nebuchadnezzar gave these three young men another chance? Was it due to the fact that they were governors of the province of Babylon and he needed them because they were very capable rulers? Or do you think that King Nebuchadnezzar wondered if they really understood his command? Most kings would have carried out the sentence at once, they would never have been given a second chance. But King Nebuchadnezzar, willing to overlook their failure to worship the Golden Image, restates his command. Now listen to him as he speaks,-

"Shadrach, Meshach and Abed-Nego, I am giving you another chance, if when I give the command and the music starts, you fall down and worship the image, then all will be well; but if you will not fall down and worship the image then I will have you thrown into this fiery furnace, who is the God who will deliver you?"

Shadrach answers, "O King, we are glad to answer your question. We know you will throw us into this fiery furnace since we will not bow down and worship this image. We worship the Living God who is able to deliver us if He so chooses, but if not, we would rather become three handfuls of ashes than to bow down and worship this false God that you have erected. We are not "yes men", we have convicions and we stand by them. There is no need for you to give us a second chance, for I am telling you now that we will not worship this image, we will not serve your false gods. We are not cringing cowards who will crawl in the dust at your every command. We will die before we will worship this golden image!"

Verses 16-18.

"Shadrach, Meshach, and Abed-Nego, answered and said to the king, O Nebuchadnezzar, we are not careful to answer thee in this matter.

If it be so, our God whom we serve is able to deliver us from the burning furnace, and he will deliver us out of thine hand, O King.

But if not, be it known unto thee, O king, that we will not serve thy gods, nor worship the golden image which thou hast set up."

You have already read the answer that Shadrach gave to the King. The King had commanded that they attend the dedication of the Golden Image, the King had commanded that they bow down and worship the image. They obeyed his first command, they attended the dedication but they could not obey his second command for they worshipped the Living God, they had no place in their hearts for the worship of an idol. So they faced death in the fiery furnace.

The prophet Job was a man of like faith. Suffering terribly in body, condemned by his friends, and urged to curse God and die by his unbelieving wife Job cries out,-

"Though He Kill me, yet will I trust Him".

God give us men and women to-day in this space age who have convictions and who will stand for what they believe, no matter what the cost!

"But, if not!"- note what is implied in the answer given by Shadrach. How our hearts are stilled by their willingness to undergo this fire test! But God delivered them, but let us remember that God does not always deliver. The prophet Jeremiah was sawn assunder, John the Baptist was beheaded, the Apostle Peter was crucified head downwards, the Apostle Paul met death with the axe. Hundreds of others since were not delivered, and hundreds more will seal their testimony with their life's blood, during the regin of the Anti-Christ. It may be, dear reader, that YOU will face this same test. If so, do you have a faith that will stand the test? Remember, if you keep the faith, you will find that in this testing hour THE FAITH WILL KEEP YOU!

Verse 19.

"Then was Nebuchadnezzar full of fury, and the form of his visage was changed against Shadrach, Meshach and Abed-Nego: therefore he spake, and commanded that they should heat the furnace one seven times more than it was wont to be heated."

What effect did the answer Shadrach gave to the King have upon him? We are told he could rule a world Empire but he could not control his temper! He was white in the face with anger, he had been gracious enough to give them a second chance to worship the image, it was a favor he had granted them, yet they had despised even this favor and had humiliated him in the presence of all his people. To think that he had men helping him rule his Empire who dared to disobey him! God's Holy Word says that his very visage (features) were changed he revealed what he had in his heart.

He now commands that the furnace heated seven times hotter than it was ever heated before. Seven is the Bible number of completeness, his order meant that the furnace was to be heated to its maximum capacity.

Do you think that the King really believed these young men would obey him and worship the image? One thing is true, if he did, and I really think he did, he was greatly surprised to learn that he had three men in his great Empire who refused to obey him and worship his image.

Heating the furnace seven times hotter would only hasten their death and put them out of pain sooner. Passion defeats its own end, it always does, it was the death of the men who threw them into the furnace. It also magnified the power of the Living God who delivered them.

Verses 20-22

"And he commanded the most mighty men that were in his army to bind Shadrach, Meshach, and Abed-Nego and to cast them into the burning fiery furnace.

Then these men were bound in their coats, their hosen, and their hats, and their other garments, and were cast into the midst of the burning fiery furnace.

Shadrach, Meshach and Abed-Nego are now bound securely they passed ropes around their clothing binding their arms and legs, they are now ready to be thrown into the heated furnace. The dedication of this great Golden Image was brought to a sudden stop, now the great image is forgotten, the over heated furnace is now the center of attraction. The great crowd is now moving toward the furnace, they watch as the three men bound, are carried to the front of the heated furnace.

Suddenly the large door of the furnace is opened, two of King Nebuchadnezzar's strong men now grasp Shadrach and with a rush he is thrown through the open door into the blazing furnace of fire the hot flaming blast enveloping the two men and their clothing ablaze they are dragged away from the entrance of the furnace. Two other men now throw Meshach through the open door of the furnace, two more men are killed by the blast of flame, and are dragged away. Then two more men grasp Abed-Nego, he too is thrown through the open door of the blazing furnace and two more men lose their lives, and killed by the flames and the excessive heat, their burned clothing smoking and still afire. The order of the King has been carried out, the three men are now in the blazing furnace.

Verses 23-25.

"And these three man, Shadrach, Meshach and Abed-Nego fell down bound into the midst of the burning fiery furnace.

Then Nebuchadnezzar the king was astonished, and rose up in haste, and spake, and said unto his counsellors, Did not we cast three men bound into the midst of the fire? They answered and said unto the King, True, O King.

He answered and said, Lo, I see four men loose, walking in the midst of the fire, and they have no hurt; and the form of the fourth is like the Son of God.

Let us consider what has happened here. Three men were cast into this heated furnace, they were securely bound with ropes but all the fire did to them was to release them from their bonds so they were free, they could walk about in the midst of the flames, unharmed. Heating the furnace seven times hotter and being delivered from this excessive heat which killed the men who threw them into the furnace only gave the Living God greater glory.

King Nebuchadnezzar naturally expected the three men to be instantly consumed by the flames but when he saw that they were no longer bound but were standing and walking about talking with each other in the midst of the flames he was astonished beyond measure, he turned to his counsellors who were with him and who were watching,- "Didn't we cast three mean bound into this blazing furnace? They answered, "True, O King! "Then the King said, "But I see four men walking about, and this fourth man looks like the Son of God"!

Do you know who this fourth person was? It was God's angel whom God sent to deliver them. Our Heavenly Father was watching this entire proceeding, God's protecting angel was with them all the while the program was under way. They had nothing to fear, God's angel would not allow any harm come to them. God's Holy Word says,

"The angel of the Lord encampeth round about them that fear him, and delivereth them."

Psalm 34:7.

"Though I walk in the midst of trouble thou wilt revive me: thou shalt stretch forth thine hand against the wrath of mine enemies, and thy right hand shall save me."

Psalm 138:7.

"Fear not: for I have redeemed thee, I have called thee by thy name; thou art mine....when thou walkest through the fire, though shalt not be burned: neither shall the flame kindle upon thee."

Isaiah 43:1-2.

I know that you can see that this heated furnace had no power whatever to harm these three men. Why? Because God's angel had protected them. Flames have no effect upon God's angels. I just mention the angel who was in the midst of the flame of the burning bush when Moses was on the desert (Exodus 3:2). Another instance was when Manoah and his wife, (they were the parents of Samson) were visited by an angel of the Lord, Manoah prepared a sacrifice and when the flame went up toward Heaven from off the altar, the angel of the Lord ascended in the flame." (Judges 13:20)

Dear reader, are you now in a furnace of affliction, going through a time of terrific testing and trial? If you have faith to believe in God's power to deliver then God's fourth man" will walk with you. Who is He? In this space age He is none other than the Blessed Holy Spirit who will give you the strength, guidance, comfort, protection and blessing you need. Believe this for it is true.

Verse 26.

"Then Nebuchadnezzar came near to the mouth of the burning fiery furnace, and spake, and said, Shadrach, Meshach, and Abed-Nego, ye servants of the most High God, come forth,

and come hither. *Then Shadrach, Meshach and Abed-Nego, came forth of the midst of the fire."*

King Nebuchadnezzar had commanded that they be bound and thrown into the burning fiery furnace, which was done; he now commands them to come out of the furnace. I hope you can form in your mind a picture of these three mean coming out of the furnace at the command of the King. They were having a blessed time in the furnace talking with the angel of God, they had no desire to leave, they would rather be in the furnace with the angel than in the palace with the King. They just walked up and down in the fire waiting for God's time to bring them out just as Jesus waited in the tomb until God raised Him. So Noah waited in the ark until God brough him forth. (Genesis 8:12-18)

Verse 27.

"And the princes, governors, and captains, and the king's counsellors, being gathered together, saw these man, upon whose bodies the fire had no power, nor was an hair of their head singed, neither were their coats changed, nor the smell of fire had passed on them."

What effect did the fire have upon these three men and upon their clothing? We are told that all the princes, the counsellors, governors, captains and all watched what happened very carefully. I am sure they examined the clothing of the men, they were surprised to learn that not one hair of their head was singed. There was not the slightest smell of fire upon any of them.

Everyone present knew that they had witnessed a miracle they all had to admit that these men served a Living God. There was no longer any worship of the Golden Image, it took such a miracle to bring an end to the worship of this mammoth idol. What happened to it? That I cannot tell you, all I can say is that we never hear of this Golden Image again.

Verse 28.

"Then Nebuchadnezzar spake, and said, Blessed be the God of Shadrach, Meshach and Abed-Nego, who hath sent his angel, and delivered his servants that trusted in Him, and have changed the King's word, and yielded their bodies, that they might not serve nor worship any God, except their own God."

King Nebuchadnezzar now admits that they have all witnessed a miracle. He believes that this fourth person walking in the flaming furnace with the three men was an angel of God who had protected them. Everyone is interested in seeing the three men who were delivered from the flaming furnace. Suppose they had bowed down and worshipped the Golden Image, or even pretended to do so, do you think that the true and Living God would have been known in Babylon? What wonderful tribute did

King Nebuchadnezzar give to them? I want you to notice that even as these three men yielded their bodies to the flaming furnace trusting God to deliver them, even so, we, in this space age, are asked, not by any earthly king, but by God to present our bodies, not to a furnace of fire but to God for service. Now read God's command,-

"I beseech you therefore, brethren, by the mercies of God, that ye present your bodies a living sacrifice, holy, acceptable unto God, which is your reasonable service.

And be not conformed to this world: but be ye transformed by the renewing of your mind, that ye may prove what is that good, acceptable and perfect, will of God.

Romans 12:1-2.

What God is asking you to do, dear reader, is that you give the Blessed Holy Spirit, who lives in the body of every true born agian believer, your body. He wants all of you, give Him your feet, your hands, your eyes, your ears, your brain, don't fit into the wicked world mold; if you will give the Blessed Holy Spirit full and complete control of your life He will renew your mind, then you will know and experience the perfect will of God.

Verse 29-30.

"Therefore I make a decree, That every people, nation, and language, which speak anything amiss against the God of Shadrach Meshach and Abed-Nego, shall be cut in pieces, and their houses shall be made a dunghill: because there is no other God that can deliver after this sort.

Then the King promoted Shadrach, Meshach and Abed-Nego, in the province of Babylon.

What decree did King Nebuchadnezzar issue? I want you to notice that the King does not demand that the people of the Empire worship the true and the Living God who delivered the three young men, his only demand is that they honor and respect Him.

Shadrach, Meshach, and Abed-Nego were now restored to their original position they held as governor of a province of Babylon. You may be sure that they were not demanded to worship the idols of Babylon after this experience.

CHAPTER IV.
THE HUMBLING OF KING NEBUCHADNEZZAR

I want you to take plenty of time in the study of this chapter because it teaches us a powerful lesson, that "Pride cometh before a fall". This entire chapter, and especially the first three verses, are part of a proclamation that became a state record, kept in the annals of Babylon, King Nebuhcadnezzar wanted all the world to acknowledge the true God of Heaven. We are told that "Honest confession is good for the soul", and King Nebuchadnezzar certainly opened his heart to us in this chapter. It was given to us AFTER his seven years of humbling, when as an insane King he lived with the beasts of the field. It is important that you remember that this chapter was given AFTER his insane experience.

Verse 1.

"Nebuchadnezzar the king, unto all people, nations, and languages, that dwell in all the earth; Peace be multiplied unto you."

You will notice that this chapter opens with a proclamation which was given to all the people of the earth. Notice the phrase 'Dwell in all the earth'. King Nebuchadnezzar was the first Gentile world ruler, Gentile world power began with him. See Luke 21:24. King Nebuchadnezzar conquered Jerusalem for the first time in the year 604 B.C., this was the time when Daniel and his three companions were brought to Babylon and when the Times of the Gentiles began. He overran Jerusalem the second time in 598 B.C., Ezekiel the prophet was brought back at this time. Many of the sacred vessels of the Temple were brought to Babylon on this second trip. The third time Jerusalem was taken was in 587 B.C. the city was completely destroyed at this time. The Temple was burned, the land was left desolate. The sacred vessels which were used in Temple worship, and which king Belshazzar used the night he held his impious feast were these vessels that were brought at this time.

Verse 2.

"I thought it good to shew the signs and wonders that the High God hath wrought toward me."

What did King Nebuchadnezzar consider to be good? He had indeed passed through a very severe testing experience. He had, through this experience, learned a much needed lesson. What do you think he learned? Let me tell you what I think he learned, I think he learned that kings are but men. After conquering all these nations and bringing them under his power he needed only to give the command and it would be carried, out. Such power makes a man independent. How proud and haughty he had become! In the chapter we just studied we hear him cry out to the three young Hebrews Shadrach, Meshach and Abed-Nego," "Who is that god that can deliver you out of my hand?" He even set his power and authority above God.

But now things have been completely changed, hs has been brought low. his spirit is changed, he admits this, he makes this confession himself. What do you think brought this confession out of him? Only one thing, his years of suffering, testing and trial. The prophet Job is another example, he was a rich man in his day and very powerful. If he had lived and died as a rich man, even though serving the Lord, most likely the world would never have heard of him. But trial, testing and extreme suffering brought out the best that was in him. It transferred his wealth from earthly, tangible, perishable things to that which has encouraged and inspired an untold mulititude of lives in all the centuries to come.

Are you passing through a difficult trying experience? This may may be God's way to enrich your life, God's way to bring you to the place where you can be of the greatest blessing to others. If you are a surrendered, born again believer then nothing can touch you save it be by God's permissive will. God will never allow you to be tested and tried above what He knows you are able to bear. He will, with the testing provide a way of escape that you will be able to bear it. Commit to memory I Corinthians 3:16.

Verse 3.

"How great are His signs! and how mighty are his wonders! His kingdom is an everlasting kingdom, and His dominion is from generation to generation."

King Nebuchadnezzar is now experiencing the joy of a changed life. He has learned that only through his trials and testings could he know the true and living God. He now tells us of his experiences. The "signs" and "wonders" of God are now clear to him. He believed his kingdom to be his greatest possession, now he has been brought to realize that there are other things of infinitely greater value. For instance, his reasoning ability, his opportunity to live in peace and harmony with his subjects, the privilege afforded to him to live life to the full, these things are of far greater worth than all the wealth of his kingdom. To be able to think clearly, to enjoy his food and shelter, to enjoy the gift of seeing and hearing, these blessings beyond compare. The truth is, we all enjoy these same blessings, how little we appreciate them until we lose them!

One more important thought is brought out in the first three verses of this chapter. King Nebuchadnezzar is brought to see and realize that even though he is the absolute ruler of a kingdom that covers the earth, yet there is one who is still higher in majesty and power than himself.

How great are His signs! How mighty is His power! How wonderful are His wonders! How enduring is His kingdom! The words of King Nebuchadnezzar sound like the ring of praise from the prophet David! Yet they come from the lips of a pagan king who had learned more through his suffering than through all his conquests.

"I Nebuchadnezzar was at rest in mine house, and flourishing in my palace:"
This verse tells us that king Nebuchadnezzar was resting. His wars of conquest were over, he had conquered Syria, Phoenicia, Judea, Egypt and Arabia. He was indeed a world ruler, independent, absolute in his authority and power, AND HE KNEW IT! His word was law, he but needed to speak and his command was instantly obeyed. But he thought only of himself, and the gratification of HIS DESIRES! He was like the rich man our Lord Jesus told us about whose crops were so abundant that he did not have the place to store them. So he said, "I will pull down my barns and build bigger, and there I will store them. Then I will say to my soul, 'Soul, thou hast much goods laid up for many years, take thine ease, eat, drink and be merry'." But God said, "Thou fool, this night thy soul shall be required of thee!
"King Nebuchadnezzar was like this rich man, he was "at rest", he had no problems to solve, but suddenly his rest was broken by a dream.

Verse 5.

"I saw a dream which made me afraid, and the thoughts upon my bed and the visions of my head troubled me."
This dream came to him suddenly and at once he is terribly afraid. But why? Why should he be afraid, he was an absolute monarch, he had been successful in all his conquests, his kingdom was not threatened he had everything that his heart desired, and yet he was greatly troubled, and all through a dream. WHY?
I am sure that it was because he believed that this dream had something to do with himself. He was unable to understand the meaning of the dream no matter how hard he tried.

Verses 6-7.

"Therefore made I a decree to bring in all the wise men of Babylon before me, that they might make known unto me the interpretation of the dream.
Then came in the magicians, the astrologers, the Chaldeans, and the soothsayers: and I told the dream before them: but they did not make known unto me the interpretation thereof."
The king at once called all his wise men to come and interpret the dream for him. So into the room they came, there were the magicians, the astrologers, the Chaldeans, and the soothsayers, they were all there. In chapter II we saw King Nebuchadnezzar call this same group, you will recall that they were unable to tell the King what he had dreamed let alone to tell him its meaning.

This so angered the King that he gave the order that they and all their families were to be killed and their possessions taken. Their lives were spared becuase Daniel and his companions had spent a night in prayer and God had given to him the dream and its interpretation. But this experience is now forgotten, but he could not forget this vivid dream he had just experienced. This dream is remembered while the first dream was not. As his wise men were seated before him, listening carefully so they will not miss a word, he told them the dream. When he finished talking he waited f·.r them to tell him its meaning. But there was nothing they could teil nim, none of the group could even imagine what the dream was about. All the king could do was to send them away.

Man has not changed for the same conditions exist today. Hundreds of people to-day consult spiritualistic mediums, astrologers, fortune tellers, magicians, etc. to get help instead of coming to the Lord. They believe the suggestions given in the newspapers and magazines who publish the reports given daily for every sign of the zodiac. They buy the many magazines on the newstands believing that they can reveal the future to them.

These so called fortune tellers can tell you nothing of the future, the money you give them is money thrown away. Put your trust in God, give the Holy Spirit, who is in the room even now as you are reading, give Him control of your life. He will instruct you and teach you in the way you should go. Stop now and turn to Psalm 32:8. If you look to man you will meet with failure, but those who give the Holy Spirit control of their lives find happiness and peace.

Verse 8.

"But at the last Daniel came in before me, whose name was Belteshazzar, according to the name of my God, and in whom is the spirit of the holy gods: and before him I told the dream, saying,-"

When the wise men were unable to interpret the dream, King Nebuchadnezzar sent for Daniel. Why didn't he send for Daniel at the beginning instead of sending for his wise men? For one thing the king was a lot older, and old men forget easily. It may be that one of his older men who remembered Daniel reminded the King of the former dream, we are not told. There is one thing we can say, King Nebuchadnezzar remembered this dream, he could not forget it. What name was given to Daniel?

I want you to remember that the god "Bel" or "Baal" as the god was called, was the most important and the most worshipped of all the Babylonian gods. Note that King Nebuchadnezzar told Daniel that the spirit of the holy gods was in him.

Verse 9.

"O Belteshazzar, master of the magicians, because I know that the spirit of the holy gods is in thee, and no secret troubleth thee, tell me the visions of my dream that I have seen, and the interpretation thereof."

King Nebuchadnezzar mentions three things regarding Daniel,-

1. He was master of the magicians. His wise men would never admit this but the King knew that it was true.

2. The spirit of the holy gods was in him. The King was a worshipper of idols, he worshipped several gods so he uses the plural term. He knew that Daniel had power with God.

3. "No secret troubleth thee". The King knew that Daniel enjoyed a deep, abiding peace which the King did not enjoy. What a wonderful testimony this was! Tell me, why should a born again believer carry a troubled heart? Are you worried? It is a sin to worry. You say, "I can't help it, if you had as many troubles as I have you would worry also." But let me say that daily fellowship with God through prayer and the reading of God's Holy Word will bring you peace in your heart. I want you to turn to Phillipians 4:6-7. Commit these verses to memory for they contain the formula for finding peace.

Verses 10-12.

"Thus were the visions of mine head in my bed; I saw, and behold a tree in the midst of the earth, and the height thereof was great.

The tree grew, and was strong, and the height thereof reached unto heaven, and the sight thereof to the end of all the earth:

The leaves thereof were fair, and the fruit thereof much, and in it was meat for all: the beasts of the field had shadow under it, and the fowls of the heaven dwelt in the boughs thereof, and all flesh was fed of it."

I would like to have you try to get a picture of this entire vision in your mind, it will help you to understand its true meaning. This large tree was located in the middle of the earth, it was a very high tree, it was so high that its top reached up into heaven, it was visible to all men no matter where they lived upon the earth. The tree was not only very beautiful, it was very productive. I want you now to write down the five things that are said about this tree.

Verse 13.

"I saw in the visions of my head upon my bed, and behold, a watcher and an holy one came down from heaven."

The King was really puzzled as to the meaning of this tree.

Suppose YOU had seen this vision, wouldn't you be wondering as to what this tree represented? While considering its meaning the King saw two angels descend from heaven, he was told that they were a watcher and an holy one. Now he is wondering about these two angels-

Verses 14-16.

"He cried aloud, and said thus, Hew down the tree, and cut off his branches, shake off his leaves, and scatter his fruit: let the beasts get away from under it, and the fowls from his branches:

Nevertheless leave the stump of his roots in the earth, even with a band of iron and brass, in the tendergrass of the field; and let it be wet with the dew of heaven, and let his portion be with the beasts in the grass of the earth:

Let his heart be changed from man's, and let a beast's heart be given unto him: and let seven times pass over him."

Notice that this order was given by one of these angels. There is another outstanding fact given to us here, THIS TREE IS NOW PERSONIFIED. Note that this angel changed the word "it" that was used in the preceding verses in describing this tree, to the word "HIS". The King is now greatly troubled for he now knows that the tree is HIMSELF. Now write down the twelve things that the angel ordered to be done. The King is now more puzzled than ever, what does all this mean? What is to happen to him?

King Nebuchadnezzar now is convinced that some terrible experience is ahead of him, for since he is the tree and the tree is to be chopped down and its branches removed, its leaves stripped and its fruit scattered, then he is to lose his throne.

What do you think the word "stump" implies? Do you agree with me that we are told that he is not to be killed but that even as the tree was to be cut down there was still life in its roots which would grow again. This he could understand but what of the other things mentioned? He had no idea what they could mean.

Verse 17.

"This matter is by the decree of the watchers, and the demand by the word of the holy ones: to the intent that the living may know that the most High ruleth in the kingdom of men, and giveth it to whomsoever He will, and setteth up over it the basest of men."

I want you now to give considerable thought to the information that is given to us here. Did you know that there is in heaven a court which is known as "THE COURT OF THE WATCHERS OR HOLY ONES"? Here we are told that the case of King Nebuchadnezzar had been given to this court, they were to pass judgment upon it.

The Book of Daniel reveals to us that there is a close connection between the earth and the great unseen spirit world which is about us. We shall see as we continue our study of this book that there are several instances given when the angel Gabriel comes to earth from this spirit world to enlighten Daniel concerning what he has seen. I want you now to turn to Ephesians 6: and consider verses 11-12, these verses tell us much concerning this spirit world.

There is a court in heaven before which the actions of "THE POWERS OF EVIL" (Satan and his Demons) as well as of earthly nations are tried. Daniel calls this court "The court of the watchers", its decrees are carried out upon the earth. This 17th verse pulls aside the veil and reveals to us the fact that our Heavenly Father governs the affairs of men and of nations, "The most High ruleth in the Kingdom of men and giveth it to whomsoever He will!"

God's court had passed the decree, while King Nebuchadnezzar was absolute in his power, now he was given a dream to teach him that his greatness was given to him by God. He did not realize this for all his thoughts and ambitions were self-centered, all he thought most important was HIMSELF. Now he is given a terrifying dream, he who terrified others, and whom no others could terrify, was made a terror to himself.

Verse 18.

This dream I King Nebuchadnezzar have seen. Now thou, O Belshazzar, declare the interpretation thereof, forasmuch as all the wise men of my Kingdom are not able to make known to me the interpretation: but thou art able; for the spirit of the holy gods is in thee."

King Nebuchadnezzar has now completed telling the dream to Daniel, nothing was held back, everything he saw and heard was given in detail. The confidence the King had in his wise men was completely gone they had failed him before, now they failed him again. He now knows that they are nothing but frauds, deceiving his subjects. The only hope the king has is in Daniel, this verse gives us the basis of his hope. Do you know what it was?

DANIEL INTERPRETS THE DREAM VISION
Verse 19.

"Then Daniel, whose name was Belteshazzar, was astonished for one hour, and his thoughts troubled him. The King spake, and said, Belteshazzar, let not the dream, or the interpretation thereof, trouble thee. Belteshazzare answered and

said. My lord, the dream be to them that hate thee, and the in-
terpretation thereof to thine enemies."

How long did Daniel sit speechless before the King? What
was his attitude of mind? What did King Nebuchadnezzar say to
him and what was his answer? There was no question whatever
in Daniel's mind as to the meaning of the dream. He sat quietly
before the King, he did not say anything, the King could see that
he was deeply moved, the King knew that Daniel realized that
something terrible was going to happen to him, he was anxious to
know what it was.

The King speaks, "Do not be afraid to tell me, Daniel, the
meaning of the dream." Daniel was wise, he is trying to tell the
King the sentence that has been passed upon him as kindly and as
tactfully as he can. He dreaded to tell the King this terrible
sentence so he said, "O King, how I wish that what is to happen to
you would be to your enemies and not to you!" Daniel did not
want King Nebuchadnezzar to go through this terrible experience. Note how tactfully he prepares the way for giving the
King the interpretation of the dream.

Verses 20-22.

"The tree that thou sawest, which grew, and was strong,
whose height reached unto the Heaven, and the sight thereof to
all the earth;

Whose leaves were fair, and the fruit thereof much, and in it
was meat for all; under which the beasts of the field dwelt, and
upon whose branches the fowls of the heaven had their
habitation:

It is thou, O King, that art grown and become strong: for thy
greatness is grown, and reacheth unto heaven, and thy dominion
to the end of the earth."

King Nebuchadnezzar is now told that he is the tree he saw in
the dream. Just as the entire world could see the tree, even so the
rule of King Nebuchadnezzar was world-wide in its outreach and
power. Great men are often represented as trees in God's Holy
Word. Here are some instances for you to look up - Ezekiel 17:5-6.
Ezekiel 31:3. Jeremiah 22:15. Psalm 1:3. Psalm 37:35.

Verses 23-25.

"And whereas the King saw a watcher and an holy one
coming down from heaven, and saying, Hew the tree down, and
destroy it; yet leave the stump of the roots thereof in the earth,
even with a band of iron and of brass, in the tender grass of the
field; and let it be wet with the dew of heaven, and let his portion
be with the beasts of the field, till seven times pass over him;

This is the interpretation, O King, and this is the decree of the
most High, which is come upon my lord the King:

That they shall drive thee from men, and thy dwelling shall be with the beasts of the field, and they shall make thee to eat grass as oxen, and they shall wet thee with the dew of heaven, and seven times shall pass over thee, till thou know that the most High ruleth in the Kingdom of men, and giveth it to whomsoever he will."

Daniel now goes into detail in explaining to the King the meaning of his dream. God's judgment upon the King is now revealed, King Nebuchadnezzar is to lose his mind and become insane; he will be taken away from Babylon, he will live in the field as an animal, eating grass like the oxen. His body will be wet with the dews of heaven, his hair will become matted until he looks like an animal. This is to continue until he learns that the true and living God controls the kingdom of men and gives power to those He chooses. He is to live with the animals for seven years. This actually happened, historians tell us that King Nebuchadnezzar was insane for seven years.

Verse 26.

"And whereas they commanded to leave the stump of the tree roots; thy kingdom shall be sure unto thee, after that thou shalt have known that the heavens do rule."

What definite promise did Daniel give to the King? He was assured that no new king would be given the throne of the Babylonian Empire, during the seven years that he was insane. He was told that he would be returned to Babylon and would again occupy the throne after he had learned that the Living God controls the Kingdoms of men and gives power to those whom He will. This promise was actually fulfilled as I have already told you. Evil- Merodach, his son, ruled the Babylonian Empire while King Nebuchadnezzar was away.

Verse 27.

"Wherefore, O King, let my counsel be acceptable unto thee, and break off thy sins by righteousness, and thine iniquities by showing mercy to the poor; if it may be a lengthening of thy tranquillity."

Daniel, as a true servant of the Living God, reveals the concern he has in his heart for this pagan King. He pleads with the King to repent of his sins and begin living an entirely different life, that if he will do this perhaps God will spare him from going insane and losing his Kingdom. He is urged to show mercy to the poor and needy, many of this great number were made poor by himself. Do you think that King Nebuchadnezzar heeded the plea of Daniel?

I thank God for the many true and faithful preachers of the Gospel we have in this space age, men who preach the Gospel without fear or favor, how they are needed! Dear pastor, do not compromise or water down your message, God desperately needs you in the community where you live. Sin of every kind is increasing and is spreading like a prairie fire fanned by a strong wind. Do not be discouraged because you do not see the results you hoped to accomplish as a result of your ministry, remember, God rewards us, not on the basis of our results but for faithful service. So carry on, in faith believing, our Living God will care for the results.

Did the King take Daniel's advice and repent of his sin and serve the Living God? Indeed, he did not. God gave him a full year to change the pattern of his sinful life. The months passed but nothing happened. Do you think that he tought perhaps Daniel was mistaken in his interpretation of the dream or that perhaps the judgment Daniel said would fall was lifted? In any event he continued on in his worldly ways with pride, vanity and self-greatness filling his heart.

Verses 28-30.

"All this came upon the King Nebuchadnezzar."

At the end of twelve months he walked in the palace of the Kingdom of Babylon.

The king spake, and said, "Is not this great Babylon, that I have built for the house of the kingdom by the might of my power, and for the honor of my majesty?"

A year passes by. One day King Nebuchadnezzar, with some of his leaders, is walking about upon the flat roof of his royal palace. His heart was inflated with pride, and pointing to the great towering walls, and the beautiful hanging gardens which were one of the wonders of the world, and the great Temple he had erected to the idol god Bel, he said, "Look about you, is not this great Babylon that I have built for the house of the Kingdom by the might of my power and for the honor of my majesty?" Note that it was "I HAVE BUILT", "MY POWER", "MY MAJESTY", he gave all the credit to himself, the Living God was not acknowledged at all. This was the place where King Nebuchadnezzar crossed the line between God's mercy and God's wrath. Daniel's plea for reptenance had gone unheeded, God's day of mercy was over, now God's judgment would fall. Now the King will reap what he had sown.

Verses 31-32.

"While the word was in the King's mouth, there fell a voice from heaven saying, O King Nebuchadnezzar, to thee it is spoken; The Kingdom is departed from thee.

And they shall drive thee from men, and thy dwelling shall be with the beasts of the field: they shall make thee to eat grass as

oxen, and seven times shall pass over thee, until thou know that the most High ruleth in the kingdom of men, and giveth it to whomsoever he will."
Even before King Nebuchadnezzar finished speaking, the truth is that while he was speaking, God's voice was heard. The stillness of death gripped the King and his leaders, and as the King heard God's sentence pronounced he vividly remembered the dream and Daniel's telling him what would happen to him. As he heard God's voice, he knew that now this sentence would be carried out.

Dear reader, I want you now to consider carefully the sevenfold judgment which is pronounced by God upon the King,-

1. *"THE KINGDOM IS DEPARTED FROM THEE!"*
Your present ruler King of the great Babylonians Empire is ended, all your possessions, your Kingdom, your gods, all is gone, it is taken from you.

2. *"THEY SHALL DRIVE THEE FROM MEN!"*
Could it be that his leaders conspired agianst him, which caused the King to lose his mind? This is possible, we are not told how it came about, all we know is that it happened.

3. *"THY DWELLING SHALL BE WITH THE BEASTS OF THE FIELD!"*
The type of insanity that afflicted King Nebuchadnezzar is a disease called "LYCANTHROPY" in which the patient imagines he is some king of beast, the King imagined he was an ox. He was not confined in a room behind bars but was allowed to roam in the fields, he forsook all society, this makes me think of the wild, demon possessed man of Gadara (Mark 5). He roamed the fields like an animal, it is possible that he went about on all fours. What a terrible punishment this was!

4. *"THEY SHALL MAKE THEE TO EAT GRASS AS OXEN!"*
For seven years he lived as an animal eating grass like the cattle.

5. *"SEVEN TIMES SHALL PASS OVER THEE!"*
Seven is God's number, as you have been reading, have you been thinking that perhaps this number of years had a prophetic significance? It certainly has, in Chapter 9 the "seven times" bring to mind the seven year ruler of the Anti-Christ who will rule the earth AFTER all the born again believers have been taken to be with our Blessed Lord. King Nebuchadnezzar is to be insane for seven years.

6. *"UNTIL THOU KNOWEST THAT THE MOST HIGH RULETH IN THE KINGDOM OF MEN!"*
The King had forgotten God, that He is the one who directs

the affairs of men. He had forgotten the day that he cried out,"
Daniel's God is the God of gods, a Lord of Kings, and a revealer of
secrets." His accomplishments and selfish pride had made him
forget God.

7. *"AND GIVETH IT TO WHOMSOEVER HE WILL!"*
He is to know and realize that it is the true and the Living God
who brought this judgment upon him, that this Supreme Ruler is
God.

I want to stop here, dear reader, for I feel I must bring God's
warning to you personally. Are you living a deliberate sinful life
and think that you can get away with it! I want you to know that
simply because God's sentence is not carried out at once that you
can escape the penalty! Consider the plain clear warning of
God's Holy Word.

*"Because sentence against an evil work is not executed
speedily, therefore the heart of the sons of men is fully set in them
to do evil."*

Ecclesiastes 8:11.

*"Rejoice, O young man in thy youth; and let they heart cheer
thee in the days of thy youth, and walk in the ways of thine heart;
and in the sight of thine eyes: but know thou, that for all these
things God will bring thee into judgment."*

Ecclesiastes 11:9.

Remember what I have told you before, I want to emphasize
this truth once again, there never has been a man born into this
world who was wise enough, smart enough, and clever enough, to
live a wicked sinful life and escape the penalty. 1. "The mills of
God grind slowly but they grind surely and they grind to powder!
2. King Nebuchadnezzar thought that he could carry on a sinful
life and escape the penalty! God's judgment fell and what a
terrible penalty he paid!

Dear reader, if you are living a sinful life, heed God's warning before it is too late!

Verse 33.

*"The same hour was the thing fulfilled upon King
Nebuchadnezzar: and he was driven from men, and did eat grass
as oxen, and his body was wet with the dew of heaven, till his
hairs were grown like eagle's feathers, and his nails like bird's
claws."*

That very hour judgment fell. His punishment came directly
from God, the devil had nothing to do with it. His mind snapped,
he was an insane man who was driven from Babylon, his reason
had fled. He now imagined he was an ox, he lived with the beasts
of the field, he eat the same grass they eat, his hair grew long, it
became matted, his nails soon became claws, day after day his

body became wet with the dews of heaven. What a price he had to pay for his wicked life!

THE KING'S RECOVERY
Verses 34-37.

"And at the end of the days I Nebuchadnezzar lifted up mine eyes unto heaven, and mine understanding returned unto me, and I blessed the most High, and I praised and honored him that liveth forever, whose dominion is an everlasting dominion, and his kingdom is from generation to generation:

And all the inhabitants of the earth are reputed as nothing: and he doeth according to his will in the army of heaven, and among the inhabitants of the earth: and none can stay his hand, or say unto him, "What doest thou?

At the same time my reason returned unto me; and for the glory of mine kingdom, mine honor and brightness returned unto me; and my counsellors and my lords sought unto me; and I was established in my kingdom, and excellent majesty was added unto me.

Now I Nebuchadnezzar praise and extol and honor the King of heven, all whose works are truth, and his ways judgment: and those who walk in pride he is able to abase."

Seven years have now passed. Everything concerning the dream and its interpretation has been fulfilled. God restored King Nebuchadneaar's sanity, his reason returned, he was no longer a beast but a man. What was the first act of the King: He now recognizes God for what He is, the Supreme Ruler of the Universe. It has taken a lot bring him to this place - there was the first dream vision of the large man image and its interpretation by Daniel; the furnace experience he had with the three young men Shadrach, Meshach and Abed-Nego who dared to face the wrath of the King and be true to God even though it led them through the door of a furnace of fire; and then finally this dream vision of the tree and the seven year sentence he just finished.

The restoration of King Nebuchadnezzar's sanity fitted him to once again take over his duties as King of the Babylonian Empire. When he became insane, why wasn't he kept in some room of the palace instead of having to live with the beasts of the field? We are not told. I am of the opinion that God hid him away as He did the prophet Elijah keeping him hidden until his sentence was completed. When he returned to the palace his mind was fully restored, his counsellors and lords rejoiced in his return. He is now a different man, now he lived to live and honor the Living God.

The God who heard and who healed King Nebuchadnezzar is just the same to-day. God never changes, He is the same - "yesterday, to-day and forever". (Hebrews 13:8). You have been reading of a healing that took place centuries ago but the same Living God is healing man and women to-day. He can and will heal you if you are in need of healing and if you have the faith to believe and meet His conditions.

King Nebuchadnezzar took up his duties as the King of the Babylonaian Empire and faithfully honored and served the Lord. We hear no more ot him other than we are told that honors were given to him. God's Holy Word tells us that he honored, praised God, this leads us to believe that he remained true to the Living God all the days of his life. Let us all hope that this was true!. He died in 561 B.C. and was succeeded by his son, Evil Merodach.

CHAPTER V.
BELSHAZZAR'S IMPIOUS FEAST.

King Nebuchadnezzar is no more, he died in B.C. 561. He was succeeded by his son Evil-Merodach, who at once freed Jehoiachin, the King of Judah, who had been kept in prision. Evil-Merodach fed this King from his own table, I want you to stop now and look up these passages which tell of this action - II Kings 25:27-30. and Jeremiah 52:31-34. Evil Merodach was a very wicked King, he was so wicked that a plot was formed by some of his men at the close of the second year of his reign, it was headed by his brother-in-law whose name was Neriglissar. Evil-Merodach was murdered and Neriglissar ascened the throne. The reign of King Neriglissar was not much longer for he was killed in battle during the fourth year of his reign. His death took place in B.C. 556. He had a son who became his successor, this son was but a small boy, he did not rule for even one year for he was tortured to death. His name was Laborosoarchod. At his death Belshazzar, the son of Evil-Merodach, was made King. Belshazzar was even more wicked than his father, we are told that there were no depths of sin that he did not experience. He was an alcoholic as well. He ruled the Babylonian Empire for 17 years, he was killed by Darius The Mede, on the night that Darius entered the city when the great feast was in progress as we shall see when studying this chapter.

As we begin the study of Chapter V we soon see that we are in the closing days of this mighty Babylonian Empire. In the dream vision given to King Nebuchadnezzar, which we studied in chapter II, we saw that the Babylonian Empire was designated as the head of gold of this great man image, and that the Empire was to be conquered and taken over by the armies of Medo-

Persia, led by Darius the Mede. The Medo-Persians were designated as the breast and arms of silver of this great image we saw in chapter II.

When King Belshazzar ascended the throne of the Babylonian Empire it was no longer the mighty nation it was in extent and power as when King Nebuchadneaar was the ruler, for many of the provinces had rebelled and had thrown off the yoke of Babylon. In the meantime Medo-Persia was growing stronger in strength and power day by day, so with this information in hand we begin the study of chapter V.

BELSHAZZAR'S IMPOIUS FEAST.
Verse 1.

"Belshazzar the King made a great feast to a thousand of his lords, and drank wine before the thousand.."

King Belshazzar made a great feast. This feast is believed to have been an annual affair, given in honor of "Bel" or Baal who was the leading Babylonian god. King Nebuchadnezzar years before had built a most magnificent temple to honor the god "BEL", this beautiful temple had eight towers, each seventy-five feet high, one rising above the other, with an outside winding stairway to each summit, where there was a chapel at the top. The total height of this temple to this god "BEL" was 660 feet. We are told that this chapel on the top contained the most expensive articles of worship of any place in the world. One golden image alone, which was 45 feet high, was said to be worth over 17 million dollars. The sacred vessels used in the worship of this god were worth over 200 million dollars.

Cyrus, the King of Persia, with his armies, had been besieging the city of Babylon for some months, and when his spies learned that this animal feast was soon to be held, and that all the activities of the city would center in its celebration, he at once decided to make this day of the feast the time for the capture of the city and the taking over of the Empire.

This seige which had been going on for months had not alarmed King Belshazzar in the least, what was there to worry about? The walls about the city were 87 feet thick, these walls were 350 feet high, they were fifty feet wide at the top and were well manned by soldiers. There was enough food and provisions in the city to last for several years, with acres of land available within the city to raise more food if that should be necessary. So let the enemy besiege the city all they pleased they were only wasting their time.

How ignorant King Belshazzar was of what was actually taking place! He did not know that King Cyrus had divided his army, half of his men were cutting a new route for the river where it ENTERED the city, the other half of his men were cutting a new route for the river where it LEFT the city. His plan was divert the course of the river so his army could enter the city by the original river bed. Everything was ready for the capture of the city the night the feast was held, the armies of King Cyrus were ready to enter the city when the signal was given, half of the army would enter where the river ENTERED the city, the other half where the river LEFT the city. King Belshazzar's entire thought and effort was given over to the feast.

How many lords of the Empire attended this feast? You can be sure that the most prominent people in the Empire were present. This feast was, indeed, the most important and outstanding event of the year. There was food of all kinds in abundance, wine flowed like water, there was plenty for everyone. King Belshazzar led all the hundreds present in drinking for he was an alcoholic. Yes, dear reader, this was SOME feast!

In the little village of Stark, Florida there is a large canvas painting depicting this feast. The canvas is around 12 by 30 feet in size, when you go to Florida be sure to stop in the village of Stark and see it, anyone in the village can tell you where it can be seen. It is well worth stopping to see.

Verse 2.

"Belshazzar, whiles he tasted the wine, commanded to bring the golden and silver vessels which his father Nebuchadnezzar had taken out of the temple which was in Jerusalem; that the King, and his princes, his wives, and his concubines, drank in them."

What command did King Belshazzar give to his servants? Everyone present was having a hilarious time eating and drinking and indulging in every gratification of the flesh, as only a drinking crowd know how to do. King Belshazzar knew that the enemy were working just outside the walls, but he did not know what they were doing and he did not care. Why should he worry? He did not believe any enemy could batter down walls that were 87 feet thick.

So in his drunken condition, and wanting to do something very unusual and sensational, he ordered his servants to bring in the sacred golden vessels which his grandfather King Nebuchadnezzar had brought from the temple in Jerusalem many years before. These were the golden vessels that were dedicated to be used only in the service of the Living God.

When the servants returned bringing these sacred vessels of pure gold he had them distributed among his lords, his princes, his wives and his concubines, then they unitedly filled them with wine and drank praising the gods of gold, silver, brass, iron, wood and stone. Such a disgraceful and unholy act had never been done before, but when a man is filled with liquor he does whatever the flesh desired. It does not take much wine to befog the mind of most men and women, and this King was no exception. Why do you think King Belshazzar and those who were with him at the feast drank wine from these holy sacred vessels? Do you think it was to celebrate what he believed to be the superiority of their gods over the Living God? Some Bible teachers think that this was the reason. What do you think?

Verse 3.

"Then they brought the golden vessels that were taken out of the temple of the house of God which was at Jerusalem; and the King, and his princes, and his wives, and concubines, drank in them."

I hope you can picture in your mind what was going on at this feast. Imagine you were there, you see King Belshazzar, his princes all dressed in their regalia, his wives, and concubines and the thousands of his lords, some eating, some drinking, some dancing, all were letting the flesh run riot. King Belshazzar orders the vessels of gold be filled with wine time and again. God is forgotten, wisdom, morality, honor and reason are all thrown to the winds, drowned in the winecup. It was indeed a feast of licentiousness, drunkeness and idolatrous worship.

Verse 4.

"They drank wine, and praised the gods of gold, of silver, of brass, of iron, of wood, and of stone."

Tell me, whom do this drinking crowd praise? I want you now to turn back to chapter III, verse 29. Note that King Nebuchadnezzar had issued a decree condemning to death anyone who would speak a word against the God of the three consecrated young Hebrews, Shadrach, Meshach and Abed-Nego, who were delivered frrm the fiery furnace. King Belshazzar had, no doubt, completely forgotten this decree, or if he remembered it, why should he obey it? He is the King of this Babylonian Empire, he can do what he pleases. I am sure that many of those present at the feast threw themselves down before their idols.

THE FINGER OF GOD WRITES.
Verse 5.

"In the same hour came forth fingers of a man's hand, and wrote over against the candlestick upon the plaster of the wall of the King's palace: and the King saw the part of the hand that wrote."

While the music, drinking and dancing were at their height, what suddenly happens? King Belshazzar, and all those present at the feast, who were drinking wine from the sacred vessels that had been dedicated to the service of the Living God, had now passed beyond the point of no return. This was the fatal moment, the turning point of this impious feast. The time had come when God said,- *"It is enough!"* Our Heavenly Father is great in mercy and slow to anger. But there is a deadline, even with our God of divine compassion. When King Belshazzar and those with him filled the golden sacred vessels with wine and began to drink out of them, they all crossed God's deadline, God's judgment would now be administered.

Suddenly a woman screams as she points to the wall. A supernatuaral hand has appeared out of space and is now writing a message in large letters upon the side of the wall, in plain sight of everyone, and in a language that none can understand. Everything stops dead still. The music has stopped, the laughing and shouting has stopped, the praising of the idols has stopped, no one moves as all watch as the finger of God is writing the message upon the wall. The drinking, dancing, lustful reveling has ended, all are asking, "what is this message that is written upon the wall, that is there before our eyes? Who can tell us what is said? They all look to King Belshazzar who is as puzzled as they are.

Verse 6.

"Then the King's countenance is changed, and his thoughts troubled him, so that the joints of his loins were loosed, and his knees smote one against another."

Note this writing upon the wall had upon the King. The fact that the writing was permanently fixed upon the wall proved to the King that this was not some hallucination of his drunken mind. Everyone present at the feast saw the handwriting, the message was there for all to see.

King Belshazzar was in a drunken condition but this hand that appeared out of space and wrote upon the wall sobered him enough to know that the Living God which he had forgotten, and which he had insulted had taken a hand in his affairs. His face was white with fear, he was gripped with sheer, stark terror: his knees knocked together, his hair no doubt stood on end. He could not read the writing on the wall but he did know in his heart that it was not a message of peace and good-will.

Listen to me, dear reader, if you, too, have been violating God's Holy Laws, and trampling under foot all his warnings and exhortations when God's judgment falls upon you, then, you too, will experience this same terror. kThe hearts of men have not changed, the drinking, dancing, cursing, sex loving crowd are JUST THE SAME TO-DAY! But let God manifest His presence and power in some way and terror will grip the group.

God does not always use an earthquake to arouse sinners. He does not need a trumpet. I want you now to turn to I Kings 19:11-12. Read these verses several times, consider what is said. Elijah soon discovered this, God did not speak through" a strong wind that rent the mountains", or through the mighty earthquake, or the raging fire, He spoke to Elijah with a still small voice.

You may sin secretly and carefully cover your tracks, you may be certain in your heart that no one will ever know about it; but unless you repent and your sin is covered by God's precious blood your covered sin will be publicly exposed and we will all have a look. I have a few more verses I want you to read and consider, read - Luke 12:2-3; I Corinthians 4:5; Ecclesiastes 8:11. Do you think you can continue to live a sinful life and escape the penalty? Dear reader, all such will pay the price!

AN INTERPRETER IS SOUGHT
Verse 7.
"The King cried aloud to bring in the astrologers, the Chaldeans, and the soothsayers. And the King spake, and said to the wise men of Babylon, Whosoever shall read this writing, and shew me the interpretation thereof, shall be clothed with scarlet, and have a chain of gold about his neck, and shall be the third ruler in the Kingdom.."

What was the first thing King Belshazzar did? As soon as the writing ended and the hand was withdrawn and disappeared, leaving the message on the wall, the King in his consternation and terror called for his wise men. You may be sure these wise men wasted no time in getting to the banquet hall, I can see them as they come trooping into the building. There they were, all standing together as a group, all dressed in the garb of their office, staring at the handwriting upon the wall before them. King Belshazzar is no longer boasting, the muic has stopped, people are standing in groups talking to each other, in low tones. All the dignity King Belshazzar had is gone, all see a man dressed in royal robes who is in deep trouble. What three things does the king promise to give to anyone who can read the writing on the wall?

Verse 8.
"Then came in all the Kings wise men,: but they could not read the writing, nor make known to the King the interepretation thereof."

These wise men studied the writing on the wall, they looked at one another, they conferred together, but none could read the message that was written on the wall before them. They were absolutely unable to tell what it was or to reveal its meaning. After telling the King that the message was in a language unknown to any of them, a message they were unable to read, they march out. This left the King more terrified than ever. Have you noticed thus far in your study of the Book of Daniel that every time these Gentile Kings were in trouble and needed help that they sent for their wise men, and EVERY TIME without a single exception, their wise men were unable to help them? This message on the wall was God's message to the King and the assembled crowd, and only God's man could reveal its meaning.

Now stop long enough to consider how many people in this space age rely on the advice and predictions of astrologers, mediums, and fortune tellers to direct their future. Are you one of this number? If so, I pity you, for your mind is blinded (II Corinthians 4:4) this group are just as powerless to help you as these wise men were to help the King in his hour of need.

Verse 9.

"Then was King Belshazzar greatly troubled, and his countenance was changed in him, and his lords were astonished."

King Belshazzar is now sobered, his desire for drink is gone. He is in great trouble. AND HE KNOWS IT. His wise men, upon whom he relied, could not help him, of course they couldn't, they were motivated and controlled by demons and demons with all their wisdom can never read the writing of the Living God! Only the Holy Spirit can reveal the deep things of God, for God's Holy Word says,-

"But the natural man receiveth not the things of the Spirit of God, for they are foolishness unto him: NEITHER CAN HE KNOW THEM, for they are spiritually discerned."

I Corinthians 2:14.

King Belshazzar grew more and more hysterical. His face white, his conscience is condemning him for what he has done. His princes, his lords, his wives and concumbines are all standing in groups the sacred vessels still in their hands. They are all puzzled at the turn of events. Fear has now gripped the entire assembly. They now know that this handwriting on the wall was not a part of the evening program, something the King had provided to entertain them, it was something supernatural, something unexpected. Now cries of terror are hear. King Belshazzar, sobered, stands looking at the writing on the wall, there it is, large and clear, he does not know what it says but he does believe that it is a message which reveals God's anger and judgment.

Verse 10.

"Now the queen by reason of the words of the king and his lords came into the banquet house: and the queen spake and said, O King, live forever: let not thy thoughts trouble thee, nor let thy countenance by changed:"

Word of this striking event had now reached the queen mother she had been told what had happened since she had not been present at the feast. She hurried at once to the banquet hall, what did she say to the King? Do you think her message brought any relief to the King?

Verse 11.

"There is a man in thy kingdom, in whom is the spirit of the holy gods; and in the days of thy father light and understanding and wisdom, like the wisdom of the gods, was found in him; whom the King Nebuchadnezzar thy father, the King, I say, thy father, made master of the magicians, astrologers, Chaldeans, and soothsayers;

If you are wondering who this queen was let me say that she was not the wife of King Belshazzar, for if she had been his wife she would have been present at the feast. She was, most likely, the wife of King Nabonidus who was the first ruler of the Empire. He was away at the time on a military expedition, King Belshazzar reigned the Empire in conjunction with King Nabonidus at the time. The queen was the daughter of King Nebuchadnezzar who had been dead for 23 years. She lived in the royal palace, she at once remembered Daniel who helped her father in his hour of need. So she asked King Belshazzar to send for Daniel. What three things did the queen say that Daniel possessed? You may recall that King Nebuchadnezzar made Daniel master of all the wise men.

Verse 12.

"Forasmuch as an excellent spirit, and knowledge, and understanding, interpretating of dreams, and shewing of hard sentences, and dissolving of doubts, were found in the same Daniel, whom the King named Belshazzar: now let Daniel be called and he will show the interpretation."

Read this verse slowly once again, consider what it says. Then make a list of the six things the queen said Daniel possessed. Take the time to consider each one of his capabilities. The queen knows that Daniel is God's man and that the message on the wall was God's message and that Daniel could read it and tell the King what it was.

Verse 13.

"Then was Daniel brought in before the King. And the King spake and said unto Daniel, - Art thou that Daniel, which art of the children of the captivity of Judah, whom the King my father bought out of Jewry?"

King Belshazzar at once sends a messenger to locate Daniel and bring him to the banquet hall. Born again believers are never found at worldly drinking parties, with which group, dear reader, do you associate? Had you lived in Babylon at this time, and had been invited to attend this feast, knowing what it was and what would be done there, would you have attended?

Daniel was probably fast asleep when he was located for it was now in the early hours of the morning, long past midnight when God's hand appeared. It was sixty-five years ago that Daniel had interpreted King Nebuchadnezzar's dream, so if Daniel was around twenty years old when he was carried into captivity then he must be an old white haired man in the late eighties.

Daniel was at once brought into the banquet hall and ushered into the King's presence. What was the first question King Belshazzar asked Daniel? This question leads us to believe that King Belshazzar did not know Daniel personally, it is possible that King Belshazzar did not even know that Daniel existed for he was now living a quiet, retired life. He was still living in Babylon, no doubt not far from the palace.

Verse 14.

"I have even heard of thee, that the spirit of the gods is in thee, and that light and understanding and excellent wisdom is found in thee."

King Belshazzar tells Daniel that he has heard of him. What three things had been told to King Belshazzar regarding Daniel? King Belshazzar was ignorant of the Living God, he was an idol worshipper, he believed that there were many gods.

Verse 15.

"And now the wise men, the astrologers, have been brought in before me, that they should read the writing, and make known to me the interpretation thereof; but they could not shew the interpretation of the thing."

What does King Belshazzar admit to Daniel regarding his wise men? What he said was not new to Daniel, he knew that these wise men were absolutely ignorant of what the message God had written on the wall was, there was nothing that they could tell the King.

Verse 16.

"And I have heard of thee, that thou canst make in-

terpretations, and dissolve doubts; now if thou canst read the writing, and make known to me the interpretation thereof, thou shalt be clothed with scarlet, and have a chain of gold about thy neck, and shalt be the third ruler in the Kingdom".

King Belshazzar was very anxious to have Daniel tell him the meaning of this message God has written on the wall. He promises Daniel three things, three great outstanding rewards if he can read the message. Consider each of these rewards.

Verse 17.

"Then Daniel answered and said before the King, Let thy gifts be to thyself, and give thy rewards to another; yet will I read the writing unto the King, and make known to him the interpretation."

What answer did Daniel give to King Belshazzar? The moment Daniel entered the banquet hall and saw the message that God had written upon the wall he knew what it was, he knew that the reign of King Belshazzar had come to an end, for the Medes were already in the city having entered through the empty river bed under the wall. Daniel knew that King Belshazzar was unable to give any honors to anyone for his doom was sealed. So Daniel tells the King that he will reveal the message to him, he does not want any reward, he can give his gifts to others if he so desires.

GOD'S MESSAGE IS REVEALED BY DANIEL.
Verses 18-19

"O thou King, the most High God gave thy father King Nebuchadnezzar a kingdom, and majesty, and glory, and honor:

And for the majesty that he gave him, all people, nations, and languages, trembled and feared before him: whom he would he slew: and whom he would he kept alive; and whom he would he set up; and whom he would he put down."

I want you to note that Daniel did nto hesitate a moment in revealing the message on the wall to King Belshazzar. In plain, straight from the shoulder words his message is given to the King. You can be sure that this banquet hall was as still as death as Daniel speaks, everyone present was anxious to hear what Daniel had to say. There is no softening or watering down of the message. What did he tell King Belshazzar that the Living God had given to his father, King Nebuchadnezzar. What effect did this gift have upon the people King Nebuchadnezzar ruled? Note that King Nebuchadnezzar was an absolute monarch, he possessed unlimited power.

Verses 20-21.

"But when his heart was lifted up, and his mind hardened in

pride, he was deposed from his kingly throne, and they took his glory from him:

And he was driven from the sons of men; and his heart was made like the beasts, and his dwelling was with the wild asses: they fed him with grass like oxen, and his body was wet with the dew of heaven; till he knew that the most High God ruled in the kingdom of men, and that he appointeth over it whomsoever He will."

What effect did this absolute power God gave to King Nebuchadnezzar have upon him? Note that not only was his mind affected, his heart was affected as well, so much so that God had to pronounce judgment upon him. Daniel knew this for he was the man who had warned King Nebuchadnezzar that God would punish him severely if he did not repent and give up his wicked, sinful ways. The sentence was actually carried out, I know that it will refresh your mind if you will stop long enough to turn back to chapter IV and begin reading verse 27.

Consider once again the warning God gives in His Holy Word,-

"Be not deceived: God is not mocked: whatsoever a man soweth, that shall he also reap.

For he that soweth to his flesh shall of the flesh reap corruption; but he that soweth to the Spirit shall of the Spirit reap life everlasting."

Galatians 6:7-8.

How this message is needed in this age in what we live! Think of the multitudes who are sowing to the flesh and never giving a second thought to what they are doing! But there is a judgment day coming, our God is not mocked!

Verses 22-23.

"And thou his son, O Belshazzar, hast not humbled thine heart, though thou knowest all this;

But hast lifted up thyself against the Lord of heaven; and they have brought the vessels of His house before thee, and thou, and thy lords, thy wives, and thy concubines. have drunk wine in them; and thou hast praised the gods of silver, and gold, of brass, iron, wood, and stone, which see not, hear, nor know: and the God in whose hand thy breath is, and whose are all thy ways, hast thou not glorified."

Daniel now drives home God's personal message to King Belshazzar. Note the four great outstanding sins King Belshazzar committed, the sins that brought God's judgment upon him,-

1. He did not humble his heart.
2. He defied the Living God.
3. He desecrated God's sacred holy vessels of gold.

4. He worshipped and praised the false gods of Babylon.

Verse 24.

"Then was part of the hand sent from Him; and this writing was written."

After Daniel had delivered his heart searching rebuke to King Belshazzar he now reveals to him the sentence God has pronounced upon him. He now reveals step by step and word for word the message the hand of God had written upon the wall.

Verse 25.

"And this is the writing that was written, MENE, MENE, TEKEL, UPHARSIN."

We are not told in what language the message on the wall was written. We know it was not written in the language of the Chaldeans for if it had the wise men of Chaldea could have read it. It may have been written in Hebrew though most Bible teachers think that it was written in Aramiac since Daniel was familiar with both languages. Yet it is possible that it was written in an entirely different language which was revealed to Daniel by the Spirit of God.

We now consider the words of this message,-

Verse 26.

"This is the interpretation of the thing; MENE; God hath numbered thy Kingdom and finished it."

The word "MENE" when translated means "numbered". King Belshazzar, you thought that you were safe, that no enemy could break through the city wall. You were prosperous, you were proud, your heart was lifted up, you thought you had nothing to fear. You did not know that your days were numbered, that your reign over the great Empire of Babylon was ended.

Verse 27.

"TEKEL; Thou art weighed in the balances and art found wanting."

The word "TEKEL" translated into the English language means "weighed and found wanting". King Belshazzar, you are proud and haughty, you have exalted yourself, you consider yourself a mighty monarch. Because of this attitude of yours you are weighed in God's balances and art found wanting.

One of the greatest sermons the late Mr. Moody preached was based upon this text, "You are weighed in God's balances and found wanting". Mr. Moody asked his hearers to imagine a large set of balances to be lowered from Heaven in which every person present would be placed upon the one side of the scale and on the other side one after another of the ten commandments were used as weights. Suppose, dear reader, you were placed upon God's scale and were weighed, would you be found wanting?

Verse 28.

"PERES; Thy kingdom is divided and given to the Medes and Persians."

The word "PERES" is a root word, the word "UPHARSIN" comes from this root. Its English meaning is "DIVIDED". Daniel said to King Belshazzar, "Your Kingdom is taken from you, it is divided, God's sentence has been pronounced, your time to meet the Living God has come, your reign as ruler of the great Babylonian Empire has ended as of to-night!

Do you think that King Belshazzar believed Daniel?

Verse 29.

"Then commanded Belshazzar, and they clothed Daniel with scarlet, and put a chain of gold about his neck, and made a proclamation concerning him, that he should be the third ruler in the Kingdom."

I want you to note that King Belshazzar made good his promise. Daniel was rewarded, the three promised gifts were given to him, they were,

1. Daniel was clothed in scarlet.
2. A chain of gold was placed about his neck.
3. He was proclaimed third ruler in the Kingdom.

Why was Daniel proclaimed third ruler in the Kingdom? Because King Nabonidus was the first ruler, and King Belshazzar was the second ruler, so he could only offer the position as third ruler to Daniel.

GOD'S SENTENCE IS FULFILLED.
Verses 30-31.

"In that night was Belshazzar the king of the Chaldeans slain.

And Darius the Median took the kingdom, being about three score and two years old."

Do you think that King Belshazzar believed that he was going to have his kingdom taken from him that night? We do know that King Belshazzar was killed that night before the break of day. While the sounds of merriment and music rang throughout the banquet hall suddenly another sound was heard, the clash of steel, the heavy tread of iron heels, soon the banquet hall was filled with armed men. There was no avenue afforded for escape, soon the hall rang with the cries of the wounded and the dying. When all voices were stilled King Belshazzar was seen lying on his throne, without crown or scepter, his royal robe of purple wrapped about him.

How did it happen? I have already told you that the armies of

Cyrus had entered the city from both the north and the south, the course of the river Euphrates had been changed so the armies were able to enter the city through the river bed. Led by the 62 year old Darius the Mede the city of Babylon was taken!

Weighed in the balances and found wanting! What a lesson there is in this for us! May God help us to live our lives in such a way that God is glorified in all we say and do. This is possible even to-day if you will give the Holy Spirit complete control of your life!

CHAPTER VI.
DANIEL IN THE LIONS DEN.

This is one of the wonderful chapters of the Bible, it contains the story of Daniel in the Lion's Den., it is a story that will never grow old.

I know you will agree with me when I say that it is one of the best known and best loved stories given in all God's Holy Word, it is a constant inspiration to everyone who reads it. You, no doubt, can remember when you heard it for the first time, it may be your mother read it to you when you were but a child, or your Sunday School teacher told the story when you were a member of her class, or you read it yourself in the McGuffy third reader when you were in school. How I wish we would publish these great Bible stories in the readers we use in our schools to-day! This story of Daniel in the Lion's den is considered to be one of the best stories in the literature of the world. Best of all it is a true story which actually happened, it shows us how faith and loyalty of a man in the Living God he served was rewarded, and how it became a powerful testimony in the land.

So let us now begin the study of this chapter-

Verse 1.

"It pleased Darius to set over the kingdom an hundred and twenty princes, which should be over the whole kingdom."

The Babylonian Empire was taken over by the Persians and Darius the Mede was placed upon the throne. After 67 years of powerful rule by King Nebuchadnezzar who was the head of gold of his great man image which we studied in chapter II, this head of gold finally gave way to the arms and breast of silver of this man image. This took place in B.C. 538. Two years later, that is in B.C. 536 King Darius died, then Cyrus the Persian took over the rule of the Empire. It was somewhere between these two dates that the events recorded in this chapter took place.

When King Darius ascended the throne the Babylonian Empire consisted of 120 provinces, with a prince controlling each province. All these princes were subject to the King, who could replace any one of them any time he desired. The Empire was later enlarged to contain 127 provinces, this information is given to us in the Book of Esther, chapter 1, verse 1. King Darius placed three men he called "PRESIDENTS" over these 120 provinces, each PRESIDENT had 40 provinces under his control. Daniel was chosen to be the first PRESIDENT, he was assigned the province in which the seat of Government was located.

Verse 2.

"And over these three presidents; of whom Daniel was first: that the princes might have give accounts unto them, and the king should have no damage."

Why was Daniel given this outstanding position? He had been a ruler in the Empire under King Nebuchadnezzar and King Nabodinus. You must remember, dear reader, that Darius the Mede was an enemy King who had conquered the former King Belshazzar, and killed him the night the great feast was held. Why did'nt King Darius kill Daniel the night he killed King Belshazzar? God had a hand in this, instead of killing Daniel or even throwing him into prison he was given the chief place of authority in the Empire.

Tell me, dear reader, why was this done?

There is but one answer that can be given. Daniel lived day by day in close fellowship with God. DO YOU? Because Daniel lived a completely surrendered life God protected him, God guided and directed his life. Even though a decided change had taken place in directing the course of Empire Daniel remained the same faithful Daniel, loyal, steadfast, and true to the Living God he served and true to those God had placed over him.

Verse 3.

"Then this Daniel was preferred above the presidents and princes, because an excellent spirit was in him; and the King thought to set him over the whole realm."

Why was Daniel preferred above all others? King Darius was a shrewd discerning man, he soon saw that Daniel possessed the oustanding ability to govern. King Darius said he preferred Daniel above all other men in the Kingdom because, as he said, "Daniel had an excellent spirit in him". What was this excellent spirit to which Daniel owed his promotion? There were several things that were outstanding in his life,-

1. DANIEL'S EXCELLENT SPIRIT WAS A SPIRIT OF SELF-CONTROL.

Daniel kept his body under complete control, turn now to I Corinthians 9:27, he kept his flesh nature under complete control. Every one of us are born with a flesh nature, its a sin nature, it hates God, Romans 8:7 says it is enmity against God. Daniel controlled all his appetites and passions, "he purposed in his heart that he would not defile himself by eating the King's meat or drinking the King's wine" See Daniel 1:8. Let me ask you, do you let the Holy Spirit control your flesh nature or do you allow it free reign to gratify every desire of your mind? This flesh nature despises everything that is righteous, holy and good.

2. DANIEL'S EXCELLENT SPIRIT WAS DUE TO HIS GIVING GOD COMPLETE CONTROL OF HIS LIFE.

God was first and foremost in Daniel's life. Much as we admire Daniel's self-control, his wisdom as a counsellor, his honesty as a judge, as well as his moral courage to stand for that which he knew was right, we still have to look deeper than this to discover the secret of his wisdom, strength and power. God was a real person to Daniel, a living and a dependable friend, one to whom he could take every problem he had to be solved, and one in whom he could trust for guidance and protection in every danger.

3. DANIEL'S EXCELLENT SPIRIT WAS DUE TO HIS DEFINITE AND UNSHAKEN FAITH IN GOD.

In all his life when troubles came, and they were many, Daniel never lost confidence in the God he served. He always took his problems to God in prayer. DO YOU? Consecrated to God as Daniel was, he still considered himself a sinner, living in the presence of a just, holy and righteous God. Because of his great outstanding christian character, his ability to advise, to direct and rule others, King Darius was planning to promote him and make him the ruler over the entire Babylonian Empire. Who dares to say that it does not pay to serve the Lord?

4. DANIEL'S SPIRIT WAS DUE TO THE FACT THAT HE GAVE GOD FULL CONTROL OF ALL THE TALENT HE HAD.

This was the reason why he was so capable, why he had so many virtues. The kings under whom he served recognized at once his ability. Every talent that God had given to him was developed and used in a maximum way.

Every person born into this world has some talent. Some of us have more, some less. Many do not know what talent they have for they have never surrendered their lives to the Lord, they live and die with the talent never known or used. When you accept our Lord Jesus as your personal Saviour, and give the Holy Spirit, who lives in your body complete control of your life, then the Holy Spirit not only reveals to you what talent you possess, he brings it forth from the depths of your personality, he multiplies it, then blesses it as our Lord Jesus multiplied the loaves and the fishes when he fed the crowd on the hillside. And as your talent is used you will enjoy a life of happiness and peace. Daniel gave God all the talent he had, you know how God blessed and used him.

A PLOT AGAINST DANIEL IS PLANNED
Verse 4.
"Then the presidents and princes sought to find occasion against Daniel concerning the Kingdom; but they could find none occasion nor fault; forasmuch as he was faithful, neither was there any error or fault found in him."

What effect did the promotion of Daniel by King Darius have upon the other leaders? They did not know the Living God that Daniel served, so it was natural for their flesh nature to assert itself. It is just the same to-day. Centuries have come and gone but the flesh nature has not changed. These leaders conferred together, trying to find some way to get rid of Daniel.

They searched Daniel's life with a fine toothed comb to see if they could find anything with which they could accuse him. But try as hard as they could they were unable to find one thing, his life, was blameless and above reproach. Let me ask you, would your life stand such a searching, such scrutiny? Believe me when I say that you must live very close to God to be able to live a life that your enemies cannot find one thing that they can use against you I do hope you are living such a dedicated and surrendered life. If not, I ask you, EVEN NOW, to open your Bible to the Book of Romans, chapter 12 and read verses one and two. Read these verses seven times a day for a week or longer. Why do I ask you to do this? Because I want the message of these two verses to grip your heart until you are willing to do what they ask. Here are these two verse,-

"I beseech you therefore, brethren, by the mercies of God, that ye present your bodies a living sacrifice, holy, acceptable unto God, which is your reasonable service.

And be not conformed to this world: but be ye transformed by the renewing of your mind, that ye may prove what is that good, and acceptable and perfect, will of God."
Romans 12:1-2.

If you will obey the command of these verses, God's blessing, rich and complete will be enjoyed, and you, like Daniel, will experience the wonderful guidance of the Holy Spirit for your life.
Verse 5.
"Then said these men, We shall not find any occasion against this Daniel, except we find it against him concerning the law of his God."

These leaders, after a most thorough search, admitted that they could not find one thing with which they could accuse him.

Why did they want to get rid of Daniel? If you want to know I'll tell you. It wasn't just jealousy and envy, they had this, they were angered because he was favored by the King. They envied him because of the wisdom he possessed and the power to rule. But there was a still deeper reason why they wanted to get him out of the way. They knew that when he was given the control of the entire Empire that he would expose any graft and dishonest dealing in the conducting of business affairs, thus their gain and profit would be cut off, their own lives would be in danger; so to make their position secure and the opportunities to get rich safe from discovery they determined to get rid of him.

Let us stop here a moment consider life as it is lived in this busy and complex space age. Do you agree with me that this same spirit of envy, jealousy and greed is prevalent to-day? Many a true and faithful minister of the Gospel has suffered the loss of position, his reputation ruined, (they could not ruin his character for character is WHAT YOUR ARE, reputation is what men SAY YOU ARE, note the difference) all because of the envy and jealousy of self-made enemies. No douby you can think of men who have had to undergo such testing and trial, perhaps even you, yourself, have had to face such an experience.

Since these leaders could find nothing with which to accuse Daniel, what course did they now persue? In their investigation of his personal life they discovered that he prayed three times a day with his window open that faced Jerusalem. How often do you pray? They now worked out a carefully laid plan which they believed would enable them to get rid of Daniel.

THE PLAN THEY PRESENTED TO THE KING
Verse 6-7.

"Then these presidents and princes assembled together to the King, and said thus unto him, King Darius .. live forever.

All the presidents of the kingdom, the governors and the princes, the counsellors, and the captions, have consulted together to establish a royal statute, and to make a firm decree, that whosoever shall ask a petition of any God or man for thirty days, save of thee, O King, he shall be cast into the den of lions."

What were the first steps taken by these enemies of Daniel? Here is an outline of the plan they prepared which they would present in person to the King,-

1. They would, unitedly, the presidents and princes, go to King Darius salute him and then present the plan.

2. They would try to convince the King that the plan they had prepared was an urgent matter, that should be taken care of at

95

once.

3. They would ask the King to issue a decree that he would be the only dispenser of favors and the only one who would grant a petition for a period of thirty days.

4. They would tell the King that they, the presidents, governors princes, counsellors and captains were all agreed on the matter.

5. They would ask that the penalty for disobedience to this decree would be death in the lion's den.

This was the plan they prepared, when they were all agreed on the plan, then the entire group came in a body to see the King. Coming in a body as they did the King naturally assumed that the plan they presented was an urgent matter. I hope you see the lie they told the King. They told him that they were all agreed on the plan, of course Daniel had not been consulted. He was absolutely ignorant of what these men were doing. Do you think that King Darius saw that this was a plan that they had prepared to get rid of Daniel? You can be sure that he did not. If they had asked King Darius to forbid anyone praying to Daniel's God under the penalty of death in the lion's den, he would have known at once that this was a plot to destroy Daniel, but the way it was worded the King did not discover what was involved.

Verse 8.

"Now, O King, establish the decree, and sign the writing, that it be not changed, according to the law of the Medes and Persians, which altereth not."

Let me explain to you the law of the Medes and Persians. I want you to know that the Empire of Babylon ruled by King Darius was far from being as absolute as it was under King Nebuchadnezzar. The "head of gold" of the dream image of chapter II was now displaced by the "Breast and arms of silver". The Medo-Persians did not give the King full absolute authority, the leaders of the provinces had a definite voice in the affairs of government. When a law was made and a decree established it could not be changed by the will and desire of the King, the law and the decree had to be carried out.

Verse 9.

"Wherefore King Darius signed the writing and the decree. To accomplish the death of Daniel these leaders finally persuaded the King to sign the decree. King Darius, flattered by these leaders and ignorant of the plan they had made to kill Daniel, signed the decree. It then became a law that had to be carried out. These leaders knew that they had to get him to sign the decree at their meeting for if his signing was delayed he would likely discover the plot and then would not sign. How happy

they were when they realized that the King had signed the decree, they could not proceed with their plan to kill Daniel.

Verse 10.

"Now when Daniel knew that the writing was signed, he went into his house; and his windows being open in his chamber toward Jerusalem, he kneeled upon his knees three times a day, and prayed, and gave thanks before his God, as he did aforetime."

What effect did this law have upon Daniel? Do you think that his knowledge of the plot changed his mode of living in any way? Had you been in his shoes what would you have done? Would you have moved to some other location in the province where you would be free from observation? Or would you have given up praying three times a day with your window open that faced Jerusalem?

Now that you have considered these questions I want you to note just what Daniel did. He knew that these leaders had plotted against him. He knew that they planned to kill him, yet he made no effort whatever to overthrow their plan. He did not go to the King with an appeal for help. He simply trusted in the God he served, he knew that God was able to protect and save him if this was God's will.

Daniel continued praying three times a day as usual. It may be that you may ask, "What did Daniel have to be thankful for, he was a captive in a heathen land, he had been made a eunuch, and now he faced a decree that had been made deliverately to end his life." Daniel always prayed to God with his window open facing Jerusalem. Now look up and read I Kings 8:45-49.

Verse 11.

"Then these men assembled, and found Daniel praying and making supplication before his God."

Daniel's enemies watched him day after day to see whether he had changed his time and place of prayer. How they rejoiced and congratulated each other when they heard him praying as he did before! Now they had the information which they knew would condemn him, now they knew that it would be an easy matter to have him thrown into the den of hungry lions.

Verse 12.

"Then they came near, and spake before the King concerning the King's decree; Hast thou not signed a decree that every man that shall ask a petition of any God or man within thirty days, save of thee, O King, shall be cast into the den of lions? The King answered and said, The thing is true, according to the law of the Medes and Persians, which altereth not."

Why do you suppose that King Darius kept lions? Do you think that they were kept just to be used to kill those they wanted to destroy? As soon as the enemies of Daniel had the information they needed after they had seen and heard him praying to his God, they hurried to the King. After they were admitted to the counsel chamber they asked him "King Darius, do you remember signing a decree some days ago?" "Yes", said the King, "I did sign a decree and it is now law." "Doesn't this decree state that no one is allowed to pray to any God except yourself, for thirty days?"

"Yes", said the King, "This is true!" "And anyone who prays to anyone else is to be thrown into the lion's den?" "Yes", answered the King, "I have signed this decree and it must be carried out for this is the law of the Medes and the Persians which cannot be changed!"

Verse 13.

"Then answered they and said before the King, That Daniel, which is of the children of the captivity of Judah, regardeth not thee, O King, nor the decree which thou hast signed, but maketh his petition three times a day."

I want you to note the sneering tone of voice these enemies of Daniel used as they accused him before the King. They said, "O King, that fellow Daniel, that Jewish captive, who is dependent upon you for his very life and for every blessing he enjoys, instead of being grateful to you he does not even regard you or pay the slightest attention to your decree, he asks favors of his God three times a day." King Darius now knows that the decree, which must be carried out, was planned by these men to kill Daniel. He now knows that Daniel must face death in the lion's den.

Verse 14.

"Then the King, when he heard these words, was sore displeased with himself, and set his heart on Daniel to deliver him: and he labored until the going down of the sun to deliver him."

King Darius is now aware of the fact that not only have they set a trap and caught Daniel, they have caught him in their rap as well. They knew that the King had the highest regard for Daniel, that he considered Daniel the ablest and most dependable of all his men. The King was deeply burdened and sorely displeased with himself for signing such a foolish and ridiculous decree, he began at once to see what he could do to save Daniel, to keep him from being thrown into the lion's den. He realized now that he should not have been so hasty in signing the decree, that if he had considered its meaning he would have known that Daniel would never have consented to such a law, but now it was too late.

No doubt he pled with his men to save Daniel. How long did he work? He knew that when the sun went down he had to sentence Daniel, he had no other choice, there was nothing more he could do.

Verse 15.

"Then these men assembled unto the King, and said, Know, O King, that the law of the Medes and Persians is, that no decree nor statute which the King establisheth may be changed."
I have the belief that the King called the men together and made a final appeal to them before the sun went down. Instead of heeding his earnest appeal for Daniel's life, they DEMANDED that the decree that the King had signed be carried out. They said to the King, "We know that you have tried your best to save Daniel but there is not one thing you can do, you know the law of the Medes and the Persians, this decree is law and must be carried out. Daniel must be thrown into the den of lions.

Verse 16.

"Then the King commanded, and they brought Daniel, and cast him into the den of lions. Now the King spake and said unto Daniel, Thy God whom thou servest continually, he will deliver thee."
The King had to admit that there was nothing more he could do to save Daniel. The sun had now gone down, the shades of night were falling, so the King sent for Daniel. When Daniel was brought and stood before him the King, knowing that Daniel was a man of prayer, said to him, "Daniel, I have no choice, I have to sentence you to be cast into the lion's den. But I know you are a man of prayer, I know that the God that you are serving so faithfully every day, He will deliver you!"

What a wonderful testimony this was coming from the ruler of the great Babylonian Empire! Do you think that King Darius believed that Daniel's God will save him?

Dear reader. I must stop here to say that there is a powerful lesson for you, yes, for all of us! Our lives carry a daily testimony to our loved ones and to others who know us, either for good or evil. If you are now living the life of a true born again believer, if you, like Daniel are a person of daily earnest prayer, then your life is carrying a testimony no one can deny. Even sinners, no matter how wicked, will honor and respect you. I need not tell you that there never was a time in the history of our nation when such a testimony was more needed! I ask you dear reader, are you living such a transparent life?"

DANIEL IN THE LION'S DEN
Verse 17.

"And a stone was brought, and laid upon the mouth of the den; and the King sealed it with his own signet, and with the signet of his lords; that the purpose might not be changed concerning Daniel".

Daniel was now led to the lion's den, the door was opened and Daniel walked fearlessly into the den of lions. Notice that the men demanded that a stone be placed against the door to make sure that Daniel could not escape through the door which opened into the den. Then the seal of King Darius and the seal of his lords was placed upon the stone. Daniel's enemies now rejoiced, they were certain that this was the end of Daniel, they would never see him again.

I do not think that King Darius even went to the Lion's den, he had given the order, his enemies would gladly see that it was carried out. I believe that one of the men carried the King's seal and placed it upon the stone. Do you think that these enemies stood as close to the door of the den as possible, waiting to hear Daniel's cry and the lion's roar as they leaped upon him and tore his body in pieces? If so, they waited in vain for when Daniel entered the lion's den God's angel unseen by human eyes, walked in with him and protected him.

Verse 18.

"Then the King went to his palace, and passed the night fasting: neither were instruments of music brought before him: and his sleep went from him."

Where did the King go and what did he do after he left the conference hall? Who do you think had the worst night, the King or Daniel? The King had no appetite for food, he refused all food brought to him. He did not want any form of entertainment, he went to bed early but he could not sleep, he rolled and tossed all night. All he could think of was Daniel, alone in that den of hungry lions. He knew that Daniel would be killed immediately unless his God protected him, and while he knew that Daniel was a man of much prayer he was not sure that Daniel would be saved from the lions, this is why he spent a night of deep concern and worry. It takes a lot of abiding faith to believe God would deliver when you hear the lions roar and know how hungry they are.

DANIEL DELIVERED
Verse 19.

"Then the King arose very early in the morning, and went in haste unto the den of lions."

As soon as it was break of day King Darius was out of bed he dressed and hurried at once to the lion's den. No affair of state could get him up at such an early hour, but now, haggard from the loss of sleep and deep anxiety, and white in the face with concern, he wonders, "Will Daniel be alive when I get there?"

And what about Daniel? You may be sure that he had a good night's sleep. Daniel knew from experience that nothing can touch a true born again believer save it be by God's permissive will. The lions were as harmless as any cat in your home. I am sure that Daniel was still asleep when the King arrived at the lion's den. We all need to learn the lesson that the Blessed Holy Spirit is with us, no matter where we may be, on land, sea or air, no matter how dangerous the situation may be in which we find ourselves. He neither slumbers nor sleeps. Daniel was as safe in the lion's den as he would be were he in his own bed at home.

Verse 20.

"And when he came to the den, he cried with a lamentable voice unto Daniel; and the King spake and said to Daniel, O Daniel, servant of the Living God, is thy God, whom thou servest continually, able to deliver thee from the lions?"

When King Darius arrived at the lion's den what was the first thing that he did? What is a lamentable voice? I want you to note carefully the question the King asked Daniel, it was not, "Daniel, are you still alive?" "No, indeed, the question the King asked was, "Daniel, you servant of the Living God, was the God that you serve so faithfully and so continually, was He able to deliver you?" His tone of voice told of his anxious concern. Someone has said that the King had tears in his voice, I am sure that he did.

Consider now the two things that King Darius said concerning Daniel's character,-

1. He called Daniel "A servant of the Living God". King Darius was most likely an idol worshipper. What a wonderful testimony this is.

2. He added, "Whom thou servest continually". Daniel's life was a testimony, a blessing and a benediction. Dear reader, I hope that you, too may give such a testimony!

Verse 21.

"Then said Daniel unto the King, "O, King, live forever."

Then the King heard Daniel say, "O, King, live forever! It was Daniel's voice, he was alive! How relieved the King was to hear his voice! He now knew that the Living God whom Daniel served had delivered him from the hungry lions.

Verse 22.

.... *"My God hath sent his angel, and hath shut the lion's mouths, that they have not hurt me: forasmuch as before him innocency was found in me; and also before thee, O,*

King, have I done no hurt."

Daniel then tells the King that God sent an angel who had shut the mouths of the hungry lions so they had no desire to harm him. Note that Daniel did not blame King Darius for throwing him into the lions' den for Daniel knew that it was his enemies who hatched up the plot, he does however, remind the King that he was an innocent man, he had not harmed anyone, nor had he wronged the King. God had indeed delivered him just as He delivered his three friends, Shadrach, Meshach and Abed-nego from the fiery furnace. Daniel was delivered by a power higher and greater than any power on earth. What effect do you think Daniel's deliverance had upon the King?

Remember, dear reader, and all of you who read these lines, GOD NEVER CHANGES! He is just the same today! He is delivering faithful needy souls even in this space age! Believe this, do not doubt! Now turn to Mark 9:23, commit this verse to memory. If you have enough faith, this promise which Jesus gave us, will meet your need!

Verse 23.

"Then was the King exceedingly glad for him, and commanded that they should take Daniel up out of the den. So Daniel was taken up out of the den, and no manner of hurt was found upon him, because he believed in his God."

King Darius was beside himself with joy over Daniel's deliverance, he at once ordered the stone removed from the entrance to the lions' den, and Daniel was brought out and taken to his home. You can image the fear and consternation that filled the hearts of his enemies when they learned that Daniel had been delivered by the Living God he worshipped, that he was alive and unharmed. What do you suppose they said? Do you think that they believed that Daniel's God had delivered him? No doubt they tried to explain it by saying that the lions were not hungry. It is always hard to get a sinner to admit that a miracle has been performed.

Now these enemies of Daniel were in serious trouble AND THEY KNEW IT! They know they face the wrath of the King for they know the King had done everything he could to keep Daniel from being thrown into the den of lions. Now the tables are turned, they wonder what the King will do to them. They did not have to wait long to find out.

Verse 24.

"And the King commanded, and they brought those men which had accused Daniel, and they cast them into the den of lions, them, their children, and their wives, and the lions had the mastery of them, and brake all their bones in pieces or ever they

came at the bottom of the den."

King Darius now issues an order, these enemies of Daniel are brought before him. Now he turns upon them, no doubt he said, "You have been saying to each other that Daniel was delivered because the lions were not hungry, now we will see whether the lions are hungry or not. You, yes, all of you, together with your wives and children shall be thrown into this same den of lions, then we will see whether you will be delivered."

The King gave the order and it was carried out, they were all one by one, thrown into the lion's den. The lions were very hungry, they leaped upon them, soon they were all torn to pieces. They did not have a Living God to deliver them, so you may be sure the lions had an ample meal. Thus were the words of King Soloman as recorded in God's Holy Word fulfilled,-

"The righteous is delivered out of trouble, and the wicked cometh in his stead."

Proverbs 11:8.

It is always very dangerous to hinder and oppose God's faithful servants. Many folk, to their sorrow, did not realize this, God's Holy Word says,-

"Touch not mine anointed and do my prophets no harm."

Psalm 105:15.

Now see also I Corinthians 16:10-11. Lord Jesus gave us this warning, consider it,-

"Judge not, that ye be not judged. For with what judgment you judge, you shall be judged: and with what measure you mete, it shall be measured to you again."

Matthew 7:1-2.

There is still more I want you to consider, these enemies of Daniel did not suffer alone. Their wives and children were killed with them. The innocent suffer with the guilty. God has declared that the sins of the fathers should be visited upon the children of the third and fourth generation. See Exodus 20:5. I do not think I need to say anything more.

THE SECOND DECREE OF KING DARIUS
Verse 25.

"The King Darius wrote unto all people, nations, and languages, that dwell in all the earth; Peace be multiplied unto you."

We now consider the second decree made by King Darius, to whom did it apply? Note that this decree encompassed the entire earth. The King wanted it to apply to all men. He wanted all men to honor and serve the Lord, the Living God.

Verses 26-27.

"I make a decree, That in every dominion of my kingdom men tremble and fear before the God of Daniel: for he is the Living God, and steadfast forever, and his kingdom that which shall not be destroyed, and His dominion shall be even unto the end.

He delivereth and rescueth, and he worketh signs and wonders in heaven and in earth, who hath delivered Daniel from the power of the lions."

I want you to note the content and the extent of this decree.

1. Daniel's God is a Living God, all other gods are idols, dead, worthless and unable to help anyone.

2. Daniel's God never changes, He is the same yesterday, to-day and forever.

3. Daniel's God rules a kingdom which shall never be destroyed, and no King can destroy it.

4. Daniel's God will rule this earth even to the end of time. King Darius looks beyond his temporal kingdom to God's eternal Kingdom which will never end.

5. Daniel's God is a God who delivers those who serve Him, keeping them from harm. He delivered three Hebrews, Shadrach, Meshach and Abed-Nego. He delivered Daniel.

6. Daniel's God manifests His power through signs and wonders and mighty miracles, both in heaven and on the earth.

7. Daniel's God delivered him, we have witnessed this wonderful deliverance with our own eyes. This is the fullest and most complete proof of His power, goodness and love.

Verse 28.

"So this Daniel prospered in the reign of Darius, and in the reign of Cyrus the Persian."

Need anyone say that Daniel prospered! Of course he did! Think of all that is contained in that one word "PROSPERED"! The prophet Daniel served five kings in his lifetime - King Nebuchadnezzar; King Evil-Merodach (his son); King Belshazzar (his grandson); King Darius, the Mede and King Cryus, the Persian. Under each King Daniel glorified God by his life.

Before we leave this chapter I want to give you the secret of Daniel's power for I know this will be helpful to you. Daniel had power not only with God but with men as well. Why was this true? Here is the secret, HE CONQUERED THE THREE GREAT BATTLES HE FACED IN HIS LIFE. Let me say that we all face these three great battles. They are,-

1. The Battle of the Flesh.
2. The Battle of the Soul.

3. The Battle of the Spirit.

His first trial, the battle of the flesh, took place shortly after he was carried into captivity and arrived in Babylon. He was one of those chosen to serve in the palace of the king, consequently he was expected to eat the king's meat and drink the king's wine. Daniel knew that some of the meat served was meat that had been offered to idols in sacrifice, and the wine that was served was likewise poured out as a libation before them. He also knew that they at times served meat which was pronounced unclean by Jewish law which was given by the God he served so his battle with the flesh consisted in his having to decide whether he would eat this meat and drink this wine and in so doing defile himself. So he requested the prince of the eunuchs to allow he and his three companions to eat food in keeping with God's demand. This request was granted.

His second battle, was THE BATTLE OF THE SOUL. Your soul is composed of three things, conscience, intellect and will. Daniel and his three companions as well as all the king's wise men, faced death if they could not tell the king what he had dreamed and its interpretation.

The intellect is involved here. The king's wise men were unable to tell the king what he had dreamed, they knew they faced death. Death stared them in the face and they were paralyzed by it. Daniel and his companions faced it also but Daniel in this battle of the soul, with a courage that was devoid of all personal fear, looked to the God he served for the answer. He knew that many lives depended upon him, he knew that only God could give his intellect the knowledge needed in this emergency. His will was determined to wait upon God until God gave him knowledge to reveal the dream and its interpretation. God did not fail Daniel. God will not fail you in this battle of the soul if you have the faith needed and will trust God completely and give Him the glory. Because of Daniel's abounding faith the knowledge of the dream and its interpretation was given to Daniel.

We come now to Daniel's third battle, the battle of the spirit. Daniel's first battle took place in the palace of the king; his second battle took place in his room where he met with the Living God and his third battle took place in the lion's den.

The battle of the spirit consisted of a threat against his faith in the Living God. The decree signed by King Darius demanded that all men abstain from prayer to anyone but the king for a period of thirty days. The penalty was death in the lion's den. Daniel conquered this battle of the spirit through his abounding faith in God. He never wavered but remained steadfast in his faith trusting God to deliver him, and his faith was rewarded as we have seen in the study of this chapter.

Dear reader, if you are going through a time of testing and trial, if you will keep the faith you will find in the emergency that THE FAITH WILL KEEP YOU! May you, too, be a person of such an abounding faith!

This ends the historical part of the book of Daniel. We now come to the prophetic portion which reveals to us the entire course of THE TIMES OF THE GENTILES from its beginning in the reign of King Nebuchadnezzar in the year 600 B.C. through to the glorious Millennial reign of our Blessed Lord Jesus.

We now begin the study of chapter VII.

.....

PART 2

THE PROPHETIC DIVISION

CHAPTERS 7-12

CHAPTER VII.
THE BEAST VISIONS

We come now to a change in this book of Daniel. All the events that preceded this seventh chapter have to do with the life of Daniel and his three companions Shadrach, Meshach and Abed-Nego and their relation to the king and to God. Daniel has, through the answers to prayer that God has given to him, been able to reveal the dream vision to King Nebuchadnezzar together with its interpretation, now in this seventh chapter and in the chapters that follow he tells us of the visions that God gave to him.

The chapters we have studied thus far have been almost entirely historical, the chapters we are now to study are prophetical. Daniel continues to reveal to us the events that are to take place; the coming events which cover the entire sweep of Gentile World power from its beginning to the end of this age.

True prophecy is two-fold, it is descriptive and predictive. The prophets were both "forth tellers" and "fore-tellers". They had both "insight" and "foresight". The messages they gave were given to them by the Holy Spirit, they were but the channels through which the message was given.

We should thank God every day that He has given to us the information concerning the coming events. We are not left in darkness and ignorance, true born again believers know, as they see these events that are recorded in God's Holy Word, fulfilled, that God is carrying out his program just as He gave it to us. Our faith is strengthened, our hopes are brightened, we are encouraged to make our lives produce for God in this age in which we live.

The visions given to Daniel which are recorded in this chapter were given to him shortly after the death of King Nebuchadnezzar and during tthe first years of the reign of King Belshazzar. Daniel was an old man when he received these visions, the Apostle John was also an old man when he received the visions which are recorded in the Book of the Revelation.

THE FOUR BEASTS
Verse 1.

"In the first year of Belshazzar King of Babylon Daniel had a dream and visions of his head upon his bed: then he wrote the dream, and told the sum of the matters."

During whose reign did Daniel have this beast vision? Note exactly what is said. This is the same King Belshazzar we learned about in chapter V. The chronological order has been disregarded deliberately in order that the historical part of the book might be a unity, standing by itself; and the prophetical part of the book, which we will now study, might not be interrupted by historical events that have to do with Daniel himself. I want you to note that Daniel gave us a detailed record of all his experiences; that he might not forget this most unusual dream he recorded it as soon as he rose from his bed.

Verse 2.

"Daniel spake and said, "I saw in my vision my night, and, behold, the four winds of heaven strove upon the great sea."

When did this dream vision take place? The four winds blowing from every direction upon the great sea and meeting upon its surface means forces stirring up the sea to its depth. Most Bible teachers say that the "great sea" mentioned is the Mediterannean sea, since this is known as "the sea of the prophets". See Ezekiel 47:10. It is called "the great sea" to distinguish it from the sea of Galilee and the Dead sea. Other prominent teachers of this age think that the term "sea" which is used here is symbolic, that it refers to the great, unorganized mass of mankind. When I was a student at Moody Bible Institute the late Dr. Gray, who was one of the leading Bible students of the world, also held this view. Now look up these Bible passages Matthew 13:47-50.; Revelation 13:1; Revelation 17:15. Now that you have looked up these references, do you agree with me that "the great sea" refers to people?

I think it would be wise to stop here, before we get into the study of the meaning of this dream vision of the beasts given by God to Daniel, to consider how far we should go in the interpretating some of God's words as being literal in its meaning and other portions as being symbolic. May I tell you how I study God's Holy Word? I believe that all of God's Holy Word is to be taken LITERALLY if what it says makes good sense. I do believe that God's Holy Word means JUST WHAT IT SAYS, UNLESS IT IS STATED THAT IT IS SYMBOLIC, OR else referred or considered after study to be so. I also believe, that all passages in God's Holy Word, that are definitely symbolic, should be interpreted by that which is literal. This is the plan I have followed in writing this book.

We can all see that this dream vision of the beasts is symbolic because God's Holy Word says so. The symbols given to us are, FOUR WINDS, THE GREAT SEA, FOUR GREAT BEASTS, TEN HORNS AND ANOTHER LITTLE HORN THAT HAD EYES AND A MOUTH AND ROSE UP IN WAR AGAINST GOD AND ALL BORN AGAIN BELIEVERS. So we must study God's Holy Word carefully, asking the Blessed Holy Spirit to give us spiritual discernment that we might know the meaning of these symbols.

Verse 3.

"And four great beasts came up from the sea, diverse one from another."

We are now ready to study the meaning of this dream vision of Daniel. He saw four great beasts that came forth out of this great sea, each beast was different from the other. Four is the number of the earth, these four beasts that Daniel saw are four kings, each a completely different person. Now note verse 17 of this chapter. Their subjects were different; their form of administration of government was different; their laws and customs were different. This is what is meant when we are told that they were diverse one from another.

THE WORLD EMPIRE OF KING NEBUCHADNEZZAR.
DANIEL 2:37-38.
Verse 4.

"The first was like a lion, and had eagle's wings: I beheld until the wings thereof were plucked, and it was lifted up from the earth, and made to stand upon the feet as a man, and a man's heart was given to it."

What strange creatures these four beasts really are! Who has ever seen a lion with wings? Or a four headed leopard? Or a beast with ten horns? We know now that these beasts are but symbols, for we are told that they represent four kings and their kingdoms. So it is natural for you to ask, "Who are these four different kings and what nations do they rule?

As we study this seventh chapter we are very soon made aware of the fact that we have in this chapter the SAME VISION that God gave to King Nebuchadnezzar only here it is expressed in another way, instead of using the image of a man with the parts of his body designating nations, God now uses BEASTS. Naturally you wonder why, you ask, "Why did God to this?"

In answer I would say that in the dream of King Nebuchadnezzar's great man image, the nations of the world are shown as he saw them. They were beautiful, mighty in power, vast and unlimited in resources. King Nebuchadnezzar was a pagan king, it was natural for him to see these Gentile nations as beauitful strong and powerful. Now in this dream image of the beasts which God gave to Daniel we are shown these same nations as they really are, greedy, selfish, ambitious, and terrible destructive. The dream vision of King Nebuchadnezzar shows these nations FROM MAN'S POINT OF VIEW, while Daniel's dream vision shows these same nations AS GOD SEES THEM. I hope you see the difference.

It may be you are asking the quesiion,- "Why does God repeat this dream vision in another form to Daniel if it covers the same ground as the dream vision of King Nebuchadnezzar which was given in chapter II?" Here is the answer - God wants us to study the information given, over and over again, until we thoroughly understand God's plan for the ages. But there is a decided difference in Daniel's beast vision, God now gives us much additional information, many more important facts are given us which were not given us in chapter II. King Nebuchadnezzar was an idolator, God would not give him the information He would give to His faithful servant Daniel, a man greatly beloved by God. How grateful we are that He has done so!

We now consider this first beast which we saw coming up out of the great sea. This beast looked like a lion but it had the wings of an eagle. The lion is known as the king of beasts and the eagle as the king of birds so we know at once that this lion is a symbol of the great Empire of Babylon of whom King Nebuchadnezzar was the head. The King of Babylon is compared to a lion in Jeremiah 4:7 and in Isaiah 5:29, he is said to fly as an eagle in Jeremiah 48:40 and Ezekiel 17:3.7. King Nebuchadnezzar was the greatest and the most powerful of all the Gentile world rulers. Dare we say that the eagle wings on this lion denote the speed with which King Nebuchadnezzar conquered the nations of the world and brought them all under his control? It would indeed seem so. But about these plucked wings? What do they mean? I believe they refer to the fact that when King Nebuchadnezzar had the entire known world under his control, he then gave all his time and energy to building palaces and making the city of Babylon the greatest city in the entire world. And from that time on the glory of the Babylon Empire began to fade, no farther extention of the Empire took place under King Nebuchadnezzar or under King Evil-Merodach his son, or under King Belshazzar, until the Empire was lost by King Belshazzar and became divided as we shall see in the days to come.

Another thought has been advanced by some Bible Teachers, they believe that the plucked wings may refer to the fact that several of the provinces such as Lydia, Media and Persia threw off the Babylonian yoke and set up kings of their own.

Then Daniel saw the lion lifted up and caused to walk on two feet instead of four. In Daniel 4:16 we read that a beast's heart was given to King Nebuchadnezzar, this I believe, refers to the humbling of King Nebuchadnezzar's pride, he had acted like a fierce and growling lion, God struck him down because of his pride, he then lived the life of a beast, he had a beast's heart in disposition and habits, and in Daniel 7:4 we are told that a man's heart was given to him. Do you think that this refers to the insanity of King Nebuchadnezzar? Most likely it does. God restored his sanity, he became a humble, pious man, and in this state he died.

THE WORLD EMPIRE OF MEDO-PERSIA. Daniel 2:39.
Verse 5.

"And behold another beast, a second, like to a bear, and it rassed up itself on one side, and it had three ribs in the mouth of it between the teeth of it: and they said thus unto it, Arise, devour much flesh."

We now consider this second beast which looked like a bear, which is next in power to the lion. There is a decided difference in movement between a lion and a bear, lion is swift in its attack, the bear is awkward and slow, it depends upon its strength and brute force to conquer its enemies. A command is given to this bear which is a symbol of the Medo-Persian Empire. Who gave the command. I believe it refers to the heavenly watchers spoken of in Daniel 4:17. We saw in this fourth chapter that this court of heaven makes the decisions which govern the actions of the leaders here upon this earth. It was these heavenly messengers who gave the command to "Arise, devour much flesh!"

Now I want to explain the meaning of this command. The Medo-Persian Empire conquered its enemies by hurling great masses of troops against them. Xerxe's expedition against Greece was carried out with a mass force of two and a half million (2,500,000) men. Naturally such a force would "devour much flesh" through exposure, disease and death.

Note that this bear "raised up itself on one side". This means that the Persian side of this dual Medo-Persian Empire, which came last, finally rose to power and became the controlling factor of the Empire. The three ribs between its teeth stood for the three kingdoms of Lydia, Babylon and Egypt who united to form a triple alliance, they tried to overcome the Medo-Persian Empire but were overcome and destroyed.

I want to add one more word regarding this bear which represents the Medo-Persian Empire. The Medo-Persian Empire was definitely inferior to the great Babylonian Empire of King Nebuchadnezzar, not in power but in wealth, in magnificience and in form of government. We shall see, as we continue our study, that these beasts do not rise all at once, they rise, one after another, they are spoken of as the first, the second and etc. They correspond to metals in the man image seen by King Nebuchadnezzar in his dream, with each beast weaker and inferior to the one that precedes it.

THE WORLD EMPIRE OF GREECE - Daniel 2:39: Daniel 8-21.
Verse 6.

"After this I beheld, and lo another, like a leopard, which had upon the back of it four wings of a fowl; the beast had also four heads; and dominion was given to it."

Daniel's dream vision now shows us a third beast which looked like a leopard. It had on its back four wings of a fowl, and it had four heads, just what does this beast represent? We find after careful study that this third beast is a symbol of the Empire of Greece, the third Empire to come upon the world scene. Daniel in Chapter II, verse 39 tells us that this beast refers to the belly and thighs of this man image of King Nebuchadnezzars' dream.

The leopard is a very lithe animal, swift, cat-like in its attack. This is a very good discription of the speed with which Alexander the Great, who with a small but well equipped army of 30,000 men conquered the forces of King Darius who had an army of 600,000 men, and in a short time brought the whole of the then civilized world under his control. The records of history tell us that Alexander the Great marched his armies more than 5100 miles in the short time of less than eight years. This is what the four wings on the leopard signified. King Alexander the Great was twice as swift as King Cyrus of Persia, since the lion which symbolized King Cyrus had but two wings and the leopard four. The leopard also had four heads, these represent the four kingdoms into which the Empire of Alexander the Great was divided after his death. We are told that he died as a result of a drunken debauch. He could conquer the then known world but he could not conquer himself. He was only a young man of 37 years when he died. His great Empire was then divided between his four leading generals, General Cassander was given Macedon and Greece in the west; General Lysimachus had Trace; General Ptolemy received Egypt and General Seleucus was given Syria.

I am wondering how many of you are like Alexander the Great, you are a slave to drink? You, too, are caught by the great unseen power of the drink habit. When you took your first drink you never for one moment ever dreamed that the day would come when you could not let drink alone. Now you are an alcoholic but even now you will not admit that this is true, but the truth is, you are a slave to drink. Unless you realize your lost condition and give the Holy Spirit the opportunity to deliver you, otherwise you are eternally lost!

THE WORLD EMPIRE OF ROME. Daniel 2:40-43; Daniel 7:23-24.

Verse 7.

"After this I saw in the night visions, and behold a fourth beast, dreadful and terrible, and strong exceedingly; and it had great iron teeth: it devoured and break in pieces, and stamped the residue with the feet of it: and it was diverse from all the beasts that were before it; and it had ten horns."

This fourth beast that Daniel saw was a monstrosity, it was so terrible in its appearance that no name could be found for it. It was incredibly strong, devouring some of its victims by tearing them apart with its strong iron teeth, and others (that is the previous beast with its powerful feet. Superlative adjectives are used to describe this beast but it was very difficult to do so).

We know from our past study that this terrible beast represents the great Roman Empire. It corresponds to the legs and the feet of King Nebuchadnezzar's man image he saw in his dream. When Rome reached the height of her power under Emperor Trajan, Rome was not only the conqueror of all the

112

land areas of the world, she was the master of all the seas as well. Yes, the entire world at that time was under the power of Rome, she ruled by brute force. In power and greatness, in extent of dominion, and in length of duration Rome was indeed diverse from all the other kingdoms.

Note that this beast which represented the Roman Empire had ten horns which verse 24 of this chapter tells us symbolizes ten kings or kingdoms. This corresponds to the ten toes of the man image of chapter II.

THE TEN HORNS AND THE LITTLE HORN
Verse 8.

"I considered the horns, and behold, there came up among them another little horn, before whom there were three of the first horns plucked up by the roots: and behold, in this horn were eyes like the eyes of a man, and a mouth speaking great things."

I want you to note how much additional information is given to us in Daniel's visions. In the man image given to King Nebuchadnezzar as recorded in Daniel, chapter II we are told that the ten toes were part iron and part clay and that the iron and the clay DO NOT MIX! I will explain the meaning of this later. In the dream vision of Daniel we are told that as he watched the actions of this terrible beast his attention was called to the ten horns. While looking at these ten horns he saw a little horn suddenly appear from among the ten horns, it kept growing larger, stronger and more powerful as he watched.

This little horn then destroyed three of the ten horns, they were pulled up by the roots. As Daniel carefully observed this little horn he saw that it had a man's eyes and a mouth that told of great things. What do you think the eyes and the mouth of this little horn signified? Did you say that you do not know? I am not surprised, for who this little horn is and what it does is given to us in verse 25 of this chapter which I will explain at length later. I must add this word, all the visions given to Daniel are given primarily to the Jewish people, though we, who are Gentiles, are involved in them as well. Before Daniel could ask God to explain to him the meaning of this little horn and its actions, he was given another vision.

Verse 9.

"I beheld till the thrones were cast down, and the Ancient of days did sit, whose garment was white as snow, and the hair of his head like the pure wool: his throne was like the fiery flame, and his wheels as burning fire."

Again I refer you to the man image seen by King Nebuchadnezzar, the record is given in Daniel, chapter II. Now turn back to chapter II and read verses 31-36. Now read again verses 34 and 35. Note that this great image was destroyed by the smiting stone which struck the image upon its feet causing it to collapse, the image was then broken into small pieces until it became like chaff which the wind carried away, scattering the chaff to the ends of the earth. Then the stone that smote the image grew larger and larger until it filled the earth.

Try to visualize if you can the destruction of this great man image. Keep this scene in your mind, now you are ready to read Daniel, chapter 7, verses 9-14. I want you to read these verses over several times until the magnitude and the solemnity of this tremendous scene becomes clear in your mind. Let me say this, dear reader, I know of no scene given us in all of God's Holy Word that is greater in its significance or more magnificent in its visualization than this scene. The smiting stone that struck the man image in Daniel, chapter II upon the feet causing the man image to collapse is here presented in definite detail in these verses 9-14 in this chapter 7. Now let me try to give you a picture of this great event as I see it and explain it as best I can,-

Remember this outstanding fact, this scene is not only a description of what Daniel saw in his dream vision given in chapter 7, it is a picture given to us of what is actually going to take place in the future when our victorious Lord Jesus is going to return to this earth with we, who are His true born again believers. You, my dear readers, if you are a true born again believer, will actually be here upon this earth with Him and all the redeemed,,you will see all these wonderful events as they happen before your eyes. Best of all, you will be living in your glorified body that is perfect in every respect. This is the body which was given to you when we were caught up to meet our Lord Jesus in the air. This will be a flesh and bones body. Think of how wonderful it will be to have a body with perfect sight, perfect hearing, perfect smell, perfect understanding, with everything perfect!

Who is this "Ancient of days"mentioned in this verse 9? I'll tell you, he is none other than our precious Lord Jesus. I want you to remember that our Lord Jesus existed long before He was born in Bethlehem of Judea. He was one with the Father IN THE BEGINNING, long before this earth, the sun, moon stars and the unnumbered host of galaxies were created. He was one with the Father and the Blessed Holy Spirit in the early hour of creation, they alone know when this took place. If there is any question in your mind concerning this statement I want you to turn to the book of Colossians, chapter one and read verses 14-16. Note especially what is said in verse 16. Now that you have read this record in God's Holy Word are you convinced that our Lord Jesus was one with the Father when this world was created? Mother, your children have, no doubt, asked you the question,-"Where did God come from when did God begin?" The words "Ancient of Days" in this verse 9 comes close to giving us an answer. "Days" always refers to a period of time, "Ancient" refers to "time in action". The Trinity, that is, God the Father, Jesus Christ the Son, and the Blessed Holy Spirit, ALWAYS EXISTED, always was, our Lord Jesus was one with the Father in the beginning.

You may ask, "How to you know that this "Ancient of Days" is our Lord Jesus? I ask you to read verse 9 carefully, consider what it says, note the description that is given. This can be no other than our Lord Jesus who called Himself "The Son of Man." (Matthew 9:6; 12:8) Now read the description given of this glorified "Son of Man" that the Apostle John saw centureis later,-

"And I turned to see the voice that spake with me. And being turned, I saw seven golden candlesticks;

And in the midst of the seven candlesticks one like unto the Son of man, clothed with a garment down to the foot, and girt about the paps with a golden girdle.

His head and his hair was white as snow; and his eyes were as a flame of fire;

And his feet like unto fine brass, as if they burned in a furnace; and his voice as the sound of many waters,

And he had in his right hand seven stars: and out of his mouth went a sharp two-edged sword: and his countenance was as the sun shineth in his strength."

Revelation 1:12-16.

When you compare this description of our Lord Jesus which was seen by the Apostle John with the description given in this verse 9 we now know that this "Ancient of Days" is our Lord Jesus. He has a four-fold purpose in leaving heaven with all the angels and the redeemed and coming back to this earth, now consider this four-fold purpose,-

1. He is coming to this earth to bring an end to the Battle of Armageddon.

2. He is coming to his earth to judge the Anti-Christ and the Fales Prophet and bring an end to their rule.

3. He is coming to this earth to judge the nations.

4. He is coming to this earth to set up His Millennial Kingdom and usher in a wonderful thousand years of peace.

Now let me explain in more detail the different things our

Lord Jesus will do when He returns to this earth. Our Lord Jesus is coming to this earth at this particular time, not as He came the first time as the Son of man to provide salvation for us; not as He will come a second time (and this may be soon), when He will raise the bodies of all true born again believers who died looking for His return; and when He will give all we who are born again believers our glorified bodies we will meet Him in the air; but this verse tells us of a time in the future when He is coming to complete the four-fold purpose I have just made clear to you.

This will be a time of judgment. This is the time when our Lord Jesus coming, not as a High Priest but as a JUDGE. You will note from the description given that He is not dressed as a High Priest but as a Judge, for He is dressed in white. This makes me think of the judges of England who wear white wigs.

Daniel was ignorant of these tremendous coming events, none of them had been revealed to him in King Nebuchadnezzar's dream man image. God wanted Daniel to know what was going to happen to the Gentile nations when our Lord Jesus returns to earth and He would set up His Millennial Kingdom. Step by step this information was to be revealed to him. As to how the Battle of Armageddon will be brought to an end, this would be revealed to him later.

I told you that our Lord Jesus will at this time come to this earth to judge the nations. This will take place in the Valley of Jehoshaphat. Now turn to the book of Joel chapter 3, read verses 1-2. This is the time when the "sheep nations" (that is the true born again Gentiles) and the "goat nations" (the unsaved Gentiles), will be separated, so that the "sheep nations" can enter and enjoy the Millennial reign of our Lord Jesus, the "goat nations" will be destroyed. This judgment of the nations will take place at the same time that our Lord Jesus restores the land given to them for an everlasting possession when God made His covenant with Abraham. Turn now to Genesis Chapter 12 and read verses 1-3 which tells of this wonderful promise which will be fulfilled at this time.

The trial and judgment of the Anti-Christ and the False Prophet will take place when our Lord Jesus returns to this earth, with we, the born again believers and a great unnumbered host of angels. Turn now to Revelation, chapter 19 and read verse 20, note that we are told here that our Lord Jesus, casts the Anti-Christ and the False Prophet into Hell after they have been tried and sentence pronounced.

I know that there are many men and women who are living in this space age who do not believe there is a Hell, but their unbelief does not change the fact. There is a Hell, GOD NEEDS A

HELL, all created personalities have a will which gives them the power of choice. You, my dear reader, have this power of choice, the soul and spirit you have, (which is the real "you"), will live on and on throughout the endless ages of eternity, somewhere, forever! There are only two places God has prepared for us. one is Heaven, the other is Hell, the place where all the wicked who have rejected God and the salvation He has provided through Christ are placed.

God cannot allow any sinner to enter Heaven so you see God needs a Hell. Hell was not created for man, it was created for the Devil and his angels, but all who do not accept the wonderful salvation God has provided for them, which is free to all, will be thrown alive into this Bible Hell. God has never sent anyone to Hell, God never will, for He is a God of love, "not willing that any should perish but that all should come to repentance." See II Peter 3:9. I pray dear reader, that you will never experience such a terrible end!

I have told you that our Lord Jesus is coming to this earth to bring an end to the rule of the Anti-Christ and the False Prophet, but I am not finished. There is still one more important reason why our Lord Jesus is returning to earth. He is coming to set up His millennial kingdom in which He will rule this earth for a thousand years. Believe me when I tell you that all life will be changed when our Blessed Lord Jesus arrives upon this earth, bringing, we, His redeemed saints, with Him. Daniel says, "I beheld, until the thrones were cast down." Verse. 9.

Who were these thrones? I believe these thrones were the thrones of the four World Empires - The Babylonian World Empire; the Medo-Persian World Empire; The Grecian World Empire and the great Roman World Empire. Some Bible teachers think these thrones may refer to the thrones of the ten kings that shall be reigning at the time our Lord Jesus returns to earth with His saints. God did not tell us, I give you what I believe.

Verse 10.

"A fiery stream issued and came forth from before him: thousand thousands ministered unto him, and ten thousand times ten thousand stood before him: the judgement was set, and the books were opened."

I want you to take plenty of time to carefully study these two verses. What a tremendous event this will be, for what we are told here is actually going to happen and the day is coming when YOU, if you are a true born again believer, (how I pray that you are) will see this prophecy given to Daniel, fulfilled. YOU WILL BE THERE, YOU WILL SEE IT WITH YOUR OWN EYES!

Now let me try to describe to you as best I can, what is actually going to happen as revealed in these two verses,-

When our Lord Jesus returns to this earth His throne is brought with Him on wheels of fire, (verse 9). His throne is surrounded with a halo which is called the righteousness of God, when our Lord Jesus takes his place upon His throne He will be dressed in white, as I have already told you, He will be dressed as a Judge, He has a red sash over his shoulder and breast, His hair will be white as wool. A great unnumbered host of angels, extending as far as eye can see, will be above and about Him. (See Revelation 5:11) thousand thousands ministered unto Him.

When this Heavenly Court begins its session the "Books" will be opened. What are these books? I believe they contain the day by day record of the infamous and impious record of the actions of the Anti-Christ and the False Prophet. They are opened as the trial begins. Dear reader, I must stop here long enough to tell you that God keeps two books, one book is the book of works, the other is the Book of Life. God has an individual book for every person born into this world, and a recording angel who keeps the record for each one of us. This book of works contains a record of every sin you have committed in your life, as well as every good deed. Do you know that the very secret thoughts of your heart are recorded in this, your book of works?

Then there came a day when you saw yourself a sinner and accepted our Lord Jesus as your own personal Saviour. On that day the Holy Blood of our Lord Jesus Christ was applied to your record which is written in your Book of works, on that day the complete record of every sin was blotted out, all your past sins will be remembered against you no more. On that day your name was written in God's Book of Life. Only Born again believers have their name written in God's Book of Life. Dear reader, is YOUR NAME written in God's Book of Life?

Verse 11.

"I beheld then because of the voice of the great words which the horn spake: I beheld even till the beast was slain, and his body destroyed, and given to the burning flame."

Sentence is now pronounced after the trial os the Anti-Christ and the False Prophet is completed. Now they will be thrown into the Lake of Fire. But even here at this trial the Anti-Christ continues to utter blasphemous words against our Lord Jesus. Daniel says, *"I beheld then because of the voice of the great words which the little horn (the Anti-Christ) spake"*. Verse 25 Sentence is carried out at once, the Anti-Christ and the False Prophet are thrown alive into the Lake of Fire. This is the end of them as far as this world is concerned. By their bodies being destroyed'does not mean that they are put out of existence, as some cults teach, we know they are alive because God's Holy Word in Revelation 20:10 tells us that after the Millennial reign of our Lord Jesus has ended, and the Devil himself is thrown into this same Lake of Fire, this beast (the Anti-Chirst) and the False prophet are still alive. Note that the word "are" is used, not the word "Were" as would be the case if the Anti-Christ and the False Prophet no longer existed. I hope this clear to you.

Verse 12.

"As concerning the rest of the beasts, they had their dominion taken away: yet their lives were prolonged for a season and time."

Most Bible teachers believe that the Beast spoken of in verse 11 which was slain refers to the Roman Empire. The Anti-Christ is never called a Beast in the Book of Daniel. The words, "the beast was slain and his body destroyed and given to the burning flame" is figurative language which tells of the end of the Roman Empire. We know that these words could not refer to the Anti-Christ who is called "the Little Horn" by Daniel and "the Beast" by the Apostle John in Revalation chapter 13 verses 1-8 for the Anti-Christ is not slain but is cast alive into the Lake of Fire as I have already told you.

We do know that the other beasts Daniel saw, that is, the lion, the bear, and the leopard which represent Babylon, Medo-Persia and Greece were not destroyed, they only had their dominion (power to rule) taken away. Persian, now known as Iran, (for the name was changed to Iran in 1935) and Greece still exist as nations to-day.

Verse 13-14.

"I saw in the night visions, and, behold one like the Son of man came with the clouds of Heaven, and came to the Ancient of days, and they brought him near before him.

And there was given to him dominion, and glory, and a kingdom, that all people, nations, languages, should serve him: his dominion is an everlasting dominion, which shall not pass away, and his kingdom that which shall not be destroyed."

This scene takes place in Heaven. Here is the order of events, which will actually take place in the days to come,- Daniel sees it as though it had actually happened,-

1. The second Coming of Christ for His saints has already taken place. The righteous dead have been raised, they, together with we, who are born again believers, have received our glorified bodies and have been caught up to meet our Blessed Lord Jesus in the air. See I Thessalonians 4:13-17 which tells of

this.

2. The Judgment of the believer is now over, the rewards have been given, soon the King of Kings and Lord of Lords will return to this earth where He will set up His Millennial Kingdom. Note that our Lord Jesus revives His Kingdom from the Father BEFORE He returns to this earth.

3. Meanwhile the Anti-Christ has been ruling the nations here upon the earth. He has massed his tremendous army of over two hundred million men, all riding upon horses, preparing for the battle of Armadgedon. This battle is NOT a war of man against man but is a war of man against God. Communism has completely dominated this earth, men everywhere curse God. I want you now to turn to Psalm 2 and read a record of what the rulers of the world under the Anti-Christ will do just before this great battle of Armageddon begins.

4. Now I want you to read slowly and carefully the entire chapter of Revelation 19. Remember, dear reader, This is a future event that is to take place, as I have told you several times. YOU will be there and take part in it, that is, if you are a born again believer and your name is written in God's Book of Life. Now for verse 9 of this 19th chapter, the marriage supper of the Lamb, (our Lord Jesus is called the Lamb), is now being enjoyed. All Heaven rings with the praises given to the Lamb, then at its conclusion, the Lord Jesus, with the great multitude of the Redeemed, so many they cannot be numbered, all clothed in white linen and all mounted upon white horses, are ready for the greatest event of all time.

Now our Blessed Lord Jesus, clothed in white, with a red sash draped over His right shoulder and breast and down over His thigh, upon which was written "King of Kings and Lord of Lords". Suddenly the heavens are rolled back as a scroll and He, with qll we who are the Redeemed, descend to this earth to bring to an end the rule of the Anti-Christ and the False Prophet, and the Battle of Armageddon. He will then set up His millennial kingdom.

Verse 15.

"I Daniel was grieved in my spirit in the midst of my body, and the visions of my head troubled me."

Daniel, in his vision saw this tremendous scene, he saw our Lord Jesus descend from Heaven to this earth bringing with Him the great multitude of the Redeemed. Daniel now knows that our Lord Jesus is going to reign here upon this earth; he knows that all nations and peoples will serve Him and that His Kingdom will endure forever, it will never be destroyed. Daniel was deeply moved by what he saw, he was troubled in his spirit. Why?

Because there was so much that he had seen in the vision that he could not understand.

Verse 16.

"I came near unto one of them that stood by, and asked him the truth of all this. So he told me, and made me know the interpretation of the things."

It was the magnitude of these events that completely overwhelmed Daniel, he wants to know the meaning of what he has seen, he wants these tremendous events to be made clear to him. The person who explained these coming events to Daniel was no doubt the angel Gabriel. Now turn to Daniel, Chapter 8: verse 16 where we are told that it was actually the angel Gabriel.

Verse 17.

"These great beasts, which are four, are four kings, which shall arise out of the earth."

This verse explains itself. As we have already seen, these four beasts symbolize the four Empires, one will follow the other.

Verse 18.

"But the saints of the most High shall take the Kingdom, and possess the Kingdom forever, even forever and ever."

What a wonderful promise is given to us! We, who are the saints which are spoken of here, will eventually possess and rule the governments of the world forever and ever! Even now, out of all the hundreds of denominations our Lord Jesus is taking a people who will love and serve Him. Those born again believers are known in God's Holy Word as "saints". We are those who are spoken of in God's Holy Word as "the church". It is not the denominational label that you carry that determines your position in God's Kingdom, it is whether you have the Holy Spirit living in your body. Turn now, if you will, to Romans 8:11, do you see that if you do not have the Holy Spirit living in your body you are NOT a true born again believer? Check your life, for this is very important. I know that we, who are born again believers are looked down upon by worldings, we are ridiculed, we are mocked, they sneer and make fun of us but the day is coming when our Lord Jesus will set up His Kingdom, and we will rule with Him, and His rule will last forever and ever! Praise the Lord for this wonderful promise!

Verse 19.

"Then I would know the truth of the fourth beast, which was diverse from all the others, exceedingly dreadful, whose teeth were of iron, and his nails of brass; which devoured, brake in pieces, and stamped the residue with his feet.;;

Daniel wants to know more about this fourth beast which was a monstrosity. He can understand the meaning of the other three

121

beasts that is the Lion, the Bear and the Leopard for their meaning was made clear, but this terrible fourth beast with its iron teeth and brass nails, what does this beast represent?

Verse 20.

"And of the ten horns that were in his head, and of the other which came up, and before whom three fell; even of that horn that had eyes, and a mouth that spake very great things, whose look was more stout than his fellows."

This terrible beast that had ten horns and the one little horn that grew stronger and stronger, this little horn that destroyed three of the ten horns pulling them up by the roots, this horn that had eyes like a man, shrewd, intelligent eyes, and a mouth that talked and boasted of its power, what about this horn? Who did it represent? Daniel was puzzled and perplexed.

Verse 21.

"I beheld, and the same horn made war with the saints, and prevailed against them."

We have already learned in our study that an Anti-Christ is coming. We now know that this little horn represents this Anti-Christ, we are now learning more about who he is, more about his character, more about what he does. We now know that he hates God and our Lord Jesus Christ, he hates God's born again believers, he wages war against them, keeping them under his power and control, and making them submit to his will under penalty of death.

Verse 22.

"Until the Ancient of days came, and judgment was given to the saints of the most High; and the time came that the saints possessed the kingdom."

This Anti-Christ will not be allowed to control the saints of God who are living upon the earth FOREVER, it will only be for a short period of time. I have already told you that we, the born again believers, shall possess and rule this earth with our Lord Jesus when He returns, but the Anti-Christ will prevail over the saints until our Lord Jesus returns to bring an end to his rule.

Verse 23.

"Thus he said, The fourth beast shall be the fourth kingdom upon earth, which shall be diverse from all kingdoms, and shall devour the whole earth, and shall tread it down, and break it in pieces."

We have already seen that this fourth beast whose looks are so terrible, represents the Roman Empire which in its day conquered and ruled the entire earth. It was indeed different from all the other Empires that preceded it, it ruled by brute force. The iron teeth identifies it with the iron legs of King

Nebuchadnezzar's man image.

Verse 24.

"And the ten horns out of this kingdom are ten kings that shall arise: and another shall arise after them; and he shall be diverse from the first and he shall subdue three kings."

As the centures pass this Roman Empire will be revived under a ten kingdom arrangement, for the ten horns on this beast represents these ten kings. There are two figures given in this verse that I want to explain, the first figure is the beast which represents this revived Roman Empire, the second figure is this little horn which represents the Anti-Christ. This Anti-Christ which I have mentioned before, is a most unusual character, much is said in God's Holy Word about him, we are told that when he appears upon the world scene he will destroy three of these ten kings, they will no longer exist.

Verse 25.

"And he shall speak great words against the most High, and shall wear out the saints of the most High, and think to change times and laws: and they shall be given into his hand until a time and times and the dividing of time."

What will be the attitude of the Anti-Christ toward God and the born again believers? When the Anti-Christ comes into power he will make a covenant with the Jews, he will aid them in the rebuilding of the Temple, I am told that much of the non-perishable material for the rebuilding of the Temple is NOW ON HAND in Jerusalem. At the end of three and a half years of his rule the Anti-Christ will break this covenant, he will enter the holy of holies of this new Temple which will have been completed and demand that he be worshipped as God. All who refuse will be beheaded. See Revelation 20:4. He will also demand that everyone living upon the earth wear his mark, a choice is given, it is either wear his name or his number. This is to be placed upon the forehead or the palm of the hand.

The Anti-Christ will also change times and laws. He will do away with all Sunday worship, every day will be alike. He will most likely change the mode of dress of both men and women, we can see from our study of God's Holy Word that the customs of the people living under the reign of the Anti-Christ will be entirely different from the way life is lived in this space age.

Some Bible Teachers tell us that the Jewish Rabbis unnerstand that the words in verse 25 "times and laws" refer to the Hebrew Sabbath and festivals and the laws which regulated them. The words "a time times and the dividing of time" from a prophetic standpoint in God's Holy Word means three and a half years. The word "time" means one year; "times" is two years and the dividing of time is a half year. Therefore a time, times and the dividing of time is 3½ years.

Verse 26.

"But the judgment shall sit, and they shall take away his dominion, to consume and to destroy it unto the end." This verse tells of the coming of our Lord Jesus to earth with all the great host of born again believers. This is the time when He will bring the reign of the Anti-Christ to an end as well as the Battle of Armageddon. This is the time when He will judge the nations separating the "sheep nations" from the "goat nations". This is the time when He will begin His millennial reign upon the earth after the Anti-Christ and the False Prophet have been tried and sentenced and then thrown alive into the Lake of Fire. This trial and sentence takes place when the Battle of Armageddon is ended. The "Times of the Gentiles", this period of time which began with the rule of King Nebuchadnezzar in B.D. 600 has now come to an end.

Verse 27.

"And the kingdom and dominion, and the greatness of the kingdom under the whole heaven, shall be given to the people of the saints of the most High, whose kingdom is an everlasting kingdom, and all dominions shall serve and obey him." This verse tells us that all the earth will now live under the wonderful and blessed rule of our Lord Jesus Christ. It will continue for 1000 years. We, who are the born again believers, will rule the world with our Lord Jesus, How wonderful this will be!

Verse 28.

"Hitherto is the end of the matter. As for me Daniel, my cogitations much troubled me, and my countenance changed in me; but I kept the matter in my heart." This closes the revelation which was given to Daniel when he was asleep. When he awoke he was white in the face for we are told that his countenance was changed. And no wonder, after experiencing such a world shaking vision! What he saw and experienced he kept in his heart, that is, he told no one about it or of what he had seen.

I know, dear reader, that there is much of what I have told you that you would like to know in greater detail. For instance, what took place upon this earth from the time that the great Empire of Rome was destroyed and the coming reign of the Anti-Christ? What is the difference between the terrible fourth beast that Daniel saw in his vision and the seven headed, ten horned beast that was seen by the Apostle John and recorded in Revelation, chapter 13? What added information can be given of this Anti-Christ who is to come at the end of this Gentile age? I shall try to answer these questions in the chapters we now will study. We turn now to chapter VIII.

CHAPTER VIII.
THE RAM AND ROUGH GOAT VISION

There are several things I want to tell you before we begin the study of thie eighth chapter. I am sure that you will agree with me that this Book of Daniel is one of the most unusual and informative books in all of God's Holy Word. Let me tell you why this is true. It is an unusual book not only in its content because it gives us a picture of world events that transpired which cover a period of time from the beginning of what is known in scripture as "The Times of the Gentiles" which began with the reign of King Nebuchadnezzar, the ruler of the Empire of Babylon in B.C. 600, until it is brought to a close by the coming of our Lord Jesus Christ to this earth with His saints.

The Book of Daniel is also an unusual book because it is written in two languages. The first part of the book, that is, chapter one and the first four verses ofchapter two, is written in the Hebrew language; then the Chaldean language, which is Aramiac, is used until the end of chapter seven. Then from chapter eight to the end of the book the writing is once again in Hebrew.

There is a reason for this. The first part of the book, which was written in Herbrew, tells us of the fall of Jerusalem when King Nebuchadnezzar carried the Jews captive to Babylon. Daniel and his three companions were among this number taken captive, these Jews were made slaves, they were kept in slavery for seventy years.

The rest of the Book, which was written in Aramiac to the end of chapter seven, has to do with the four great world Empires of Babylon, Medo-Persia, Greece and Rome. This part also deals with what we call "The Timms of the Gentiles", its beginning, its power and glory, and on and on to its final end.

The reason the Book is written in Hebrew from chapter eight to its close is because this part of the Book deals with the Jews, with the church and the born again believers and the events that will take place during the end time. These events narrow down from world wide prophecies to those concerning the Jews in the centuries between the exile and the coming of our Lord Jesus to bring an end to the rule of the Anti-Christ and the setting up of the millennial kingdom. We shall see that much of what you wanted to know is made clear as we study these last five chapters.

DANIELS VISION OF THE RAM.
Verse 1.
"In the third year of the reign of King Belshazzar a vision appeared unto me, even unto me Daniel, after that which appeared unto me at the first."
I suggest that you read this entire chapter before you begin its study, I want you to get all the events recorded firmly fixed in your mind. Note the definite time that is stated when this vision was given to Daniel. There is no guesswork, it was in the third year of the reign of King Belshazzar. The first year of the reign of King Belshazzar was the year 540 B.C. therefore the third year would be 537 B.C. It is believed that Daniel was around twenty years of age when he was carried captive to Babylon from Jerusalem by King Nebuchadnezzar, this was in 606 B.C. If this be true then Daniel was in his late eighties when this vision was given to him. The words "Which appeared to me from the first" no doubt refers to the vision given to him which is recorded in chapter VII.

Verse 2.
"And I saw in a vision; and it came to pass, when I saw, that I was at Shushan in the palace, which is in the province of Elam; and I saw in a vision, and I was by the river of Ulai."
Just as the time is stated in verse one as to when this vision was given to Daniel, so in this verse two we are told where Daniel was when this vision was given to him. He was at Shushan, the place where the King of Persia had his summer home. It was the capitol of the province of Elam. Stop now and turn to Jeremiah chapter 49 and read verses 34-39.

This city of Shushan was also the home of Nehemiah, and the events recorded in the Book of Esther took place here as well. The river Ulai which is mentioned here divided Shushan from Elymais, Eulues is another name given to this same river.

Verse 3.
"Then I lifted up mine eyes, and saw, and behold, there stood before the river a ram which had two horns: and the two horns were high; but one was higher than the other, and the higher came up last."
I want you to keep in mind the golden-headed man image which God gave to King Nebuchadnezzar and which is recorded

in chapter II, and also the vision of the four beasts given to Daniel and recorded in chapter VII, and now this present vision. Every one of the visions given by God to Daniel had to do with the nations of Babylon, Medo-Persia, Greece and Rome. You are already familiar with chapter VII which we have just studied, in which Daniel saw four great beasts who represented these four Empires.

In the vision given to Daniel and recorded in this chapter VIII the prophet Daniel sees, not four beasts but only two, a Ram and a He Goat, as only two Empires are involved, the Empire of Medo-Persia and the Empire of Greece. Babylon is no longer mentioned, it has run its course and was now soon to be taken over by Medo-Persia.

Verse 20 of this chapter VIII tells us that this Ram which was seen by Daniel represents Medo-Persia, the angel Gabriel makes this clear. The two horns upon the Ram represent the two kingdoms, the one was Media, the other Persia. Media was represented by the shorter horn, Persia the other. Persia came into power last, under the reign of King Cyrus and those who followed him. Persia became the greater and the most powerful of the two united kingdoms, hence is said "to be higher".

I hope you have noticed that this Ram which represents Medo-Persia corresponds to the Breast and Arms of silver of the man image given to King Nebuchadnezzar and recorded in chapter II, as well as the Bear of Daniel's vision given in chapter VII "the Bear which raised up on one side". Do you see now how our Heavenly Father is gradually giving to Daniel added information of events to come, and to us as well, in making clear the meaning of the vision?

Verse 4.

"I saw the Ram pushing westward, and northward, and southward: so that no beasts might stand before him, neither was there any that could deliver out of his hand; but he did according to his will, and became great."

The Ram in this vision is seen to be pushing forward in three directions, west, north and south. This means that the armies of Medo-Persia were on the march. Daniel saw that this Ram was exceedingly strong, it forced everything out of its way, none could stand against it or help its victims. The Ram did as it pleased, and it grew stronger with every conquest. The armies of King Cyrus represented by this Ram, were sweeping everything before them.

In chapter VII we saw a Bear with three ribs between its teeth. This Bear likewise represents the Empire of Medo-Persia whose armies are now driving forward conquering everything before them. Babylon, Lydia and Egypt were the three nations represented by the three ribs in the mouth of the Bear. These three nations had formed a Triple Alliance, they put forth their best effort to stop this fast growing power of Medo-Persia but were unable to do so. These three nations were defeated as I told you in our study of chapter VII. This Ram, which represented Medo-Persia, pushed forward west, north and south conquering all the territory covered. Medo-Persia now controlled all the land from India to Ethopia, over 127 provinces. Note that this is mentioned in the Book of Esther, chapter 1, verse 1.

The Ram now became the insignia of the Empire, coins recently unearthed show a Ram lying down on one side of the coin, there is a Ram's head on the other side. Thus does archaeology verify and confirm the statements given in God's Holy Word.

DANIEL'S VISION OF THE ROUGH HE GOAT
Verse 5.

"And as I was considering, behold, an he goat came from the west on the face of the whole earth, and touched not the ground: and the goat had a notable horn between his eyes."

Note the word "considering", Daniel was giving a great deal of serious thought to what God was revealing to him in this dream vision. Do you agree with me that God is, in this space age, through the many disastrous earthquakes, unusual weather conditions, unrest and upsets, broken homes and lies, famine, pestilence, drug addiction, wars among the nations and etc. calling us to consider and observe these things in the light of God's Holy Word? Surely in the light of these events you must be convinced that God is behind these things now taking place in the world. He is carrying out His pre-determined plan. The poet Lowell expressed his belief of this in these words,-

"Truth forever on the scafford, wrong forever on the throne. Yet that scafford sways the future, and behind the dim unknown Standeth God within the shadow, keeping watch upon His own."

The Prophet Daniel now sees a He-Goat in his vision, we are told in verse 21 of this chapter that this Rough He-Goat represents the Empire of Greece, or perhaps I should say the King of Greece for the King represents the Empire. The goat has always been the insignia of the Grecian or Macedonian people. The goat was the insignia of the nation dating back to King Caranus, the first king, who with his people were seeking a home. The King was advised to take a herd of goats for his guide, so later, seeing a herd of goats escaping from a storm he followed them and the place where they stopped for shelter he established the city of Edessa, this city became the seat and headquarters of his Empire. He named it Aegea or goat town, the sea about it he called the Aegean sea or the goat sea. It carries the name to this day.

Alexander the Great, ruler of the Greek Empire called his son Alexander Aegus, the son of a goat, this shows the important place the goat occupied in the history of Greece. God referred to Alexander the Great as "The Goat". This name was given long before the legend was established. Hence we see, once again, that our Heavenly Father knows the end even from the beginning.

This Goat (Alexander the Great), came from Europe which is west of Asia. This is what is meant by the words "He came from the west". The words "he touched not the ground" means that the armies of King Alexander the Great moved so swiftly that they carried everything before Them. The wings on the Leopard beast in the vision we studied in chapter VIII illustrate the same point.

Verses 6-7.

"And he came to the ram that had two horns, which I had seen standing before the river, and ran unto him in the fury of his power.

And I saw him come close unto the Ram, and he was moved with choler against him, and smote the Ram, and brake his two horns: and there was no power in the Ram to stand before him, but he cast hom down to the ground, and stamped upon him: and there was none that could deliver the Ram out of his hand."

These verses tell in a few words of the defeat and the complete overthrow of the Empire of Medo-Persia by King Alexander the Great. The Rough He-Goat (Alexander the Great) rushed furiously at the town-hroned Ram (Medo-Persia), he broke off both his horns which left the Ram helpless. The Rough He-Goat now knocked him down and trampled upon him, for there was no one who could or would help him. The Armies of King Darius of Medo-Persia were defeated and completely routed by Alexander the Great at Granicus in Phrygia.

King Alexander the Great then attacked the armies of King Darius on another front and defeated them, this took place at the Straits of Issus in Cilicia; the final defeat and the destruction of the armies of King Darius took place on the plain of Arbela in Syria, Medo-Persia as an Empire was so completely defeated by Alexander the Great that the nation ceased to exist anymore as an Empire.

Let me add this additional word which I want you to know. King Darius, using spies, tried to bribe the generals of King

Alexander the Great, he tried to get one of the friends of Alexander to kill him. When King Alexander heard of this, he, who was already enraged because of the Persian invasions of Greece, and their terrible cruelties of the Greek people determined that he would not rest until King Darius was killed and the Empire of Medo-Persia was brought under his control. This is what is meant when God's Holy Word says, "the He-Goat was moved with choler (fierce anger) against the Ram". The words "none could deliver the Ram out of his power" means that all the immense Armies of Medo-Persia could not save the Ram from the armies of Alexander. Stop here and note what is said in Psalm 33:16.

Then King Darius was treacherously murdered by one of his generals, thus what he planned for Alexander the Great happened to himself. The saying, "Chickens always come home to roost" illustrates this truth. You may recall that Haman, in the Book of Esther, planned to hang Mordecai the Jew then later, this same Haman was hanged himself upon the very scaffold he had erected to hang Mordecai. "Be sure your sin will find you out". Numbers 32:23 says God's Holy Word. "Whatsoever a man soweth, that shall he also reap." Gelatians 6:2.

Verse 8.

"Therefore the He-Goat waxed very great; and when he was strong, the great horn was broken; and for it came up four notable ones toward the four winds of heaven."

Medo-Persia was now so completely conquered that the Empire disappears from the world scene. Greece (The Rough He-Goat)ruled by Alexander the Great, has now become the great ruling World-Empire. This Empire corresponds to the Belly and Thighs of brass of the man image of Daniel, chapter II, as well as the four headed Leopard Daniel saw in his vision which is recorded in chapter VII. History tells us that Alexander the Great sat down and cried because there were no more worlds to conquer.

But while Alexander could conquer nations he could not conquer HIMSELF. I have told you this before, I emphasize it now, what a lesson we can learn from this! God's Holy Word says, "He that ruleth his spirit is greater than he that taketh a city" Proverbs 16:32. King Alexander the Great died as a result of a drunken debauch, aggravated by a fever. He was only 32 years old, the age when our Lord Jesus BEGAN his ministry. Thus the horn of this great Rough He-Goat was broken at the height of his power.

The "four notable ones that came up toward the four winds of heaven" were King Alexander's four leading generals. After the death of Alexander which took place in B.C. 323 his brother,

Philip Aridoeus was proclaimed King of the Empire of Greece but his reign was very short, for he was murdered, as were King Alexander's two infant sons Alexander Aegus and Hercules. King Alexander's four leading generals were represented by the four notable horns that came up out of the place where the one great horn had been. (verse 5). Daniel saw in this vision that these four notable horns pointed toward the four winds of heaven which represented the four directions of the compass which are north, south, east and west, in other words these four generals now governed the entire earth. They were also represented in Daniel's vision as a leopard which had four heads.

We see now that within a short period of years after the death of Alexander the Great the Empire of Greece was divided as follows:

General Seleucus ruled the provinces of Syria and Babylon in the west.

General Lysimachus ruled Thrace and the northern provinces.

General Cassander ruled Macedonia and the western provinces.

General Ptolemy ruled Egypt and the southern provinces.

Verse 9.

"And out of one of them came forth a little horn, which waxed exceeding great, toward the south, and toward the east, and toward the pleasant land."

Bible students are not agreed as to whom is meant by this little horn which came out of one of the four horns of this Rough He-Goat which is mentioned in this verse. Who is this little horn? Who does it represent? Schofield Bible thinks that it refers to King Antiochus Epiphanes who was the 8th king of Syria. Others think that the Roman Empire is meant, still other Bible Teachers believe it refers to the Anti-Christ who is to come, after all true born again believers are caught up to be with our Blessed Lord Jesus (I Thessalonians 4:13-17.) I hold to this view because I believe that it is proved by verse 23 of this same chapter.

Let me stop here long enough to say that while the first three World-Empires of Babylon, Medo-Persia and Greece succeeded each other without a break, there was a considerable period of time between the ending of the Empire of Greece and the taking over of the Empire by the four generals and the "latter time of their kingdom", the period when the Anti-Christ shall be revealed and "The Times of the Gentiles" brought to and end.

Dear reader, I cannot believe that Antiochus Epiphanes is this little horn that is mentioned. It is true that he hated the Jews, that he cruelly persecuted them, he conquered Jurusalem, he profaned the Temple of God by sacrificing a sow upon the altar and sprinkling its broth all over the Holy Place. You can image how this angered and insulted the Jews! He also demanded that they worship the idol God Jupiter, he set up a statue of this idol in the Holy Place. There is much more that could be given that this wicked King accomplished, it is true that in many respects he answers to the description given in verses 9 and 10 but the angel Gabriel tells us that this little horn is not to rise "until the latter time" *when the transgressors have come to the full" (verse 23)*. You see these four Kingdoms are to be a definite part of the ten kingdom revived Roman Empire which will come into existence at the closing period of "The Times of the Gentiles". Since this little horn is not to rise until this latter time, as the angel Gabriel tells us, then we know that Antiochus Epiphanes is NOT this little horn.

I know there are those who will not agree with me. I have no quarrel with anyone. I am trying as best I can to give you what I believe is taught in God's Holy Word. If you want to believe that Antiochus Epiphanes is this little horn, God Bless You, go ahead and believe it. But do consider carefully what I am trying to give you.

There is still more what I consider proof that Antiochus Epiphanes is NOT this little horn. He was but one of twenty-six kings who ruled Syria during these years. This little horn is a separate and a distinct personage. Verse 10 tells us that this little horn became very great, this could never be said of Antiochus Epiphanes. Verse 25 says that this little horn is to "stand up against the Prince of Princes". This Prince of Princes is our Lord Jesus Christ. Antiochus Epiphanes was dead and buried 160 years before our Lord Jesus Christ was born, so it could not have been him. Then too, we are told that this little horn is to be "broken without hand" (verse 25). To know what this means turn to II Thessalonians 2:8. Since Antiochus Epiphanes dies a natural death in B.C. 164 how could he be the little horn? This convinces me that he was only a type.

We know now by what the angel Gabriel has told us that this little horn represents the coming Anti-Christ who will come into power at the time of the end. Notice these words, "the time of the end." The real meaning of these words is that this is the time when the Anti-Christ will rule the world, the time when Gentile world-power will be ended. So you can see that Daniel's vision of the Ram and the He-Goat go far beyond the age in which he lived, it extended on for many centuries, on and on, past this age in which we are now living, on to the final end of "The Times of the Gentiles".

We are told that this little horn became "exceedingly great" toward the south (this refers to Egypt and the area assigned to General Ptolemy), and toward the east (this refers to the area assigned to General Seleucus), and toward the pleasant land. The words "pleasant land" in God's Holy Wrrd always means Palestine. For proof turn now to Psalm 106:24; Jeremiah 3:19; Daniel 11:16.

Verse 10.

"And it waxed great, even to the host of heaven: and it cast down some of the host and of the stars to the ground and stamped upon them."

This is one of the difficult verses of this prophecy to understand. The words "host of heaven" are found but three times in God's Holy Word, in Deuteronomy 4:19 and Jeremiah 8:2. They always refer to angels. We know that the little horn mentioned in verse 9 is the coming Anti-Christ and this verse 10 refers to him, could it be that this Anti-Christ had conflict with some of these angels of God who surround us (Psalm 91:11) and overcame them? Give this some thought.

Verses 11-12

"Yes, he magnified himself even to the prince of the host, and by him the daily sacrifice was taken away, and the place of his sanctuary was cast down.

And an host was given him against the daily sacrifice by reason of transgression, and it cast down the truth to the ground; and it practised and prospered."

We are considering now this little horn who became exceedingly great and powerful. I do believe that these verses definitely refer to the coming Anti-Christ who will come to power AFTER our Lord Jesus Christ has come to earth and taken all the

We are considering now this little horn who became exceedingly great and powerful. I do believe that these verses definitely refer to the coming Anti-Christ who will come to power AFTER our Lord Jesus Christ has come to earth and taken all the born again believers to be with Him. You see, dear reader, that Daniel's vision of the Ram and the He-Goat go far beyond the time of the reign of Antiochus Epiphanes as I have already told you, he is but a type of this coming Anti-Christ, this personage that is spoken of in these verses. This Anti-Christ is also called "The Beast" in Revalation 13.

That this personage (the little horn) is the Anti-Christ is proven by verses 23-25 of this chapter for the angel Gabriel tells us so. Consider these verses at length for they are important. This Anti-Christ even has the boldness to challenge the "Prince of the Host", for this is no other than the Archangel Michael who commands God's great army in Heaven. We are now told that this Anti-Christ stopped the Jews from offering the daily sacrifices which were offered to the Living God, he defiled the place of the sanctuary (the Temple of God) which he helped the Jews build, he entered the Holy of Holies in the Temple and demanded that all the people worship him as God.

"A host was given him" means that our Heavenly Father did not allow the Archangel Michael with the great army of the Host of Heaven to destroy the Anti-Christ for his time had not yet come. As a result the Anti-Christ gave the people of the world over to carry on every kind of sin, truth, morality and righteousness all were done away with completely.

Verses 13-14

"Then I heard one saint speaking, and another saint said unto that certain saint which spake, How long shall be the vision concerning the daily sacrifice, and the transgression of desolation, to give both the sanctuary and the host to be trodden under foot?

And he said unto me, Unto two thousand and three hundred days; then shall the sanctuary be cleansed."

The vision is now almost complete, The Prophet Daniel hears a conversation between two of God's messengers (they were angels, see Hebrews 1:13-14.) What question did one angel ask of the other? I know this question asked may not be clear to you, let me word the question into modern English so you can understand what is asked, the question asked is,- "How long will God allow the Anti- Christ to deny the Jews, who are God's chosen people, permission to carry on their sacrifices, how long will the Anti-Christ be allowed to desecrate the Temple of God and to destroy the host? (the Jews).

We are now dealing with the time when the Anti-Christ is in power. It is the end time, the closing days of Gentile world power, known as "The Times of the Gentiles". The question asked in verse 13 is now answered, the first messenger (an angel) is now told that this little horn who is the Anti-Christ will be allowed to do what he will for Two Thousand Three Hundred Days. Verse 26 of this chapter calls these days "evenings and mornings" when we consider them as actual days, which we should do, we have 1150 days or about 3½ years. These days begin when the Anti-Christ brings an end to the offering of the daily sacrifice in the Temple. We know that this coming Anti-Christ will rule this world for seven years, he will come to power AFTER we, who are the born again believers are taken out of this world to be with our Lord Jesus when He returns. The Anti-Christ will then make a covenant with the Jews, he will aid them in the rebuilding of the Temple, but in the middle of his seven year rule he will break his covenant with them, and as I have told you before he will not allow them to continue offering the daily sacrifice, he will enter the Holy of Holies and desecrate it with his presence, then he will demand that he be worshipped as god, all who refuse to worship worship him will be beheaded.

This will usher in the greatest time of trouble this world has ever known, it is called "The Great Tribulation". This is clearly spoken of in Matthew 24 verses 21-22. I ask you to consider these verses. This time of trouble will last for 1150 days or three and a half years. We are now told that the sanctuary (the temple) will NOT be cleansed and the "daily sacrifice" renewed until this period of days has ended.

Verses 15-16.

"And it came to pass, when I even I Daniel, had seen the vision, and sought for the meaning, then, behold, there stood before me as the appearance of a man.

And I heard a man's voice between the banks of Ulai, which called, and said, Gabriel, make this man to understand the vision."

The vision given to the Prophet Daniel is now ended, no further information was given to him. He now wants to know and understand the meaning of what he has seen and heard. This verse says that Daniel "sought for a meaning" God knowing this, for God knows the inmost thought or our hearts, sent a personality that we are told looked like a man. Who was this person? Was it our Lord Jesus? Or was it the Archangel Michael or the angel Gabriel? The answer to these questions is now given, it was the angel Gabriel. The person across the river asked the angel Gabriel to reveal to Daniel the meaning of the vision.

Verse 17.

"So he came near where I stood: and when he came, I was afraid, and fell upon my face: but he said unto me, Understand, O son of man; for at the time of the end shall be the vision."

What does the angel Gabriel do? What effect did his approach to Daniel do to him? What name did he call Daniel and what message did he give to him? It is important that you know why God gave Daniel this vision, God wanted Daniel to know and record the events that were to come, the events that are to take place as the "TIMES OF THE GENTILES" come to a close. Note the words "the time of the end." This is not the time when the world will come to an end, it is the time when Gentile World Power will come to an end. This world will continue on and on for a thousand and more years longer when our Lord Jesus begins

His wonderful reign. The words "the time of the end" are mentioned many times in the Book of Revalation. It is this space age, dear reader, the age in which we are living to-day.

Verse 18.

"Now as he was speaking with me, I was in a deep sleep on my face toward the ground: but he touched me, and set me upright."

We are not suprised that Daniel was overcome by what he has seen. Suppose that you had received this vision and then you had the angel Gabriel come to you and you heard one tell the angel Gabriel to explain the vision to you and you realized its significance, wouldn't you be overcome? I think the words "a deep sleep" mean that Daniel fell to the ground in a dead faint, when he came to, he was too weak to stand, this experience was too much for him. You must remember that Daniel was an old man. What does the angel Gabriel do to Daniel? What does he say to him?

Verse 19.

"And he said, Behold, I will make thee know what shall be in the last end of the indignation: for at the time appointed the end shall be."

The Prophet Daniel is now brought to a realization that God is telling him what is going to happen, not only in the immeidate future but in the centuries to come. The angel Gabriel says to him, "Daniel , I was sent by God to tell you what is going to happen in the last and final days of this Gentile age. It will be at a time of terrible suffering and sorrow for all who are living upon the earth in those days.

Daniel has, thus far, in the vision given to King Nebuchadnezzar and recorded in chapter II, been given knowledge of events to come which cover the entire course of "THE TIMES OF THE GENTILES" from their beginning to their end.

Verse 20.

"The Ram which thou sawest having two horns are the Kings of Media and Persia."

The Angel Gabriel now explains in detail the vision God gave to Daniel. The Ram with the two horns represents the Empire of Medo-Persia. The two horns represent King Darius of Media and King Cyrus of Persia.

Verse 21.

"And the rough Goat is the King of Grecia: and the great horn that is between his eyes is the first King."

The rough He-Goat Daniel saw in his vision represents the Empire of Greece. The horn this He-Goat had between his eyes represents King Alexander the Great, who was the first King of the Great Grecian Empire.

Verse 22.

"Now that being broken, whereas, four stood up for it, four Kingdoms shall stand up out of the nation, but not in his power." The four Kingdoms that shall stand up are the four divisions of King Alexander the Great's Empire which was taken over by his four generals after his death and the extermination of his family. I have told you of this division earlier in this chapter. These generals are not of the family of Alexander, nor do they have his strength, or ability or military genious. This is the meaning of the words, "not of his power."

Verse 23.

"And in the latter time of their Kingdom, when the transgressors are come to the full, a King of fierce countenance and understanding dark sentences, shall stand up." I want you to note the words, "In the latter time of their Kingdom". All the events that precede this latter time took place during the height and glory of the Kingdoms of Medp-Persia and Greece and the centuries that followed. But now we are concerned with the events that are to take place in this space age and beyond, for verses 23 to the end of Chapter VIII deal with the closing days of the "TIMES OF THE GENTILES", the coming of the Anti-Christ and life as lived under his rule, for this Anti-Christ is the little horn mentioned in verse 9.

The words, "when the transgressors are come to the full" refers to the conditions which will exist in this space age, and the years before and during the reign of the Anti-Christ. Look at life as it is being lived to-day, the broken homes and lives, the increase of divorce, the increase in crime, the increase in drug addictions, the increase of rebellious youth, doesn't it seem to you that "transgressors have come to the full"? Many changes in living will occur, God's Holy Word gives us many signs which tell us that we are fast coming to the end of the TIMES OF THE GENTILES.

I want you to turn now to the 24th chapter of Matthew, I want you to take the time to read slowly the entire chapter. I want you to consider all the signs that are given which will be fulfilled BEFORE the Anti-Christ appears. We are told that wars, rumors of wars, nation rising against nation, pestilences, famines, and earthquakes are to come, do you agree with me that all of these signs are now being fulfilled in this space age in which we live? Now turn to II Timothy chapter 4, we read here of what God's Holy Word tells shall take place in our church life just before our Lord Jesus returns to earth, there will be a wide spread departure from the faith, there will be much activity by seducing spirits (demons) free love, doctrines of devils (modern spiritualism). II Timothy chapter 3 tells us still more of the conditions which will exist in this day, and II Thessaloians chapter 2 tells us what will take place when this man of sin (the Anti-Christ) is revealed. Consider all these signs carefully, note that they are taking place before our eyes, NOW! Surely the return of our Lord Jesus who is coming to take all ture born again believers to meet Him in the air is near! Are you ready to meet Him if He should come today?

The "King of fierce countenance" spoken of in this verse 23 is this Anti-Christ. He will, no doubt, be a man who has a striking personality, a man whose features will be powerful and imposing, will create fear in the hearts of men just by his looks. He will be shrewd, very wise and skillful in all affairs of world government. I think this is what it means when it says he understands "dark sentences".

Verse 24.

"And his power shall be mighty, but not by his own power: and he shall destroy wonderfully, and shall prosper, and practise, and shall destroy the mighty and holy people."

This verse gives us more information regarding this coming Anti-Christ. "His power shall be mighty, but not by his own power", these words tell me that the power the Anti-Christ has, is power which is given to him by the devil. We know that the devil is an imitator, our Lord Jesus is God who left Heaven to come to earth and live in a human body, even so the Anti-Christ will be a man, motivated and controlled by the devil. Now turn to Matthew 24, verse 15, this tells us that this Anti-Christ is going to enter the Holy of Holies of the Temple in Jerusalem and demand that he be worshipped as God.

This Anti-Christ, through the power given to him by the devil, will be able to "destroy wonderfully". This means that he will kill all who oppose him, none dare withstand him, he despises and hates all who love the Lord, who honor and serve Him. All such are killed.

Verse 25.

"And through his policy also he shall cause craft to prosper in his hand; and he shall magnify himself in his heart, and by peace shall destroy many: he shall also stand up against the Prince of princes; but he shall be broken without hand."

This coming Anti-Christ will usher in a great industrial age. I believe everyone will have his social security card and number, there will be short hours and big pay. There will be no unemployment problem under his rule, everyone will marvel at the wisdom and power of the Anti-Christ. This is what it means when we are told "he shall cause craft ot prosper".

This verse says, "he shall magnify himself in his heart," he boasts of the power which he possesses, he is just the opposite of our Lord Jesus who humbled Himself, who took the form of a servant, who became obedient unto death, even to death upon the cross. Turn now to chapter 2 of the Book of Phillippians, write down the seven steps taken by our Lord Jesus.

This Anti-Christ will "stand up against the Prince of princes" This prince is our Lord Jesus. The Anti-Christ will have such power that he is ready to face our Lord Jesus in battle. "He shall be broken without hand" tells us that this Anti-Christ will, with his assistant the False Prophet, be captured by our Lord Jesus and thrown alive into the lake of Fire. See Revelation 19, verse 20. This will take place when our Lord Jesus returns to earth with all we, who are His born again believers. If you, dear reader, are a born again believer, you will see our Lord Jesus bring and end to the Battle of Armageddon, you will see Him bring an end to the terrible reign of the Anti-Christ and the False Prophet.

Verse 26.

"And the vision of the evening and the morning which was told is true: wherefore shut thou up the vision; for it shall be for many days."

The vision of the morning and the evening refers to the two thousand three hundred days spoken of in verse 14. This has to do with the time when Jerusalem will be trodden down by the Gentiles. See Luke 21, verse 24. When the Anti-Christ takes over control of this world he will make a covenant with the Jews, he will aid them in the rebuilding of the Temple. But at the end of three and a half years he will break this covenant, he will bring in the greatest time of trouble this world has ever known. I have told you this before, I will deal with these coming events more in detail in the coming chapters. Note that the words "for many days" are used again here.

Daniel is told that the events revealed to him in the vision will actually come to pass. However centuries are to pass BEFORE this Anti-Christ will come upon this world scene. Daniel is commanded to tell no one of what he has seen and what has been told to him.

Verse 27.

"And I Daniel fainted, and was sick certain days; afterward I rose up, and did the king's business; and I was astonished at the vision, but none understood it."

As a result of what Daniel has seen and heard in this vision Daniel fainted, experiencing all this was more than his old worn out body could bear. He was sick for some days, than he arose from his sick bed and continued his government task. He did not understand all that was revealed to him in this vision, there was too much involved in it.

The reason the angel Gabriel did not give Daniel a full understanding of the vision is because he had been given all he could take.

CHAPTER IX.
THE PROPHECY OF THE SEVENTY WEEKS

This ninth chapter of the Book of Daniel is one of the most important chapters in the book because it gives the date when the seventy weeks begin. The world powers recede from view, this chapter explains the vision given to Daniel of the seventy weeks, it tells of the salvation promised by the Messiah. The Jews naturally expected this salvation would be given to them when they returned to Jerusalem AFTER the 70 years of captivity had ended, it was promised to them by the earlier prophets who were ignorant of God's plan in its completeness. They did not know that seventy times seven years would have to pass before this salvation would be given.

The vision of the seventy weeks, which is recorded in this Chapter IX was given in the third year of the reign of King Belshazzar, this was in B.C. 528. It was in the same year that the events given in this ninth chapter took place, in fact, less than a year passed by between these two chapters. This 9th chapter contains much additional information concerning the person and the work of the coming Anti-Christ who will rule the entire world after all the born-again believers have been caught up to be with the Lord Jesus when He returns.

This chapter also contains the prayer of the Prophet Daniel for his people, this prayer is one of the most wonderful prayers that ever came from the heart of man. It is a prayer which expresses such humiliation and consecration of life that we cannot read it without being deeply moved, at least I was.

I hope, dear reader, that you will give much careful study to this chapter, you will find it will be worth all the time you spend upon it. Note especially the vital prophetic information given to us, do not leave this chapter until you have mastered its message to its smallest detail.

I want to add one more word, I am sure that you have already realized that in this book of Daniel, the story of the four great Empires, each following the other, and the events which follow which take us to the end of the age (not the end of the world), are repeated over and over, but each time these past and coming events are given, additional information is given to us. You will find this true once again in this chapter.

Verse 1.

"In the first year of Darius the son of Ahasuerus, of the seed of the Medes, which was made King over the realm of the Chaldeans;"

In chapter V, verse 31 we are given the first reference to Darius, the Mede. We are told in this verse 1 that he was the son of King Ahasuerus, that the time was B.C. 538, it was the last year of the reign of King Belshazzar and the beginning of the reign of King Darius. The vision we considered in chapter VIII was given to the Prophet Daniel while King Belshazzar was still upon the throne. The King was killed the same night that he held the terrible feast, the time when he profaned the Holy golden vessels of God that had been used in the Temple at Jerusalem. It was the night that the handwriting was written upon the wall. That night King Darius took over the reign of the Empire of Babylon. It was during the close of this year that the vision of the seventy weeks was given to the Prophet Daniel and explained in this chapter.

Verses 2-3.

"In the first year of his reign I Daniel understood by books the number of the years, whereof the word of the Lord came to Jeremiah the prophet, that he would accomplish seventy years in the desolations of Jerusalem.

And I set my face unto the Lord God, to seek by prayer and supplications, with fasting, and sackcloth and ashes ..."

Much more important information regarding these coming events is given to us in this second verse ...

1. DANIEL WAS A BUSY MAN, HE WAS THE PRIME MINISTER OF THE GREATEST EMPIRE ON EARTH IN HIS DAY. Yet in spite of the fact that he carried the load of state affairs, he still took the time to study God's Holy Word and to pray three times a day. See Daniel 6:10. Dear reader, it may be that you feel you are too busy to read your Bible, and pray three times a day as Daniel did, so you do not do so. But be honest with me, you really could if you so desired. The truth is, you put other things first! This is probably the main reason why you are living an empty life, why you are defeated by the enemy, why you do not have the power to overcome temptation. Pay the price and you, too, will be rewarded with God's favor and blessing for our Heavenly Father is not a respecter of persons. I want you to turn to Colossians chapter 3 and read verse 25.

2. DANIEL WAS A STUDENT OF PROPHECY.
He not only studied the revelations God gave to him in these visions which were explained to him by the Angel Gabriel, he studied the revelations God gave to the other prophets as well. We know he had a copy of the book containing the prophecies of the prophet Jeremiah, which he, no doubt, brought with him from Jerusalem when he was carried into Captivity, also a copy of the Pentateuch, most of the Psalms and the books of Micah, Isaiah, Joel, Obadiah and perhaps others. The Jews believed in the prophecies of Jeremiah, they believed God gave him the messages he recorded, and the prophet Daniel agreed with them in this. Note the words in this verse "understood by books", this refers to the Scriptures which he possessed. He not only studied God's Holy Word, HE BELIEVED IT! He knew that it was given to us by God. This cannot be said of many people who are living today, I ask you, dear reader, do you believe that our Bible is God's Holy Word?

3. DANIEL KNEW THAT HIS PEOPLE, THE JEWS, WOULD BE KEPT IN CAPTIVITY FOR SEVENTY YEARS.

This was made clear to him by the prophet Jeremiah. Now I want you to read this prophecies for yourself,-

"And this whole land shall be a desolation, and an astonishment: and these nations shall serve the King of Babylon seventy years.

And it shall come to pass, when seventy years are accomplished, that I will punish the King of Babylon, and that nation, saith the Lord, for their iniquity (sin) and the land of the Chaldeans, and will make it perpetual desolations."

"Thus saith the Lord of Hosts, the God of Israel, unto all who are carried away captives, whom I have caused to be carried away from Jerusalem unto Babylon;

Build ye houses, and dwell in them; and plant gardens, and eat the fruit of them;

Take ye wives, and beget sons and daughters; and take wives for your sons, and give your daughters to husbands, that they may bear sons and daughters; that ye may be increased there, and not diminished.

And seek the peace of the city whither I have caused you to be carried away captives, and pray unto the Lord for it: for in the peace thereof ye shall have peace.

For thus saith the Lord of Hosts, the God of Israel; Let not your prophets and your diviners, that be in the midst of you, deceive you, neither hearken to your dreams which ye cause to be dreamed.

For they prophesy falsely unto you in my name: I have not sent them, saithtthe Lord.

For thus saith the Lord, That after seventy years be accomplished at Babylon I will visit you, and perform my good word toward you, in causing you to return to this place."

Jeremiah 29:4-10.

Daniel knew that the time was near at hand when the captivity of his people would be ended, he was greatly burdened for he knew how wicked they were. He knew that God would keep His word, he knew that his people, the Jews, would be allowed to return to Palestine, he knew all too well the sinful life they were living. They were now living with a people who worshipped heathen gods, Daniel knew that many of his people had completely forgotten the Living God. Some of them were actually worshipping the pagan gods of the Babylonians. They certainly were not in any condition of mind or heart to receive God's blessing.

But his is not all that Daniel knew regarding his people. He knew they were sinners even BEFORE they were carried into captivity they had forgotten God, they were living very sinful lives even while living in Palestine, this is the reason why God's judgment had been pronoucned upon them, why they were carried into captivity by the Babylonians. They deserved punishment, they had it coming to them. Because of their sinful living and God's judgment upon them Jerusalem had become a reproach among the nations.

There is a powerful warning in this for us. How long do you think our Heavenly Father will allow us to continue plunging into deeper sin day after day before His judgment will fall upon us? We, like these Jews, have forgotten God, look at our nation today! Multitudes are living but to gratify the pull and desires of the flesh. Look at the home life of our nation, divorce has become so common that those who have studied the situation tell us that in some areas of our nation we have more divorces than marriages! This is a sex age, books and magazines are filled with sex, motion pictures and television reek with sex, sloppy sex, illicit sex, perverted sex, pre-marital sex, crime and sex, need I say more!

Juvenile delinquency has reached the stage where state and national leaders tell us that they are now unable to cope with the problem. Crime has reached an all time high and is increasing daily. God's Holy Word is sneered, mocked, ridiculed, rejected in hundreds of homes, in schools, colleges and universities, you know that I am telling you the truth! How long, yes, I ask you, how long will God let this go on before His judgment will fall! "The wages of sin is death." Romans 6:23. No nation or individual can glory in sin, reveling in it, and think they can escape! God's judgment will fall, the penalty will have to be paid! God's Holy Word says,-

"Be not deceived: God is not mocked; for whatsoever a man soweth, that shall he also reap.

For he that soweth to his flesh shall of the flesh reap corruption; but he that soweth to the Spirit shall of the Spirit reap life everlasting."

Galatians 6:7-8.

Dear reader, are you one of this large number who have forgotten God?

Yes, the Prophet Daniel was greatly burdened because of the sins of his people. He uses every means he knows of to get God to forgive their sin. He prays, he pleads with God, he fasts, he puts sackcloth (a coarse burlap kind of cloth) upon his body and puts ashes upon his head. He falls upon his face and with heart-broken cries of agony he prostrates himself before God in earnest entreaty. Daniel identified himself with the sins of his people, note how completely he does this. His prayer should move a heart of stone, it came from the very depths of his being.

Verses 4-5.

"And I prayed unto the Lord my God, and made my confession, and said, O Lord, the great and dreadful God, keeping the covenant and mercy to them that love Him, and to them that keep His commandments:

We have sinned, and have committed iniquity, and have done wickedly, and have rebelled, even by departing from thy precepts and from thy judgments:"

I want you to note how Daniel honors God, he reminds God that He always keeps His promises with those who merit them. His prayer is divided into three parts,-

1. HE CONFESSES THAT THEY ARE ALL GREAT SINNERS.

He tells God that they have failed competely in serving Him. That they have not acknowledged His covenant mercies and blessings, (verses 4-10).

2. HE CONFESSES THAT THEY DESERVED THE CURSE GOD PRONOUNNED UPON THEM BECAUSE OF THEIR DISOBEDIENCE. (verses 11-15).

3. HE PLEADS WITH GOD ASKING HIM TO SHOW MERCY.

He asks God to be no longer angry with His people and against Jerusalem. (verse 15-19;)

Daniel's prayer is like the prayer of Moses. I would like to have you now turn to Exodus 32:32 and read this prayer of Moses.

Listen to the heart-cry of Moses as he realizes that the anger of God against the sinning people was so great He would destroy them, every one. Moses asks God to destroy HIM rather than all the people. Daniel's prayer is like the prayer of Solomon which was given at the time the Temple was dedicated. Now stop and read Solomon's prayer which is recorded in I Kings 8:47-53. Daniel's prayer is like the prayer of the Apostle Paul for his people. I know it would be helpful if you read the prayers of these men of God, Paul's prayer is recorded in Roman's 9:1-5.

Note the agony Daniel manifests in his prayer as he takes to himself the sins of these wicked, backslidden idol worshipping Jews, - WE have sinned; WE have committed iniquity; WE have done wickedly, WE have rebelled against Thee. Daniel admits to God that they have not only neglected and forgotten God's mercies and manifold blessings and precepts, they have forgotten His judgments as well.

Verses 6-14.

"Neither have we hearkened to Thy servants the prophets, which spake in thy name to our kings, our princes, and our fathers, and to all the people of the land.

7. O Lord, righteousness belongeth unto Thee, but unto us confusion of faces, as at this day; to the men of Judah, and to the inhabitants of Jerusalem, and unto all Israel, that are near, and that are far off, through all the countries whither Thou hast driven them, because of their trespass that they have trespassed against Thee.

8. O Lord, to us belongeth confusion of face, to our kings, to our princes, and to our fathers, because we have sinned against Three.

9. To the Lord our God belong mercies and forgivenesses, though we have rebelled against Him;

10. Neither have we obeyed the voice of the Lord our God, to walk in His laws, which He set before us by his servants the prophets.

11. Yea, all Israel have transgressed thy law, even by departing, that they might not obey Thy voice; therefore the curse is poured upon us, and the oath that is written in the law of Moses the servant of God, because we have sinned against Him.

12. And He hath confirmed His words, which He spake against our judges that judged us, by bringing upon us a great evil: for under the whole heaven hath not been done as hath been done upon Jerusalem.

13. As it is written in the law of Moses, all this evil is come upon us: yet made we not our prayer before the Lord our God, that we might turn from our iniquities, and udnerstand Thy truth.

14. Therefore hath the Lord watched upon the evil, and brought it upon us: for the Lord our God is righteous in all His works which He doeth: for we obeyed not His voice."

I think it would be helpful and very profitable to you if you would stop and read through once again Daniel's prayer from its beginning to its end. I want you to become fully aware of the fact that this prayer emphasizes the sins of God's people as well as the Holiness and righteousness of God. I must now ask you this question, "Could this prayer of Daniel be applied to the people of America? Have we sinned? Have we forgotten God? Have we done wickedly? Have we listened to the pleadings and warnings of the Blessed Holy Spirit as they have come to us through the messages of Spirit-filled men of God, speaking from pulpits, over radio and television through great mass meetings and in many other ways? Have we obeyed God? Do you think we can escape the judgment of God if we continue in our sinful ways?"

Daniel admits that the evil that has come upon them has been justly deserved, he drags out into the open the plain, undeniable facts concerning their sin. He admits that they have no ground for expecting any mercy from God for they were undeserving. Consider now verse 14 - "Therefore hath the Lord watched upon the evil and brought it upon us!"

Do you agree with me that too many of our people who are living wicked, sinful lives, think we can and will escape punishment because it is not visited upon us? Surely you know the law of God, that we reap what we sow; that we reap more than we sow and that the kind of seed we sow makes no difference. The harvest time is almost here, in fact it is now beginning. We are reaping broken homes, juvenile deliquency, increased crime, wars, pestilence, drouth, famine, disease, death! May God have mercy upon us!

Verses 15-19.

"And now, O Lord our God, that hast brought Thy people forth out of the land of Egypt with a mighty hand, and hath gotten Thee renown, as at this day: we have sinned, we have done wickedly.

O God, according to all Thy righteousness, I beseech Thee, let Thine anger and Thy fury be turned away from Thy city of Jerusalem, Thy Holy mountain: because for our sins, and for the iniquities of our fathers, Jerusalem and Thy people are become a reproach to all that are about us.

Now therefore, O our God, hear the prayer of Thy servant, and his supplications, and cause Thy face to shine upon Thy sanctuary that is desolate, for the Lord's sake.

O my God, incline thine ear, and hear; open thine eyes and behold our desolations, and the city which is called by Thy name:

for we do not present our supplications before Thee for our righteousness, but for Thy great mercies.

O Lord, hear; O Lord, forgive; O Lord, hearken and do; defer not, for Thine own sake, O my God: for Thy city and Thy people are called by Thy name."

Daniel now makes an impassioned plea for His people, he makes it, not on the ground of their merit, for he openly admits that they fully deserve God's judgment. He pleads God's promises, God brought them safely out of Egypt. He had delivered them before, time and again, therefore He was sure God would keep His word and deliver them again. He pleads the promise God gave them through His prophet Jeremiah that He would restore them to their own land.

He pleads God's righteousness and mercy, he tells God that the glory He has gained through Israel would be lost if He should turn His face from them. He makes a final plea with all the fervor and passion of his great heart, that God's sanctuary, the Holy of Holies in the Temple which lies in ruins, shall be re-established and once again filled with the glory and majesty of God's presence.

Verses 20-21.

"And whiles I was speaking, and praying, and confessing my sin and the sin of my people Israel, and presenting my supplication before the Lord my God for the holy mountain of my God,

Yea, whiles I was speaking in prayer even the man Gabriel, whom I had seen in the vision at the beginning, being caused to fly swiftly, touched me about the time of the evening oblation."

We must stand in silence and in awe before this mighty man of God. I want you to visualize him, falling on his face before God, clothed in sackcloth and with ashes upon his head, tears running down his face. We cannot help but being moved deeply by his prayer, because we can read it it our own needs as individuals and as a nation. I make it my own personal prayer, I hope you do as well!

THE INTERRUPTED PRAYER

As we continue the reading of this chapter we note that as Daniel was praying, pleading with God asking for mercy for his people and for Jerusalem, suddenly his prayer was interrupted by the appearance of the Angel Gabriel who come to give Daniel God's answer. We are told that he flew swiftly from Heaven, like a flash of lightning, see Ezekiel 1:14, he arrived at the time the evening sacrifice was offered in the Temple of God, Daniel still observed the set time of the Temple service.

The answer to Daniel's prayer was sudden, it was definite and sure. God always answers the prayers of His born again believers when they ask in faith believing. God's Holy Word says,-

"And it shall come to pass, that before they call I will answer; and while they are yet speaking, I will hear.

Isaiah 65:24

"Call unto me and I will answer thee, and shew thee great and mighty things, which thou knowest not."

Jeremiah 33:3

Dear reader, God will answer your prayer also if you will meet God's conditions and ask in faith believing. There are unlimited resources available to you, sufficient to meet your every need, be it physical, material or spiritual. How much faith do you have? If you will use what faith you have, God will give you more.

We met the Angel Gabriel for the first time when Daniel received the vision recorded in chapter VIII. This is, no doubt, what Daniel means when he says in verse 21,- "Whom I had seen in the vision at the beginning." This, I believe, assures us that Daniel is to be given additional information regarding the coming events which are mentioned in the previous vision.

Verses 22-23.

"And he informed me, and talked with me, and said, O Daniel, I am now come forth to give thee skill and understanding.

At the beginning of thy supplications the commandment came forth, and I am come to shew thee; for thou art greatly beloved: therefore understand the matter, and consider the vision."

The Angel Gabriel now tells Daniel why he has left Heaven and come to him, it was to give him the understanding of the vision given to him and recorded in chapter VIII. Dear reader, I want you to know that wisdom, skill and understanding come, not from man BUT FROM GOD. God heard Daniel's prayer the moment it was uttered, so He sent the Angel Gabriel immediately with command to reveal to Daniel what events were to take place BEFORE the "TIMES OF THE THE GENTILES" were ended. Now stop and read once again Luke 21:24. I want your mind to be clear regarding these events.

Let us stop once again before we begin our study of Daniel's vision of the seventy weeks and give some thought to what the Angel Gabriel said regarding the Prophet Daniel. His message to Daniel is given in these four words, "THOU ART GREATLY BELOVED". What a world of meaning is contained in these four words! Daniel is not only "beloved of God" (and blessed is the

148

man of whom this can be said!) he is GREATLY BELOVED"
Think how this message, coming directly from God, must have
thrilled his heart! Think of it, here is a man of this earth, born in
sin, yet so completely surrendered to God in every avenue of his
life that he so moved the great heart of God that He sent the Angel
Gabriel to earth to tell Daniel how greatly he was loved and
esteemed! We know that God is not a respecter of persons, I have
already told you this, God is also a respecter of CHARACTER!
Enoch walked with God and God took him to Heaven.
Abraham was said to be a friend of God and you, too, can be
beloved of God if you, like Enoch, like Abraham, like Solomon,
like Daniel will put God FIRST and will give the Blessed Holy
Spirit who is there where you are this very moment as you are
reading, and who is living in your body if you are a born again
believer, complete control of your life! You are greatly needed
there where you live and work, you are very important in God's
sight, He has a plan for your life and a work for YOU to do, so why
delay any longer? Give the Holy Spirit complete control of your
life NOW! Not to-morrow, not some time in the future, but NOW!
Turn now to Romans 12:1-2. I asked you before to obey this
command, have you done so? I want every reader of this book on
Daniel to live a happy, victorious, overcoming life, this is the
burden of my heart. I know the joy and the peace you will experience day by day if you give the Holy Spirit complete control
of your life.

THE SEVENTY WEEKS
Verse 24.

*"Seventy weeks are determined upon thy people and upon the
holy city, to finish the transgression, and to make an end of sins,
and to make reconciliation for iniquity, and to bring in
everlasting righteousness, and to seal up the vision and
prophecy, and to anoint the most holy."*
Tremendous prophetic issues are now presented by the Angel
Gabriel. I want you to take your time in studying these last four
verses of this chapter. Why do I ask this? Because some of the
greatest events this world is going to experience are mentioned
and explained, events which concern we who are living in this
space age. I hope I can make these events clear to you.
The Prophet Daniel knew that he was carried into captivity
in the year BC. 606. He knew that he had been in captivity 68
years and that the Jews were only to be kept in captivity 70 years,
that only two years remained, this had been made clear to him by

the prophecy God gave to Jeremiah. He knew also that their freedom would be given to them by King Cyrus, the Prophet Isaiah had prophesised this,-

"Who saith of Cyrus, He is my shepherd, and shall perform all my pleasure: even saying to Jerusalem, Thou shalt be built; and to the Temple, Thy foundation shall be laid."

Isaiah 44:28.

But now, in the visions he had received of the four wild beasts, the Ram, and the Rough He Goat, he was told that four world-wide Empires were to come and go and his people would be scattered and live for centuries among the nations of the world before they would be restored in their own land and become recognized as one of the nations of the world. Only one nation, the Babylonian Empire, had come and gone, how could he reconcile what was told him already with what had been written in the Scriptures he brought with him from Jerusalem when he was carried into captivity? No wonder Daniel was puzzled and perplexed.

Then suddenly, while he was praying the Angel Gabriel appears. After telling Daniel that he was greatly beloved of God he tells him that he was sent by God to reveal to him the meaning of the vision of the seventy weeks. This vision of the seventy weeks is a very important revelation for it explains the events that are to come. It makes clear to us another important truth that this "seventy weeks" only covers the period of time when the Jews are LIVING IN Palestine. It does not cover the period of time when the Jews are scattered among the nations of the world. It continues again when these Jews who were scattered among the nations of the world have returned to their own land, when Israel is recognized as one of the nations of the world. These "seventy weeks" cover the time from the giving of the decree to "restore and rebuild Jerusalem" until the coming of Christ with His saints at the close of "the times of the Gentiles".

We are told in this verse 24 that the purpose of the "seventy weeks" is six-fold,-

1. To finish the transgression.
2. To make an end of sin.
3. To make reconciliation for inquity.
4. To bring in everlasting righteousness.
5. To seal up the vision and the prophecy.
6. To anoint the most holy.

Let me now try to explain each of these six things individually,-

1. TO FINISH THE TRANSGRESSION.

It is important for us to know that these things I have just mentioned have to do ONLY WITH THE JEWS AND JERUSALEM. The "seventy weeks" have nothing whatever to do with the Gentiles or the church, only with the Jews and Jerusalem. Our Lord Jesus came to provide salvation for all men, that is, to remove from God's sight our sins. Psalm 51 says, "Hide they face from my sins, and blot out all mine iniquities." *We know that our Lord Jesus, through His death, made an end to sin." But this man, after He had offered one sacrifice for sins forever, sat down on the right hand of God."* **Hebres 10:12.**

The transgression of the Jews was their rejection of our Lord Jesus as their Messiah. Before the great tribulation period which takes place the last three and a half years of the reign of the Anti-Christ, the Jews will recognize our Lord Jesus as their Messiah and with joy they will accept Him. Now read what God's Holy Word says,-

"For I would not, brethren, that ye should be ignorant of this mystery, lest ye should be wise in your own conceits; that blindness in part is happened to Israel, until the fullness of the Gentiles be come in.

And so all Israel shall be saved; as it is written, There shall come out of Sion a deliverer, and shall turn away ungodliness from Jacob:

For this is my covenant unto them, when I shall take away their sins.

As concerning the gospel, they are enemies for your sakes: but as touching the election, they are beloved for the father's sakes.

For the gifts and calling of God are without repentance."
Romans 11:25-29

The Jews will continue to refect our Lord Jesus until the Anti-Christ enters the Holy of Holies of the temple and demands that he be worshipped as God. Then they will recognize him for what he is and their blinded eyes will be opened.

2. TO MAKE AN END OF SIN. (offerings)

Here again it is the sin of Israel which is meant. It is this sin of the rejection of our Lord Jesus as their Messiah. When our Lord Jesus died upon the cross no more sin offerings were needed, for he became the sin offering. He offered Himself ONCE FOR ALL! At His death the veil of the Temple was rent in twain, showing that a priest was no longer needed to go behind the veil to make atonement for the sins of the people. Please turn now and read Hebrews 9:12, note carefully what it says.

3. **TO MAKE RECONCILIATION FOR INIQUITY.**

The literal meaning of these words is- "To make atonement or expiation for sin". Our Lord Jesus died to provide salvation for Jews as well as for Gentiles, however the Jews to-day are still living in unbelief. They will continue so until the day when through terrible persecution by the Anti-Christ they will come to know Him whom they have pierced. A Jew to be saved must confess his sin and must accept Christ as his Saviour, just as a Gentile must do, if he would be saved. When he does this he becomes a member of God's church which is composed of both Jews and Gentiles. Note God's Holy Word regarding this,-

"For ye are all the children of God by faith in Christ Jesus.

For as many of you as have been baptized into Christ have put on Christ.

There is neither Jew nor Greek, there is neither bond nor free, there is neither male or female: for ye are all one in Christ Jesus."

Galatians 3:26-28.

"Ye have put on the new man, which is renewed in knowledge after the image of Him that created Him:

Where there is neither Greek nor Jew, circumcision nor uncircumcision, Barbarian, Scythian, bond nor free: but Christ is all, and in all.

Colossians 3:10-11.

4. **TO BRING IN EVERLASTING RIGHTEOUSNESS**

There can be no "everlasting righteousness" in this world until our Lord Jesus returns from Heaven bringing we, who are His born again believers with Him. We will see Him bring an end to the battle of Armageddon, we will see Him throw the Anti-Christ and the False Prophet alive into the Lake of Fire. We will see the devil chained and thrown into the bottomless pit, which is also known as the Abyss. He will then judge the nations and at its close usher in the wonderful Millennial Kingdom, and a thousand years of everlasting righteousness will begin. At this time our Lord Jesus will make a new covenant with the House of Israel. Read what God says,

"But this shall be the covenant that I will make with the House of Israel; After those days, saith the Lord, I will put my law in their inward parts, and write it in their hearts; and I will be their God, and they shall be my people.

And they shall teach no more every men his neighbor, and every man his brother, saying, Know the Lord: for they shall all know me, from the least of them unto the greatest of them, saith the Lord: for I will forgive their iniquity, and I will remember their sin no more."

Jeremiah 31:33-34.

5. **TO SEAL UP THE VISION AND PROPHECY.**
The Angel is telling Daniel of these six things which are to be accomplished during this 490 year period. These six things, as I have told you, definitely have to do with Daniel's people the Jews and the city of Jerusalem. I think I should at this time tell you what happened when the 70 years of the Babylonian captivity ended. King Cyrus issued a decree which enabled Ezra the Priest to go to Jerusalem and rebuild the Temple of God and lay the foundation for a future Jewish state. When Ezra the Priest left Babylon he took over 40,000 Jews with him, who returned to their own land. Not all the Jews wanted to leave Babylon, many were satisfied to live where they were, they were now worshipping the idols of Babylon.

Ezra was given the authority to create laws, set up magistrates and judges, and execute punishment even unto death, in other words to restore the Jewish state, civil as well as religious, according to the law of God and the ancient customs of the people. I suggest you stop and read the entire story, it is given in the Book of Ezra, chapter 7. Now that this was done there was no longer any necessity for future visions or prophecies, for they will be unnecessary in that day.

6. **TO ANOINT THE MOST HOLY.**
Most Bible teachers believe that the most Holy or Holy of Holies that will be anointed is not our Lord Jesus Christ but is the new Temple which will be builded during the reign of the Anti-Christ. This Temple was greatly polluted when the Anti-Christ entered the Holy of Holies and demanded that he be worshipped as God. This Temple will be anointed by our Lord Jesus Christ when He sets up His Millennial reign after the land has been cleansed and order has been restored. I hope you are aware of the fact that these six things are to take place in the future.

Verse 25.

"Know therefore and understand, that from the going forth of the commandment to restore and rebuild Jerusalem unto the Messiah the Prince shall be seven weeks, and three score and two weeks: the street shall be built again, and the wall, even in troublous times."

There are several matters I want to explain to you as we get further into this study of the seventy weeks. There are questions I know you want to have answered, "What do we mean by the seventy weeks?" What people are involved in this study? When do the seventy weeks begin? When do they end?"

Let me try to answer these questions. The seventy weeks are a period of time that has to do with a definite series of events connected with the Jews and Jerusalem. The period of time known as "THE TIMES OF THE GENTILES" is not involved at all in the events that take place during the seventy weeks period. It is important that you know this. The seventy weeks covers the period of time when the Jews are living in Palestine, it does not cover the time when the Jews are scattered among the nations, but it does cover the period of time again AFTER they have returned from their wanderings and are now living in Palestine.

We use the Bible term "seventy weeks" but these words really should be written "seventy sevens". The word "weeks" is used because we do not have a word in the English language which will exactly express the meaning of the original word which is given to us in the Hebrew language, so the translators just used the word "weeks", for it is the best word they could use, as the Hebrew word signifies a period of "seven". Whether the "seven" are days, weeks or years is to be determined by the Bible passages in which the word is used.

The number "seven" is indeed a Bible number. God rested on the seventh day. The number "seven" is composed of the divine number three- Father, Son, and Holy Spirit: and the world number which is four - we have spring, summer, fall and winter. Six is the number of man and etc. In the Book of Revelation we read of 7 churches, 7 seals, 7 trumpets, 7 people, 7 vials, 7 dooms and 7 new things. Yes, seven is indeed God's perfect number.

In studying prophecy we come across such divisions of time as "hours" "days" "weeks" "months" and "years"; times, time, and half a time". If we are to understand the meaning of these terms we must interpret them according to the Bible rule for their use. God has given us the "key", it is clearly given to us in God's Holy Word. We turn to the Book of Numbers, chapter 14 verse 34 where we read,-

"After the number of the DAYS in which ye searched the land, even FORTY DAYS, EACH DAY FOR A YEAR, shall ye bear your iniquities, even forty years."

Now we know that this judgment was literally fulfilled for the children of Israel wandered in the wilderness for FORTY YEARS, a YEAR for EVERY DAY that the spies searched out the Land of Caaanan. We now turn to the Book of Ezekiel where we read,-

"And when thou hast accomplished them, lie again on thy right side, and thou shalt bear the iniquity of the house of Judah, FORTY DAYS. I have appointed thee EACH DAY FOR A YEAR.
Ezekiel 4:6.

So we see now from what God has given us in His Holy Word that His unit of measurement for time is "A DAY STANDS FOR A YEAR". Applying this unit of measurement to the seventy

154

weeks we find that in seventy weeks we have 490 days, so considering "a day for a year" we have 490 years.

Now this seventy weeks or 490 years are divided into three periods, we are told that there are to be definite events take place in each period, I am now giving you these three periods, they are,-

1. 7 weeks or 49 years.
2. 62 weeks or 434 years.
3. 1 week or 7 years.

This gives us a total of 70 weeks or 490 years. We are told in this verse 25 "that from the going forth of the commandment to restore and to build Jerusalem unto Messiah the Prince shall be "seven weeks and three score and two weeks", so adding 7 to 62 we have 69 weeks or by the Bible rule of a year for a day we have 7 times 69 which gives us 483 years.

WHEN DID THE SEVENTY WEEKS BEGIN?

Let me say here that Bible teachers are not agreed as to when the seventy weeks begin. It is generally believed that the seventy weeks began when a decree was issued for the restoring of the walls and the rebuilding of the city of Jerusalem. But there were three decrees issued and a command was also given to Nehemiah to rebuild the walls of Jerusalem. But each decree given was separated by a number of years, let me now mention these decrees,-

The first decree was given by King Cyrus for the rebuilding of the Temple in Jerusalem, This decree was given in 536 B.C. Turn to the Book of Ezra chapter 1, read verses 1-4. '

The second decree was issued by King Darius for the continuation of the rebuilding of Jerusalem and the Temple, this date was 19 years earlier or B.C. 519. See Ezra chapter 6, verses 1-12. The third decree was given to Ezra the Priest by King Artaxerxes, the date was B.C. 457. Sixty-two years had passed when this decree was given. The Book of Ezra tells us of this decree, see chapter 7. Then this same King Artaxerxes commissioned the young man Nehemiah in the year B.C. 444. See Nehemiah, chapter 2.

I have already told you that this seventy weeks was divided into three periods, let me explain to you what is going to take place in each period,-

The first period of 7 weeks or 49 years is the time when the city of Jerusalem will be rebuilt.. When these decrees were given the city of Jerusalem was rebuilt and the Jewish state was organized. But the problem we face here is, did the seventy weeks begin with the first decree or the second decree or the third decree, or was it when Nehemiah was commissioned? This is the problem to be solved. There is a difference of opinion here, some Bible teachers say the seventy weeks began with the decree given by King Artaxerxes to the Priest Ezra in B.C. 457, others think it was the time permission was given to Nehemiah who is right?

Let me tell you now of this second period of years, this was a period of 62 weeks or 434 years, this refers to the period of the passing centuries from the rebuilding of Jerusalem to .... this is the question, which decree is the right one?

I want to tell you now of this third period of 7 years. There is no problem here. We know that this is the period of the last week of the 490 years, the last 7 years, known as Daniel's seventieth week. This is the end time when the Anti-Christ will rule the earth. This period begins after our Lord Jesus has taken all the born again believers to be with Him. This period will be divided, at the end of the first three and a half years the Anti-Christ will stop the offering of the daily sacrifice, he will enter the Holy of Holies of the Temple and demand under penatlty of death that he be worshipped as God.

Now let me bring you a recap of what I have been trying to tell you, for I want this entire matter to be clear in your mind. We want to find a starting point for the seventy weeks if we can,-

1. We find at the commencement of the seventy weeks period a decree is given to restore and rebuild Jerusalem. Seven weeks or 49 years were given for this work of restoration. As we reach the end of this first period of 49 years we are to find Jerusalem rebuilt and the walls restored.

2. From this point 62 weeks or 434 years later or 69 weeks from the beginning of the seventy weeks we are to see the coming of the Messiah, the Prince.

3. One more week is given to us which completes the seventy weeks. In the middle of this week the Messiah is to be cut off and the sacrifice and oblation to cease, thus we have 7 plus 62 plus 1 which makes 70 weeks.

Now the question is, which of these decrees is the starting date for the 70 weeks of years? I find that the only date that will harmonize with all these events is the date of the decree given to Ezra the Priest, B.C. 457. What happened then? Let me say that 49 years later Nehemiah tells us in chapter 13, reading verse 23 to the end of the chapter that the restoration of the Temple and the establishment of the statehood of the Jews in Jerusalem and Judea was completed.

Then 69 weeks or 483 years were to pass, at the end of that time Messiah the Prince would appear. Beginning with the year B.C. 457 the period ends in A.D. 27. Did the Messiah appear? Yes,

He appeared for Luke 3: verses 21-22 tell us that this was the time when Jesus was baptized and He began His ministry. Now note this important fact, as He entered Galilee preaching the Gospel of the Kingdom, He said, "THE TIME IS FULFILLED", the time He mentioned is the end of the 69 weeks mentioned by Daniel which were to extend to the time when the Messiah the Prince was to appear.

Verse 26.

"And after threescore and two weeks shall Messiah be cut off, but not for Himself: and the people of the prince that shall come shall destroy the city and the sanctuary; and the end thereof shall be with a flood, and unto the end of the war desolations are determined."

We are now told that the Messiah shall be "cut off" but not for Himself. This means that our precious Lord Jesus is to be crucified, He will die to provide salvation for all men. The date is not given in God's Holy Work, it is said to be after this period of 62 weeks or 434 years. It is the first outstanding event to take place, then later we are told that Jerusalem is to be destroyed. Our Lord Jesus told His disciples of this coming destruction of the city, He know it would take place, now turn to Matthew 24:2 and read the Prophecy given by Jesus. His prediction was literally fulfilled in A.D. 70 when the Roman Emperor Titus destroyed the city. He burned the Temple, the very stones of the Temple were pried apart to get the gold that ran into the cracks when the Temple was burned.

The "people of the prince that shall come" are the Romans. The "prince that shall come" is the Emperor Titus. He was the one who destroyed the sanctuary (the Temple). The last part of this verse, "unto the end" has to do with that period of time extending from the destruction of Jerusalem to the Second Coming of our Lord Jesus to this earth with all the born again believers and a great unnumbered host of angels. The length of time is not given, it has already extended nearly 2000 years. How much longer it will extend is known only by our Heavenly Father but I personally believe His coming is very near, the many signs given in Matthew 24 which I gave you in chapter IX tell me that this is so.

It is during this present space age, which is known as "the church age" that the Blessed Holy Spirit is calling out a people "unto His name". All who have accepted our Lord Jesus as their personal Savior are born-again believers, you will find them carrying different denominational labels, some are Catholics, some are Jews, some do not belong to any church. It is these born again believers who are called in God's Holy Word "the church",

"The Body of Christ", or "The Bride of Christ". Now turn to the Book of Ephesians, chapter 5 and read verses 1 - 10.

When the Body of Christ is complete our precious Lord Jesus will return. The trumpet of the Lord will sound, then, in the twinkling of an eye all the righteous dead will rise first, they will be given their glorified bodies, then we which are alive and remain will also receive our glorified bodies, then we will be caught up with them to meet our Lord Jesus IN THE AIR, from that time on we will forever be with our Lord. Read once again I Thessalonians 4:13-18. When we, who are "the born-again believers" are caught up to be with the Lord, then the third period of 7 years will begin.

VERSE 27.

"And he shall confirm the covenant with many for one week: and in the midst of the week he shall cause the sacrifice and the oblation to cease, and for the overspreading of abominations he shall make it desolate, even until the consummation, and that determined shall be poured upon the desolate."

This third period of one week or 7 years is a period of time that is definitely known. It begins the very moment all true born again believers are taken out of this world to be with our Lord. See II Thessoalonians 2:7-8. This 27th verse of Daniel, chapter IX deals with this period.

The "he" of this verse 27 is this coming Anti-Christ, he is the "little horn" we read about in Daniel, Chapter 2 and in chapter 7. Let me now give you a little more information regarding this coming Anti-Christ,-

1. He will be a literal World-Ruler governing this entire earth.

2. He will be the Devil living in a human body just as our Lord Jesus was God living and working in a human body.

3. He will "confirm the covenant with many for one week" this means the Anti-Christ will make a covenant with the Jews, he will aid them in the rebuilding of the Temple on its original site, and help them reestablish the Temple sacrifices. The one week mentioned in this verse means 7 years.

4. The Anti-Christ will break this covenant with the Jews when three and a half years have passed, he will then begin the greatest time of trouble this world has ever known. This is known as "the great tribulation". He will demand that all living persons wear his mark, now read Revelation 13: verses 16-18. He will enter the Holy of Holies and demand that all worship him as God under the penalty of death. Now read II Thessalonians 2: 3-4. Daniel 12:11; Matthew 24: 15-28.

CHAPTER X.
DANIEL'S LAST VISION

This chapter, together with the two chapters which follow, tell the story of Daniel's last and final vision. In this tenth chapter we are given a picture of our glorified Lord Jesus, we see Him as He is now in Heaven seated beside the Father, just as the apostle Paul and the Apostle John saw Him centuries later.

VERSE 1.

"In the third year of Cyrus king of Persia a thing was revealed unto Daniel, whose Name was called Belteshazzar; and the thing was true, but the time appointed was long: and he understood the thing, and had understanding of the vision."

Some time has passed since the vision recorded in chapter 8 was given to the Prophet Daniel. This was the third year of the reign of King Cyrus and the first year of the reign of Darius the Mede. When the Empire of Babylon was overthrown by the Medes and Persians in the year B.C. 538 Cyrus allowed his nephew Darius to occupy the throne which Darius occupied until his death two years later, when he was murdered by one of his generals.

Daniel was an old man at this time, he was over 90 years old. The words "And the thing was true but the time appointed was long" refer to the vision given to Daniel, and recorded in chapter 8. Daniel now understands this vision, for God sent the angel Gabriel to him for this very purpose. See verses 11 - 14 of this tenth chapter. The words "and the time appointed was long" reveal that this vision given in chapter 8 covered an undetermined period of years, stretching centuries far ahead into the future.

VERSE 2.

"In those days I Daniel was mourning three full weeks."

When Daniel realized all that was to happen to his people in the centuries to come, he was so burdened and heavy of heart in his concern for his people, the Jews, that he could not rest. Dear reader, have you ever been so burdened, so concerned for the welfare and salvation or possibly the health of your loved ones that you did not want any food or drink and sleep fled from your eyes? Daniel had been in mourning for three full weeks.

VERSE 3.

"I ate no pleasant bread, neither came flesh nor wine in my mouth, neither did I anoint myself at all, till three whole weeks were fulfilled."

In chapter 9 we heard the heart cry of Daniel as he poured out his heart in prayer to God for his people, confessing their sin: King Cyrus issued a decree allowing the Jews to return to

Jerusalem and to rebuild their Temple. In the Book of Ezra, chapter 1 verses 1-2 it is recorded that King Cyrus said he had been commanded by God to build Him a Temple in Jerusalem. When the decree was issued some forty thousand Jews returned to Palestine, this was a small number compared with the total number of Jews living in Babylon. The larger number were content to remain where they were, many were worshipping the false gods of Babylon. I told you this in chapter 9.

The Temple that was built in Jerusalem by Zerubbabel at this time cannot be compared with the magnificent Temple that was built by King Solomon. But this is not all. Daniel was the prime minister of the Empire, he was in a position to know that the Jews who returned to Palestine were being opposed by powerful enemies who were seriously hindering their work of reconstruction. This is one of the reasons why Daniel was in mourning for his people. He knows how to pray so he holds on to God in prayer until the answer comes. For three full weeks Daniel did not eat any meat or drink any wine, he did not wash or shave, he did not anoint his head which was an outward sign that he was fasting. He wore hair-cloth next to his body all the time, he put ashes in his hair.

VERSE 4.

"And in the four and twentieth day of the first month, as I was by the side of the great river, which is Hiddekel."

On what day of Daniel's prayer and fasting did the answer come? Where was Daniel at the time? You may recall that the vision given to Daniel which we studied in chapter 8 was given to him while he was sitting on the banks of the river Ulai. Now he is in another beauty spot, he is at the junction point of the Tigris and the Euphrates, both rivers were joined not far from the Persian gulf. God's Holy Word calls it the river Hiddekel which in Syriac language is known as the Euphrates; in the Vulgate, the Greek language and the Arabic, it is known as the Tigris river, hence most Bible students believe Daniel's prayer was made at the junction of these two rivers. Daniel not only prayed at home, he loved nature and often walked along the banks of nearby rivers. Daniel was not alone, there were other men with him.

VERSES 5-6.

"Then I lifted up mine eyes, and looked, and behold a certain man clothed in linen, whose loins were girded with fine gold of Uphaz:

His body also was like the beryl, and his face like the appearance of lightning, and his eyes like lamps of fire, and his arms and his feet in color like to polished brass, and the voice of his words like the voice of a multitude."

Daniel withdrew himself to a secluded spot where he can be alone to pray. As he prays he becomes conscious of the fact that he is not alone. He knows that someone is near him, as he looks up opening his eyes he sees a man so glorious and wonderful in appearance that he knows at once that this is a heavenly being who has come from Heaven. Daniel falls on his face before Him. I want you to note the appearance of this glorious person who I believe was none other than our Precious Lord Jesus. He was clothed in white linen, which is the kind of clothing we will all wear when we are in Heaven. He had a belt of the purest gold about His waist, his skin was lustrous and glowing, His face blazed with light, His eyes flashed fire, His arms and feet were the color of polished brass, His voice was loud, clear and vibrant with life.

What a wonderful description this is of our Lord Jesus! Now turn to Acts 9:1-7 and read the description of the Apostle Paul's meeting with the risen Christ; when you finish the reading of Paul's experience turn to the Book of Revelation, to chapter 1, read verses 13-18. Here the Apostle John gives us his description of our wonderful glorified Lord Jesus. I want you to note that Daniel, the Apostle Paul, and the Apostle John all fell to the ground in a faint when they saw Him the wonderous glory of our risen Lord Jesus was almost more than the physical body could stand. And just think, we too shall see Him one day as He is!

VERSE 7.

"And I Daniel alone saw the vision: for the men that were with me saw not the vision; but a great quaking fell upon them, so that they fled to hide themselves."

The men who were with Daniel did not see our Lord Jesus. He was not visible to them. I do believe that they heard His voice, this so terrified them that they ran and hid themselves. The men who were with the Apostle Paul likewise heard the voice of the Lord Jesus though they did not see HIm. The Apostle John was alone on the island of Patmos when our Lord Jesus appeared to him.

VERSES 8-9.

"Therefore I was left alone, and saw this great vision, and there remained no strength in me: for my comliness in me was turned into corruption, and I retained no strength.

Yet heard I the voice of His words: and when I heard the voice of His words, then was I in a deep sleep on my face, and my face toward the ground."

When the men with Daniel fled, he was left alone. So great was the effect of the presence of our Lord Jesus that his strength was gone, none remained. He was pale and weak as a result of this experience. In the presence of our Lord Jesus Daniel realized how corrupt the flesh really is. When he heard the wonderful voice of the Lord Jesus speaking to him he fell in a dead faint, falling upon his face.

VERSE 10.

"And, behold, an hand touched me, which sat me upon my knees and upon the palms of my hands."

When our Lord Jesus appeared to Daniel He was not alone. I am sure it was the Angel Gabriel who was with him, see verse 16 of chapter 8. It was, no doubt, the hand of the Angel Gabriel that was placed upon Daniel and who lifted him up, speaking to him words of comfort and assurance. I want you to note that in all the visions given to the Prophet Daniel it was the Angel Gabriel who gave him the explanation of these events which were to take place in the future. Now read verse 16 of this chapter where we are told that this Angel Gabriel was like the "similitude of the sons of men". So we know that this angel who was with our Lord Jesus was the Angel Gabriel.

VERSE 11.

"And he said unto me, O Daniel, a man greatly beloved, understand the words that I speak unto thee, and stand upright: for unto thee am I now sent. And when he had spoken this word unto me, I stood trembling."

Daniel is told once agian that he is a man "greatly beloved". Oh what wonderful words these are, how his heart must have been thrilled to hear them! Daniel was a man whose whole desire was to live for God. He was a man born in sin just as we are yet so completely surrendered to God that he could be used as a channel through which God could reveal the entire sweep of Gentile World Power from its beginning until its close, when the Anti-Christ and the False Prophet are thrown into the Lake of Fire and the Millennial reign of our Precious Lord Jesus begins. Daniel is encouraged and told to stand upon his feet, he is told that now additional information is to be given to him. At these words Daniel stands upon his feet, he is still trembling from head to foot.

VERSE 12.

"Then said he unto me, Fear not, Daniel: for from the first day that thou didst set thine heart to understand, and to chasten thyself before thy God, thy words were heard, and I am come for thy words."

What command is given to Daniel? The Angel Gabriel says to him, "Daniel, from the very first day that you began to fast and to pray, and you wanted to fully understand the visions which were given to you; to grant your desire our Heavenly Father sent me to reveal to you the meaning of these visions."

Let me stop here for a moment to say that all too often we think of God as one who stands over us with a cruel whip, trying to force us to do His will, and throwing us into Hell if we do not obey. This is not the picture our Heavenly Father has given to us in His Holy Word. God is love, if He loved us enough to give us His Son to die for us, sinful as we are, do you think he treasures and fosters feelings of anger and vengeance against us? He has given us a will to act, we are all given the power of choice. We must, each and all, decide whether we will accept or reject His love. If we reject His offer of mercy and His undying love, then we are lost, and no one is to blame but ourselves.

Let no one dare to say that God sends men to Hell. You send yourself when you REJECT our Heavenly Father's wonderful offer of salvation with all its blessings. For God CANNOT admit sinful men into Heaven without a change of heart, for to do so would make a Hell out of Heaven. In this verse we see the Angel Gabriel encouraging Daniel, revealing to Him God's great love for us. He is not scolding or pronouncing judgment against him.

VERSE 13.

"But the prince of the kingdom of Persia withstood me one and twenty days: but, lo, Michael, one of the chief princes, came to help me; and I remained there with the kings of Persia."

This verse should be prayerfully studied for it gives us a picture of what goes on behind the scenes when we pray in faith believing. Daniel is told that his prayer was heard from the very first moment he prayed, yet for three weeks Daniel continued to fast and pray not knowing that his prayer had been heard and answered.

How often this is true with the saints of God to-day! How little we know of what takes place behind the scenes in this great unseen world about us! Now turn to Isaiah, chapter 65, read verse 24 which says,-

"Before you call I will answer; and while you are yet speaking, I will hear".

What a joy it is to our hearts to know and realize this wonderful promise is true, and and that it is for us! While we live in a material world we little realize that there is a great, unseen world about us that our human eyes cannot see. This unseen world is so vast it is beyond our ability to comprehend its magnitude. It is in this unseen world where the devil, called Satan and his demons hold sway. There is only one devil in God's Holy World, he is called, "The Prince off this World" (John 14:30); "The Prince of the pwer of the air" (Ephesians 2:2); "The God of this age" (II Corinthians 4:4); and "The Rullr of

163

Wickedness" (Ephesians 6:12). The devil rules this great unseen world, he has it well organized.

Do you know that this world in which you live is organized into principalities? Let me try to give you a picture of this great unseen world as I see it,-

1. This world is divided into principalities, it may be that each nation is a principality, God's Holy Word does not tell us.

2. The Devil is the head, the ruler of this great unseen world.

3. Each principality is governed by an evil prince who is directly responsible to the Devil.

4. Under the control of this evil prince are an unnumbered host of demons, who are about us everywhere. There are so many that legion of 8000 can live in the body of an unsaved person. See Mark 5:9.

5. These demons are disembodied spirits, see my book on "Demons, Their origin, their work and their end" for information concerning them.

Now let me try to explain what I have just told you. The Devil has his seat, or throne in Pergamos, which is located upon this earth. See Revelation 2:13. He travels up and down this earth going from one principality to another. Read Job 1:7 also Job 2:2 and I Peter 5:8. Read also Ephesians 6:12, this verse throws much light on the dividing of this earth into principalities. We are not told how much of this world's territory is covered by each principality, only that they exist and that each is governed by an evil prince.

This prince of the kingdom (principality) of Persia could not be King Cyrus, how could King Cyrus hold back God's answer to the prayer of Daniel? Who was this prince? Let me tell you, he was the Devil's representative for this principality in this great unseen world. He could not be seen by human eyes yet he was there, a prince so powerful that he could withhold the answer to Daniel's prayer for 21 days. He was a prince so powerful that it was necessary for our Heavenly Father to send the Archangel Michael to come to help the Angel Gabriel overcome him. How this prince, this representative of the Devil, hated Daniel! a man greatly beloved of God! This prince knew that the answer to Daniel's prayer made it possible for Daniel to receive the information concerning the events which were to take place in the future, and the Devil did not want this information to be released. Finally this prince was defeated and Daniel was given the answer to his prayer. This should encourage you, dear reader, for if you pray in faith believing, you, too, can prevail in prayer, God will see that you receive the answer given. We are told that "the

earnest, effectual prayer of a righteous man, availeth much".
(James 5:16).

VERSE 14.

"Now I am come to make thee understand what shall befall thy people in the latter days: for yet the vision is for many days."
The Angel Gabriel now tells Daniel that he has been sent by God to reveal to him what will happen to the Jews in the future years. Daniel is told that in the visions given to him, the events revealed to him for the fulfillment of the prophecy, reach far into the future, they are many years away.

VERSE 15.

"And when he had spoken such words to me, I set my face toward the ground, and I became dumb."
The Prophet Daniel was so moved by what the Angel Gabriel had told him that his power of speech left him, he was unable to talk, he was literally spell-bound.

VERSES 16-17.

"And, behold, one like the similitude of the sons of men touched my lips; then I opened by mouth, and spoke, and said unto him that stood before me, O my Lord, by the vision my sorrows are turned upon me, and I have retained no strength.

For how can the servant of this, my Lord, talk with this, my Lord? for as for me, straightway there remained no strength in me, neither is there breath left in me."
The Angel Gabriel now touches Daniel's lips, he is now able to speak. He says to Gabriel," My Lord, these experiences you have told me which are to befall my people are too much for me, I am so weak, my strength is gone, I can hardly breathe." No doubt Daniel's age had much to do with his weakness for he was an old man, well past 90 years.

VERSES 18-19.

"Then there came again and touched me one like the appearance of a man, and he strengthened me.

And said, O man greatly beloved, fear not: peace be unto thee; be strong, yea, be strong. And when he had spoken unto me, I was strengthened, and said, Let my Lord speak; for thou hast strengthened me."
The Angel Gabriel now takes Daniel by the hand and says, "Daniel, you are greatly loved by God, have no fear, calm yourself, be strong, yes, Daniel, be strong!" Twice this command is given to Daniel. And as strength is given to him Daniel says, "Speak, I am now strong enough to hear the message you have to give to me!"

VERSE 20.

"Then said he, Knowest thou wherefore I come unto thee?

And now will I return to fight with the prince of Persia; and when I am gone forth, lo, the prince of Grecia shall come."

The Angel now asks Daniel, "Do you know why God sent me to you? I was sent, not only to do battle with this representative of the Devil, this prince of Persia, who kept back God's answer to your prayer for 21 days; but also to reveal to you the meaning of the visions God gave to you. My battle with this prince of Persia is not over, I will have to continue my battle with him when I leave you then the head of the principality of Grecial will come to hinder.

VERSE 21.

"But I will shew thee that which is noted in the scripture of truth; and there is none that holdeth with me in these things, but Michael, your prince."

Note the words in this verse "the scripture of truth". What do they mean? Do they refer to the visions given to Daniel which were to be put into book form? I believe it does. I believe Daniel wrote down these visions just as we have them before us to-day. The reference given here to the Archangel Michael as "your prince" I do believe is to make clear to us that the Archangel Michael is the one chosen by God to be the special representative to look after the Jewish people. Chapter 12: verse 1 proves that this is true.

Consider the words, 'there is none that holdeth with me in these things but Michael". Do you think that the Angel Gabriel is implying by these words that only he, the Archangel Michael, Daniel and God know of these events that are to come? It seems to me that this is what the Angel Gabriel had in mind.

CHAPTER XI.
THE HISTORY OF THE KINGS OF THE NORTH AND THE SOUTH

This eleventh chapter of this Book of Daniel is, I do believe, the most difficult chapter to explain in this entire book. The first part of this eleventh chapter up to, and including verse 35 deals with events which were to take place in the immediate centuries to come, and were actually fulfilled as we shall see in studying the chapter. From verse 36 to the end of the chapter we are given added information regarding the coming Anti-Christ and the events which will take place during the LAST DAYS OF "THE TIMES OF THE GENTILES".

This eleventh chapter is but a continuation of the prophecies given in the preceding chapters. This is God's plan, He reveals coming events by progression. First we see the Gentile nations as MAN sees them, this is clearly shown in chapter two. Then we see these same nations as they are SEEN BY GOD, this is shown in chapter 7. Some information regarding the character and actions of the coming Anti-Christ is given in these earlier chapters but much additional information is given in these two closing chapters of the book. In the preceding chapters figures and symbols are used. But in these two closing chapters the events which are to come are revealed just as they are to occur. Make note of this fact as we study these chapters.

VERSES 1-2.

"Alos I in the first year of Darius the Mede, even I, stood to confirm and strengthen him.

And now will I shew thee the truth. Behold, there shall stand up yet three kings in Persia; and the fourth shall be far richer than they all: and by his strength through his riches he shall stir up all against the realm of Grecia."

The person giving the information which is stated in these two closing chapters is the Angel Gabriel. He tells us that he was sent to strengthen and help King Darius the Mede in the first year of his reign and to show Daniel more of what is to take place in the days to come. Four kings were to rule the Empire of Medo-Persia, each following the other. In the golden-headed man image of chapter 2 the Empire of Medo-Persia is designated by the breast and arms of this image. Three of these kings in the order of their reign were,-

1. Ahasuerus, known in history as Cambyses, the son of Cyrus, he reigned from B.C. 529 - B.C. 522;

2. Artexerxes, known in history as Pseudo-Smerdis, the Magian, who we are told was an imposter. He reigned from B.C. 522 - B.C. 521.

3. Darius Hystaspes, he married the daughter of King Cyrus, his reign continued from B.C. 521 - B.C. 485.

King Artaxerxes reigned seven months; and King Darius Hystape (not Darius the Mede) thirty-six years.

The fourth King mentioned was Xerxes who was the son of Darius. He was noted for his riches, not his leadership. He was a fighter, his military strength consisted of five million, two hundred eighty-three thousand, two hundred and twenty men. Besides these the Carthaginians furnished him with an army of three hundred thousand men and twelve hundred and seven ships with three banks of rowers each. As he marched through one country after another he swept everything before him, forcing all able bodied men of these countries to join him.

"And a mighty King shall stand up, that shall rule with great dominion, and do according to his will."

The mighty King spoken of in this verse was Alexander the Great. Nine kings, each following the other, succeeded King Xerxes; under the masterful leadership of Alexander the Great the Empire of Medo-Persia was overthrown, now the Empire of Greece dominates the world scene. This Empire of Greece is the belly and thighs of the golden-headed man image of chapter 2, also Daniel's vision of the Ram and the Rough He-Goat (Daniel 8:3-8) also Daniel 8:20-22. The time was B.C. 335.

VERSE 4.

"And when he shall stand up, his kingdom shall be broken, and shall be divided toward the four winds of heaven; and not to his posterity, nor according to his dominion which he ruled: for his kingdom shall be plucked up, even for others beside those."

The kingdom of Alexander the Great was broken, (Daniel 8:22). We have already seen in our study of chapter 8, that Alexander the Great died an alcoholic, he could conquer nations but he could not conquer himself. I want you to note what God's Holy Word says regarding the Empire of Greece at his death; it was to be divided, each of his four leading generals took a part, thus four kingdoms now come into existence. Judea, in Palestine was considered the center of Alexander the Great's Empire of Greece, therefore all distances given in God's Holy Word were reckoned from Jerusalem in Judea. General Cassander took Greece and all the countries WEST of Palestine, so he became known as KING OF THE WEST. General Lysimachus took Trace and all the territory that lies north of Palestine, he was known as KING OF THE NORTH. General Seleucus took Syria and Babylon which lies mainly east of Palestine, so he was known as KING OF THE EAST. General Ptolemy I took Egypt and the country lying south of Palestine, so he was known as KING OF THE SOUTH. We have now identified these kings.

It was not long before these kings were fighting with each other. King Cassander, the King of the West, was soon conquered by King Lysimachus, the King of the North. King Cassander had his kingdom taken from him. Then King Seleucus, the King of the East, in a war with King Lysimachus, conquered him and added his entire kingdom to his own.

VERSE 5.

"And the king of the south shall be strong, and one of his princes; and he shall be strong above him,,and have dominion: his dominion shall be a great dominion."

Now King Seleucus has become so powerful that he controls three-quarters of the original territory governed by Alexander the Great. Meanwhile King Ptolemy I, the King of the South, has also been very busy. He annexed many of the islands and coastal cities to Egypt, this is what verse 5 means when it says, "he became strong". So King Ptolemy I is spoken of in this prophecy as "THE KING OF THE SOUTH". King Seleucus is now known as "THE KING OF THE NORTH", because the territory he governed lay north of Palestine.

But another of the princes of King Alexander the Great is now mentioned in this verse. This prince is none other than this King Seleucus, the KING OF THE NORTH. This King Seleucus at first was but a satrap serving under King Ptolemy I. The governor of a province was called a satrap, so we see that this man Seleucus at first was but a minor ruler. He was appointed vice-gerent of Babylonia but was driven out by Antigonus, he fled to Egypt where he was favorably received by King Ptolemy I and made one of his princes. King Ptolemy I helped him recover his province, he enlarged it until it extended to India, he then conquered Syria, Media, Babylon, Assyria, so was called Seleucus Nicator which means "conqueror". So we could read verse 5 this way, - "And the King of the South shall be strong and one of his (Ptolemy I) princes, even he (Seleucus Nicator) shall be strong above him (that is above Ptolemy I his former master) and have dominion, his dominion shall be a great dominion."

VERSE 6.

"And in the end of years they shall join themselves together; for the king's daughter of the south shall come to the king of the north to make an agreement: but she shall not retain the power of the arm; neither shall he stand, nor his arm: but she shall be given up, and they that brought her, and he that begat her, and he that strengthened her in these times."

The years pass, I want you to notice the words "in the end of years". We are dealing now with the descendants of the King of the North and the King of the South. These kings fought each other during the years. Ptolemy Philadelphus II is now the King of Egypt and known as the King of the South, he ruled from 285 - 246 B.C. Antiochus Theos is the King of Syria and is known as "THE KING OF THE NORTH". Tired of fighting each other they agreed to "join themselves together". Ptolemy Philadelphus II, the King of the South, asked Antiochus Theos, the King of the North, to divorce Laodice, his wife, setting her and her two sons aside, and then marry Berenice, his daughter, promising him a large fortune in money as a dowry, if he would do this. Antiochus Theos agreed, Laodice, his wife and her two sons were abandoned, he then married Berenice, the daughter of Ptolemy Philadelphus II and he received the large dowry which had been promised him.

All things seemed to go well for a time but Antiochus Theos was not happy. Ptolemy Philadelphus II died, so Antiochus Theos divorced Berenice and restored Laodice and her two sons to their former position as his wife and sons, for he loved Laodice. She and her two sons were at once restored to the favor and power of the Kingdom. This is the meaning of the words "she shall not retain the power of the arm" that is, she (Berenice) shall not reign as queen in the Kingdom of the North.

Queen Laodice, now restored to her former position, and knowing how changeable and easily influenced her husband Antiochus Theos was, fearing that he might once again divorce her and reinstate Berenice, so to protect herself and her two sons she murdered her husband by putting poison in his food. She then placed her son, Seleucus Callinicus upon the throne. He is now King of the North.

Queen Laodice did not stop here, she determined to get rid of Berenice also, so she had her murdered as well. She not only killed Berenice, she killed all her servants and the members of her court who went with her when she was divroced by Antiochus Theos, and who fought to defend her. This is the meaning of the words in verse 6 "she (Berenice) shall be given up, and they that brought her (that is, her servants and the members of her court) and he that begat her, and he that strengthened her in these times" (this was, no doubt, those who tried to keep her from being murdered, her son, who also was murdered).

VERSE 7.

"But out of a branch of her roots shall one stand up in his estate, which shall come with an army, and shall enter into the fortress of the King of the North, and shall deal against them, and shall prevail:

This branch out of the same root was the brother of Berenice, his name was Ptolemy Euergetes III, he reigned from 246 - 222 B.C. As soon as his father Ptolemy Philadelphus II died he took over the throne, thus becoming the King of the South. As soon as the news of the murder of his sister Berenice reached his ears he at once raised a tremendous army, he declared war on Seleucus Callinicus, the son of Queen Laodice, who was now King of the North. Ptolemy Euergetus III soon captured Syria, Cilicia, in fact he captured most of the territory of Seleucus Callinicus the King of the North. He killed Queen Laodice, her murders were now avenged. "The wages of sin is death." Romans 6:23.

VERSES 8-9.

"And shall also carry captives into Egypt with their gods, with their princes, and with their precious vessels of silver and of gold; and he shall continue more years than the King of the North.

So the King of the South shall come into his kingdom, and shall return into his own land."

Ptolemy Euergetes III now returned to Egypt bringing many captives with him, a wealth of money and the 2500 idol images of Egyptian gods which King Cambyses had formerly taken from Egypt. The Egyptians worshipped idols, cats were held in high veneration, the Egyptians were very happy indeed to get back the images of their gods. The Egyptian priests gave Ptolemy the name of Euergetes III which means "benefactor". Ptolemy Euergetes III, the King of the South, outlived Seleucus Callicus, the King of the North, by several years, for King Seleucus Callicus was killed by a fall from a horse.

Verse 10.

"But his sons shall be stirred up, and shall assemble a multitude of great forces; and one shall certainly come, and overflow, and pass through; then shall he return, and be stirred up, even to his fortress."

Note that the first part of this verse speaks of "sons", the plural noun is used; the last part of this verse uses but the singular, but one son is mentioned. King Seleucus Callicus had two sons, they were Seleucus Ceraunus III and Antiochus Magnus. Seleucus Ceraunus was the older of the two, he ascended the throne after the death of his father, he ruled from 226-223 B.C. The one ambition of these brothers was to attack and conquer the King of the South and win back the territory taken from their father. But because Seleucus Ceraunus was weak in body and lacking in leadership, and because the Kingdom was financially bankrupt, so much so that he could not pay his soldiers, two of his generals poisoned him. I have already told you he only reigned three years.

After his death his brother Antiochus Magnus III took over the Kingdom. He was a much stronger man, more capable in leadership. He is the "one" in this verse who should "overflow" and "pass through". Antiochus Magnus III raised a huge army, he led his armies in person, he retook Seleucia, and Syria, he overcame the Egyptian general Nicolaus, he even planned to enter Egypt itself. Antiochus Magnus III certainly came, he overflowed the land, he passed through Palestine, retook the captured territory, he came even to the frontiers of Egypt, there he stopped. This was in B.C. 218.

"And the King of the South shall be moved with choler (anger) and shall come forth and fight with him, even with the King of the North: and he shall set forth a great multitude; but the multitude shall be given into his hand."

Meanwhile Ptolemy Euergetes III, King of the South, died. We are told that he was murdered by his own son. His son, Ptolemy Philopater IV now ascended the throne. The war with Antiochus Magnus III, King of the North, continued on. Ptolemy Philopater IV was "moved with choler", this means that he was greatly enraged because of the losses he sustained. Syria and most of the territory his father had taken from Antiochus Magnus III was lost and now his own country was in danger of an invasion. He knew that Antiochus Magnus III, the King of the North, was marching against him, this verse 11 says "with a great multitude", (this consisted of sixty-two thousand foot soldiers, six thousand mounted horsemen, and one hundred and two elephants). This verse 11 says "the multitude shall be given into his hand". This means that this huge army shall be captured by Ptolemy Philopater IV, the King of the South.

This battle was fought at a place called "Raphia", which was not far from Gaza, this was in 217 B.C. Antiochus Magnus III, King of the North was badly defeated, he had over 10,000 of his foot soldiers killed, literally thousands were wounded, 3000 of his horsemen were killed, 4000 of the foot soldiers were taken captive. Ptolemy Philopater IV lost only 700 horsemen and 1500 foot soldiers.

VERSE 12.

"And when he hath taken away the multitude, his heart shall be lifted up; and he shall cast down many ten thousands: but he shall not be strengthened by it."

Ptolemy Philopater IV returned home with his captives, this is what "taken away the multitude" means. He had the opportunity to capture the entire Empire of Antiochus Magnus III, King of the North, but with his heart lifted up with pride because of his great victory, and anxious to return home to continue his wicked, licentious life he made a dishonorable peace with Antiochus Magnus III.

These battles were fought in Palestine, Ptolemy Philopater IV "was not strengthened" by this great victory. Because he failed to take advantage of his opportunity, and because he lived such a wicked, sensual life his subjects turned against him. When he entered the city of Jerusaleum he offered sacrifices, he wanted to enter into the Temple but the Jews would not allow him to do so, for this was contrary to their religion and their laws. This greatly angered him so he began at once to severely persecute the Jews, we are told that in Alexandria where many of the Jews lived, having been there since the days of Alexander the Great and where they enjoyed all its prvileges, Ptolemy Philopater IV killed 40,000 of them. Instead of strengthening his Empire of the South he nearly destroyed it.

VERSE 13.

"For the King of the North shall return, and shall set forth a multitude greater than the former, and shall certainly come after certain years with a great army and with much riches."

I want you to notice that the events mentioned in this verse 13 are to take place "after certain years". I want you to be aware of the fact that this prophecy was given to the Prophet Daniel by the Angel Gabriel, these events we are now studying are taking place in the 490 years period. These present events continue up to and including verse 4 of Chapter 12.

The peace that Ptolemy Philopater IV made with Antiochus Magnus III continued for fourteen years. Then Ptolemy Philopater IV died, largely because of the wicked, sensual life he lived, a life no physical body can endure for very long. He left a five year old son to succeed him called Ptolemy Epiphanes V. He ruled Egypt from 203-181 B.C.

Antiochus Magnus III, in the meantime, had built up his Kingdom, he had greatly increased in wealth, and realizing now that he could possibly take over the entire Empire of the King of the South, he organized "a great army", much greater than his former army, and when all was ready he marched against Egypt, believing that he could easily defeat the army of the child King.

VERSE 14.

"And in those times there shall many stand up against the King of the South: also the robbers of thy people shall exalt themselves to establish the vision; but they shall fall."

The Empire of the King of the South was now in real danger. Agathocles, the prime minister of the Empire, controlled the child King. He managed the affairs of the Empire. He was so dictatorial in his ministry that the people rebelled against him, they not only murdered him, they killed his entire family, his mother, sister, and all their associates.

Meanwhile Antiochus Magnus III, King of the North, was approached by King Philip of Macedon who suggested that they work together in conquering the Empire of the King of the South. This was agreed, they formed a criminal alliance, King Philip of Macedon was to receive Syria, Libya and Cyrenia as well as Egypt; Antiochus Magnus III was to receive all the rest.

When these plans were completed, they began their conquest. It did not take long for Antiochus Magnus III to conquer Syria and take over Palestine. The words "the robbers of thy people" refers to the Jews who turned from their religion and joined Ptolemy Epiphanes V. They were called "robbers" because by their actions they brought upon the Jews terrible suffering thus "establishing the vision" which had prophecied. These Jews hoped to build a Temple in Egypt like the Temple in Jerusalem.

When Antiochus Magnus III and King Philip of Macedon captured Palestine these robber Jews left Ptolemy Epiphanes V and joined Antiochus Magnus III. Scopas, the general who was directing the armies of Ptolemy Epiphanes V, while Antiochus Magnus III and King Philip of Macedom were busy fighting in other parts of the Empire, he recaptured Syria and Palestine, he brought these robber Jews under control who had joined Antiochus Magnus III, this is what is meant when this verse 14 says "they shall fall". General Scopas placed guards about the entrances to Jerusalem, then he returned to Egypt.

Another nation now comes upon this world scene, it is the nation of Rome. You will recall that Rome was the legs and feet of the Golden Headed man image of Chapter 2. We shall hear more of this Empire of Rome in the days to come. Rome was small and weak at first, but Rome grew larger and stronger gradually as she took to herself more and more territory, before long she was making herself heard in the affairs of the nations.

VERSE 15.

"So the King of the North shall come, and cast up a mount, and take the most fenced cities: and the arms of the South shall not withstand, neither his chosen people, neither shall there be any strength to withstand."

Antiochus Magnus III, the King of the North, was now determined to recapture Palestine and Syria from the hands of Ptolemy Epiphanes V, the King of the South. Scopas, the general in charge of the armies of the Empire of the South, opposed him. The armies clashed at the beginning or source of the Jordan river. General Scopas was defeated, he took refuge with his army of 10,000 men in Sidon, the strongest city both in situation and in its defenses in the entire area. The city was besieged by Antiochus Magnus III, Egypt then sent three of their ablest generals together with the strongest forces they could muster, they were sent to Sidon to deliver General Scopas, but they were not able to do so. Lack of food forced General Scopas to surrender, he and his men were allowed to leave the city of Sidon stripped and naked. Now Antiochus Magnus III took the rest of the fenced cities, he swept everything before him, in fact Ptolemy Epiphanes V, his ablest generals and his chosen people were not able to withstand him.

VERSE 16.

"But he that cometh against him shall do according to his own will, and none shall stand before him: and he shall stand in the glorious land, which by his hand shall be consumed."
Antiochus Magnus III, the King of the North, as I have just told you, overran the armies of Ptolemy Epiphanes V, he did as he pleased, nothing stopped him. "The glorious land" is Palestine, the homeland of the Jews. Antiochus Magnus III, the King of the North, now had complete control of Palestine. The Jews helped him, they gave him and his armies food and other assistance so he was able to take the garrison that King Ptolemy Epiphanes V's general Scopas had left in Jerusalem.

The words "which by his hand shall be consumed" is translated in the margin to read "shall be perfected under him". Antiochus Magnus III helped the Jews in every way he could, he brought back to Palestine those Jews who were living in other lands and who wanted to return. He also removed the demand for tribute money which the priests and Levites had to pay to Ptolemy Epiphanes V.

VERSE 17.

"He shall also set his face to enter with the strength of his whole kingdom, and upright ones with him; thus shall he do: and he shall give him the daughter of women, corrupting her: but she shall not stand on his side, neither be for him."
Antiochus Magnus III planned to enter Egypt, now that he had conquered Palestine, the way was clear for him to do so. "He set his face to enter" means that he brought the full striking power of his Kingdom with him. "The upright ones" spoken of here, was the name given to the leader of the Jews who helped him. But those in charge of the affairs in Egypt, learning of his plans, immediately sought help from the Romans who were becoming stronger day by day. They agreed to help Egypt, so when Antiochus Magnus III learned of this alliance he at once changed his plans, he decided to use strategy and wile in taking over the Kingdom of the South. He has a daughter called Cleopatra who was noted for her beauty.

Antiochus Magnus III now had a meeting with the leaders in Egypt, he suggested that they arrange a marriage between his daughter Cleopatra and Ptolemy Epiphanes V. The lad was only seven years old, Cleopatra was also a very young girl. This why this verse 17 calls her "a daughter of women". She was called this because she was cared for daily by her mother and grandmother.

The leaders in Egypt agreed to the arrangement and Ptolemy Epiphanes V and Cleopatra were married five years later. Antiochus Magnus III was happy for he was sure that he could now take over the Kingdom of the South using Cleopatra. He would "corrupt" her, that is, use her to influence her husband. But his plans resulted in failure, for Cleopatra told her husband of her father's plan to take over the Kingdom, so he was warned and all the efforts of Antiochus Magnus III came to naught. Cleopatra even joined her husband in sending congratulations to the Romans on their victory over his father.

VERSE 18.

"After this shall he turn his face unto the isles, and shall take many: but a prince for his own behalf shall cause the reproach offered by him to cease; without his own reproach he shall cause it to turn upon him."

When Cleopatra warned her husband of her father's intentions this so angered her father that he determined to defeat, not only the Romans but he would conquer Egypt as well. With a fleet of 300 vessels he assailed the coasts and the isles of Asia Minor. He was badly defeated at Magnesia, this was in B.C. 190 by Scipio Asisticus, he is the prince mentioned in this verse 18.

Crushed and broken by this tragic defeat he hurried home, and at Antioch he sent a committee to seek terms of peace. The Romans demanded that he give up all territory he held in Europe, also Asia on the European side of the Taurus; he was to pay 15,000 talents, 500 talents were to be paid immediatley, 2500 talents were to be paid when the peace pact was ratified by the Roman Senate, and 1000 talents each year for the next twelve years. The Romans demanded that turn over to them his fleet of 300 ships, they did however allow him ten vessels for his own personal use.

VERSE 19.

"Then he shall turn his face toward the fort of his own land: but he shall stumble and fall, and not be found."

Antiochus Magnus III was now in deep trouble. His treasury was empty and he had to raise this tribute money. Where could he get it? He marched into his Eastern Provinces to try to collect all the money he could from those who were in arrears in the payment of taxes, then he decided to plunder the Temple of Belin Elymais. This so angered the people that they rose up en masse and killed him. This verse 19 says- "he stumbled and fell and was not found."

VERSE 20.

"Then shall stand up in his estate a raiser of taxes in the glory of the Kingdom: but within few days he shall be destroyed, neither in anger or in battle."

At the death of Antiochus Magnus III his son Seleucus Philopater IV ascended to the throne. He was now the King of the North. He inherited the huge debt his father had incurred, the country was bankrupt, so he became "the raiser of taxes". He reigned about twelve years. With the tribute money nearly due, and not knowing which way to turn he decided to send his treasurer to Jerusalem, which is called in this verse 20 "the glory of the Kingdom". He was told to seize all the money deposited in the Temple treasury in Jerusalem, but "within a few days he died" having been poisoned, it is believed that this was done by HELLIODOROUS, his treasurer, who hoped to reign in his stead.

VERSE 21.

"And in his estate shall stand up a vile person, to whom they shall not give the honor of the Kingdom: but he shall come in peaceably, and obtain the Kingdom by flatteries."

The next King of the North was Antiochus Epiphanes IV. God's Holy Word tells us that he was "a vile person". He was the younger son of Antiochus Magnus III. They "did not give him the honor of the Kingdom" because his nephew Demetrius was the rightful heir. Antiochus Eipiphanes IV was in Athens, Greece, on his way home from Rome when his father died When he arrived home he found that Heliodorus, the treasurer, had declared himself to be king. But Antiochus Epiphanes IV "came in peaceably, for he obtained the kingdom "by flatteries". He flattered King Eumenus who was the ruler of Pergamus, and Attalus was his brother, they gave him their assistance. He flattered the Romans, he sent capable men to get their good-will, he paid them the money which was past due. He flattered the Syrians, so they flattered him. They called him "Epiphanes" which means "Illustrious".

Yes, Antiochus Epiphanes IV was indeed "a vile person", he reveled in all the passions of the flesh. He visited the taverns, he associated and drank with the lowest of the low, he sang debauched and sexy songs with them. But he was no man's fool, while he was selfish, self-centered and cruel he did not lack courage and ability. We are told that there was nothing too low or too wicked for him to do.

VERSES 22-23.

"And with the arms of a flood shall they be overflown from before him, and shall be broken; yea, also the prince of the covenant.

177

And after the league made with him he shall work deceitfully: for he shall come up, and shall become strong with a small people."

The "arms of a flood which were overflown from before him" were those who were his competitors for the Kingdom. Heliodorous and several others were soon "broken", that is, they were put down, removed, this was through the efforts of King Eumenes and his brother Attalus. As soon as Antiochus Epiphanes IV arrived home from Athens, Greece, these aspirants to the throne gave up the attempt.

"The Prince of the Covenant" was Onias, the High Priest. Jason the Priest then gave Antiochus Epiphanes IV a large sum of money, so he removed Onias and gave the place to Jason. Then a wicked Priest by the name of Menelaus gave him a still larger sum of money so he acted "deceitfully", he removed Jason. Then he "broke the league" he had made with King Eumenes and his brother Attalus when he persuaded the Romans to recognize him.

He was a very shrewd King for he led Rome and the other nations to believe he only had a small army while all the while he was becoming "strong with a small people". You see, at first there were but few of the leaders of the Empire who were with him, that is, who wanted him to become King, for there were others who also wanted to become King and each had their supporters. But when King Eumenes and his brother Attalus promoted him, then the last of the opposition was removed and he became strong.

VERSE 24.

"He shall enter peaceably even upon the fattest places of the province; and he shall do that which his fathers have not done, nor his fathers' fathers; he shall scatter among them the prey, and spoil, and riches: yes, and he shall forecast his devices against the strongholds, even for a time.

Antiochus Epiphanes IV now "entered peaceably" two of the richest provinces, they were Coelesyria and Palestine. This verse 24 says "he shall do that which his fathers have not done, nor his fathers' fathers". Just what did he do? What does this mean? I'll tell you, it means that he was very extravagant in his giving; he took the money and gifts he obtained from the spoil of the Temple and the riches he took from his enemies and gave them to whom he would, he scattered the "spoil" among his friends.

Let me try to explain the words, - "he shall forecast his devices". The guardians of the young King Ptolemy Philometer V demanded from Antiochus Epiphanes IV that he restore to them the two rich provinces Coelesyria and Palestine but he refused to do this for he knew that sooner or later he would have to fight a war with the King of the South so "he forecast devices", that is, he worked out plans to prevent war for the present, at the same time he visited the strongholds and places on the frontier to see that they were ready in case of an attack. He did this for a time, that is, he spent several years in getting ready for a war with Egypt.

VERSES 25-26.

"And he shall stir up his power and his courage against the King of the South with a great army; and the King of the South shall be stirred up to battle with a very great and mighty army; but he shall not stand: for they shall forecast devices against him.

Yea, they that feed of the portion of his meat shall destroy him, and his army shall overflow: and many shall fall down slain."

Several years passed, the day finally came when Antiochus Epiphanes IV felt that he was ready to invade Egypt. He entered Egypt with a large army. But meanwhile the generals of Egypt were not idle either, they, too, had organized a mighty fighting force. They met at a place called Pelusium, there were great losses incurred by both armies, but the armies of Egypt were defeated. Antiochus Epiphanes IV was soon master of all of Egypt except Alexandria. The Reason this became possible was because Ptolemy Philometer V was betrayed by the ministers and officers of his staff who "fed of the portion of his meat". They gave Antiochus Epiphanes IV the secrets of the state. Antiochus Epiphanes IV treated Ptolemy Philometer V with consideration, he made a favorable peace with him.

VERSE 27.

"And both these kings' hearts shall be to do mischief, and they shall speak lies at one table; but it shall not prosper: for yet the end shall be at the time appointed."

When Antiochus Epiphanes IV captured Egypt and he concluded a peace with Ptolemy Philometer V, his brother Ptolemy Physcon was then proclaimed king. Let me stop here and say that these kings were related. Anchiochus Epiphanes IV was the uncle of both Ptolemy Philometer V and Ptolemy Physcon. When Ptolemy Physcon ascended the throne Antiochus Epiphanes IV pretended to take the part of Ptolemy Philometer V against his brother, leading him to believe that he had his interests at heart, then Antiochus Epiphanes IV put forth the effort to capture Alexandria so he would be master of all the territory of the King of the South but his effort was not successful.

Because of his attack upon Alexandria Ptolemy Philometer

179

V knew that he could not trust his uncle; he now knew that his pretended interest in his welfare was but vain and idle words. He at once went to his brother Ptolemy Physcon, they considered carefully the entire situation of affairs in Egypt. They then agreed that they would reign jointly. They were now united, they knew they could not trust their uncle Antiochus Epiphanes IV so this prophecy was fulfilled, "These kings (Antiochus Epiphanes IV and Ptolemy Philometer V) hearts shall be to do mischief (against each other) and they shall speak lies (to each other) at one table.

VERSE 28.

"Then shall he return into his land with great riches; and his heart shall be against the holy covenant: and he shall do exploits, and return to his own land."

Antiochus Epiphanes IV then started his return trip home, while returning toward Syria he received a report that was widely circulated that he had been killed in a battle in Egypt. He also learned that Jason the Priest whom he removed in favor of the Priest Menalaus had raised an army and had attacked Jerusalem intending to oust the Priest Menalaus and recover his Priestly office by force. When Antiochus Epiphanes IV heard of this, having learned that the Jews rejoiced when they heard that he had been killed, he regarded this as a revolt and he determined at once that he would have his revenge. He killed 40,000 Jews living in Jerusalem, he sold as many more into slavery, then he went to the Temple and he killed a sow, he boiled the meat then sprinkled the broth all over the altar and the Holy of Holies, this fulfilled the prophecy given in this verse 28 "his heart shall be against the holy covenant." (How he hated the Jews!). He then carried away all the golden vessels and sacred treasures, he replaced Menalaus the Priest who had to flee when Jason attacked Jerusalem. Antiochus Epiphanes IV, his revenge now complete, continued his march home, he finally arrived at Antioch.

VERSE 29.

"At the time appointed he shall return, and come toward the south; but it shall not be as the former, or as the latter."

It was in the spring of B.C. 168 that Antiochus Epiphanes IV leanred that the two brothers Ptolemy Philometer V and Ptolemy Physcon were reigning jointly over Egypt. They knew of the treachery of their uncle Antiochus Epiphanes IV, when they learned that he was once again preparing to attack Egypt they at once appealed to Rome to come and help them. Antiochus Epiphanes IV did not know this, he marched unhindered into

Egypt, Memphis yielded to him without a struggle, he continued on until he was on the outskirts of Alexandria. But, as this verse 29 says, "but it shall not be as the former or as the latter", that is, he did not have the same success as he had when he conquered the Egyptian army at Pelusium.

VERSE 30.

"For the ships of Chittim shall come against him: therefore he shall be grieved, and return, and have indignation against the holy covenant: so shall he do; he shall even return, and have intelligence with them that forsake the holy covenant."

Antiochus Epiphanes IV was now ready to attack Alexandria, he believed that he could sweep everything before him. Then he learned that the Roman fleet was in the harbor with legates fromt he Roman Senate. What a shock this was to him! He went at once to salute them! They gave him a letter from the Senate in which he was commanded to leave his nephews alone and be satisfied to rule his own Kingdom. If he refused he would have to deal with Rome, Antiochus Epiphanes IV knew what this meant.

So he told legate Popilious that he would consult with his leaders and let Rome know his decision. At this word Popilious drew a circle in the sand about Antiochus Epiphanes IV and said,- "I want your answer now before you step out of the circle, this will be the answer I will report to the Roman Senate!" Antiochus Epiphanes IV knew there was only one course open to him so he said to Populious, "If it will so please the Senate I will depart and return home!"

And this is what he did, Enraged beyond measure he went at once to Palestine and vented his hate upon them, for he hated the Jews with all the power of his being. He sent his general Appollonius to Palestine with orders to destroy Jerusalem. He set fire to the city, he killed many of its inhabitants, he killed many of the poor Jews who had come from the country to worship the Lord in the Temple. Those who could fled for their lives to the country. Antiochus Epiphanes IV published a decree ordering that all Jewish worship of God must cease immediately. He consecrated the Temple to the worship of the idol god Jupiter. He built a castle fortress on a hill overlooking the Temple and filled it with Syrian soldiers to see that his orders were obeyed.

VERSE 31.

"And arms shall stand on his part, and they shall pollute the sanctuary of strength, and shall take away the daily sacrifice, and they shall place the abomination that maketh desolate."

The arms in this verse 31 refer to military power and might. I want to stop here before we continue furthr with our study to say that all I have tried to explain to you, that is, the events that have already taken place and that are recorded in verses 21-31 were wars that had to do with the Kings of the North and the Kings of the South, they extended from B.C. 536 to B.C. 164, a period of 372 years. I want you to remember that while you have been reading of these events that actually took place, all of these events were given to Daniel a great many years before they actually occurred. These events, recorded in verses 2-31 are actually the most prophetic foreview given in all God's Holy Word. You will note that details are given in this prophecy that only our Heavenly Father could give us before they actually happened.

THE TIME BETWEEN THE REIGN OF ANTIOCHUS EPIPHANES IV AND THE COMING OF CHRIST.
VERSES 32-33

"And such as do wickedly against the covenant shall he corrupt by flatteries: but the people that do know their God shall be strong, and do exploits.

And they that understand among the people shall instruct many; yet they shall fall by the sword, and by flame, by captivity, and by spoil, many days."

You can image the feelings of these poor persecuted Jews who had to experience the severe persecutions and the terrible suffering inflicted upon them by Antiochus Epiphanes IV. All Jewish worship of the Living God had been abolished. Jerusalem was filled with heathen Temples. Antiochus Epiphanes IV had done everything in his power by flatteries and threats to corrupt the true believers and to get them to sacrifice to these heathen false gods.

But there were some Jews who did "wickedly", they "forsook the covenant" they worshipped these idols being influenced to do this by "flatteries". But all Jews who were true believers, who knew the Living God they worshipped, were strengthened in their faith, verse 33 says "they were made strong", they did "exploits". This means that they, boldly, like Daniel and his companions, stood openly for their convictions, and in these days of testing and trial they boldly encouraged the weaker brothers. This is what it means when it says they did "exploits".

These were the days when an aged Priest named Mattathias and his sons, who from the years B.C. 166-147 fought to restore the national life of Israel. They were known as "THE MACCABEES". This good Priest Mattathias, driven to desperation by the terrible persecutions carried out by Antiochus Epiphanes IV, he rallied all the believers he could. He was forced to flee to the mountains where he and his followers carried on, determined to hold to the faith of Israel. Two years later the aged Priest Mattathias died, his third son Judas, who was known as "the Hammer" led this group of Jewish believers.

Judas was a shrewd and clever leader, he carried on a guerilla warfare defeating and routing every army sent against him, and in B.C. 165 he recaptured Jerusalem, he destroyed all the heathen temples, he purified the Jewish Temple and restored the daily sacrifice. Antiochus Epiphanes IV, heart-broken at the news of the Maccabean revolt in Palestine, retired to a place called Tabae where he died in B.C. 164.

Judas, the leader of the Maccabees, was killed in battle in B.C. 160, he was succeeded by his brother Jonathan who was a High Priest. Meanwhile the Syrians were engaged in a civil war, they were fighting among themselves, so there was a time when there was peace in Judea. This gave Jonathan the time he needed to strengthen his position, he made a treaty with the Romans and the Spartans. He was suddenly betrayed and murdered by a Syrian general, this was in B.C. 143. His younger brother Simon who was the last of the sons of the faithful old Priest Mattathias then carried on.

Simon had two sons, one of these sons, and Simon himself, were treacherously murdered by his son-in-law in B.C. 135. His other son, known as John Hyrcanus, scaped, he became the High Priest of Israel, he had a long and prosperous reign. There were others who followed him. It was some time later that the Maccabeans, falling into disfavor with the people, were succeeded by an Idumaen, who was known as Antipater, this was in B.C. 43, he, too, was murdered this same year.

We are now told that Mark Anthony, the Roman, hearing that Antipater was murdered, visited Syria. He appointed two of Antipater's sons Phasaelus and Herod (later known as Herod the Great) to govern the Jews. The reign of Herod the Great was from B.C. 37 to B.C.4. He was the ruler in Judea when the Lord Jesus was born in Bethlehem of Judea. I hope you will turn now to Matthew 2:1-15 and read the story of His birth. We have now covered the period of years from Antiochus Epiphanes IV to the birth of Christ.

It was during this period of years extending from the Prophet Malachi to Matthew, known as the silent years, that God raised up a new group of spiritual leaders to whom He gave wisdom and understanding. They "understood" the prophetic message, they "instructed" many of the people. These were the folk like Simeon and Anna, who waited for "the consolation of Israel". You can read about this in Luke 2:25-38. During this period of years from Malachi to Matthew there were ten state persecutions, these faithful believers in the Living God suffered all manner of torture, with but little intermission, for over 300 years.

THE PERIOD OF YEARS BETWEEN THE MINISTRY OF JESUS AND THE COMING REIGN OF THE ANTI-CHRIST
VERSES 34-35.

"Now when they shall fall, they shall be holpen with a little help: but many shall cleave to them with flatteries.

"And some of them of understanding shall fall, to try them, and to purge, and to make them white, even o the time of the end: because it is yet for a time appointed."

Prophecy was fulfilled when our Lord Jesus was born in Bethlehem of Judea. EVERY PROPHECY RELATING TO THE BIRTH OF JESUS WAS FULFILLED TO THE VERY LETTER. He was offered to the Jews as their Messiah but they would not accept Him, he was rejected and crucified. One day, talking to His disciples, He told them that the Temple where they were sitting would be leveled to the ground.

"And Jesus went out, and departed from the Temple: and His disciples came to Him for to shew Him the buildings of the Temple.

And Jesus said unto them, See ye not all these things? Verily I say unto you, There shall not be left here one stone upon another, that shall not be thrown down."

Matthew 24: 1-2

Forty years after Jesus was crucified and rose from the dead this was in A.D. 70, Jerusalem was captured by the Roman Emperor Titus. The Temple was burned and leveled to the ground, the very stones were pried apart to get the gold that ran in the cracks when the Temple was burned. Thus was fulfilled the prophecy that was given in verse 33 "they shall fall by the sword, and by flame, by captivity and by spoil, many days." These many days are the days in which we are now living. This period of time has been going on over 1900 years, but all signs points to the soon return of our Lord Jesus to earth, then we, who are born again believers will meet Him in the air.

Meanwhile the Jews have been widely scattered throughout the nations of the world. The Jews have suffered untold persecution, their homes have been burned, their possessions taken, untold numbers have been killed, Hitler murdered around two million of them in his gas ovens, this has happened as this verse says, "many days". They have been flattered, told what a wonderful people they are, they have been given great promises but were given but a small part of the territory God promised to Abraham, BUT THE DAY IS COMING WHEN GOD'S PROMISE WILL BE COMPLETELY FULFILLED! THE DAY IS COMING WHEN THE JEWS WILL ACKNOWLEDGE THE LORD JESUS AS THEIR MESSIAH, THEIR LORD AND SAVIOUR! From time to time the Jews have been "holpen" (helped) with a little help. "Our nation has been helping them in many ways, we have given them war material, we are training their pilots, meanwhile Russia has been giving the Arab nations war material as well. I do believe that the day is not far off when there will be a full scale war between the Arabs and the Jews, even now sporadic fighting is going on.

THE TIME OF THE END
VERSES 36-38.

"And the King shall do according to his will; and he shall exalt himself, and magnify himself above every god, and shall speak marvelous things against the God of gods, and shall prosper till the indignation be accomplished: for that that is determined shall be done.

Neither shall he egard the god of his fathers, nor the desire of women, nor regard any god: for he shall magnify himself above all.

but in his estate shall he honor the God of forces: and a god whom his fathers knew not shall he honor with gold, and silver, and with precious stones, and pleasant things.

These verses are definitely prophetic, they clear up things that have been puzzling Bible Students in their study, that is, the reference to the King who suddenly appears upon the world scene. I want you to know that these verses lead us to believe that this King is the one of whom we have met before, he is not a new person who needs to be introduced. Notice that verse 36 does not say "a" King but it does say "the" King. Some Bible Students claim that there are three Kings mentioned in this Book of' Daniel,-

1. The "little horn" of the fourth wild beast. See Daniel 7:8.
2. The "little horn" that came up on one of the four horns of this Rough He-Goat. See Daniel 8:9-12. They believe that this horn represents Antiochus Epiphanes IV.
3. The "wilful King" of this chapter 11 who represents the coming Anti-Christ.

This is the belief that some Bible Students have but we see as we study this chapter that these three personages, that is, the two "little horns" and the "wilful King" all appear and reign at the same time which is known as "The time of the end." All three manifest the same character and disposition and all three are destroyed in the same manner so we can only conclude that they are one and the same person. Who is this "wilful King"? He is none other than the coming Anti-Christ!

This wilful King will do what he pleases, note the seven things that are said concerning him,-

1. He shall exalt and magnify himself above every god. (Consider the difference between him and the Lord Jesus.)

2. He shall speak marvelous things against the God of gods. That is against our Heavenly Father.

3. He shall prosper until the indignation (this is the Great Tribulation) be accomplished. In other words God will allow him to carry on until God's plan for the "Time of the End" is completed.

4. He will have no regard for the God of his Fathers, that is, the God of Abraham, Isaac and Jacob, the Living God, Our Heavenly Father. This seems to be proof that the Anti-Christ will be a Jew since Jesus was a Jew. Note his name "ANTI-CHRIST". The word "ANTI" means "against" hence the word Anti-Christ means "against Christ". To get the Jews to accept him he would have to be a Jew.

5. He shall not regard "The desire of women." What does this mean? Does it mean that he will be a homo-sexual, that he will have no interest in women? Some Bible students think that he will be ruthless in his treatment of women, note the passage in Matthew 24:19-21 which says,-

"Woe to them that are with child, and to them that give suck in those days!

But pray ye that your flight be not in the winter, neither on the Sabbath day:

For then shall be great tribulation, such as was not since the beginning of the world to this time, no, nor ever shall be."

Matthew 24:19-21.

The Jewish people are still looking for the Messiah, to them he has not yet come. Every Jewish girl hopes to be the mother of the Messiah, could it be that the meaning of the phrase "he shall not regard the desire of women" means that he will completely ignore and disregard the desire of the Jewish women? The Jews will be looking forward to the coming of the Messiah when the Anti-Christ appears. One thing we know that is, that the Anti-Christ will not accept or acknowledge the Son for God's Holy Word says, - "He is Anti-Christ that denieth the Father and the Son." I John 2:22.

6. He shall honor the God of forces. His only god will be the god of armed might. The Anti-Christ will expect the "god of this world" who is Satan, to give him all the Kingdoms of this world. Satan offered the Kingdoms of this world to the Lord Jesus but He refused the offer.

"Again, the devil taketh Jesus up into an exceeding high mountain, and sheweth him all the kingdoms of the world, and the glory of them;

And saith unto him, All these things will I give three, if thou wilt fall down and worship me.

Then saith Jesus unto him, Get thee hence, Satan: for it is written, Thou shalt worship the Lord thy God, and him only shalt thou serve."

Matthew 4:8-10.

The Lord Jesus knew that our Heavenly Father would give Him all the Kingdoms of this world. He knew that after He had been crucified and rised from the dead and provided salvation for all men, then the Kingdoms of this world would be given to him. Proof of this is also given in the following prophecy-

"I saw in the night visions, and, behold, one like the Son of man came with the clouds of Heaven, and came to the Ancient of Days (this is God the Father) and they brought him near before him.

And there was given him dominion, and glory, and a Kingdom, that all people, nations, and languages, should serve him: his dominion is an everlasting dominion, which shall not pass away and his Kinndom that which shall not be destroyed."

Daniel 7:13-14.

I want to give you still another prophecy,-

"And the seventh angel sounded, and there were great voices in Heaven, saying, The Kingdoms of this world are become the Kingdoms of our Lord and His Christ; and he shall reign forever and ever."

Revelation 11:15.

7. He will honor a strange god with gold, silver and precious stones and pleasant things. Just what god will this Anti-Christ honor? IT IS NONE OTHER THAN SATAN HIMSELF!

VERSE 39.

"Thus shall he do in the most strongholds with a strange god, whom he shall acknowledge and increase with glory: and he shall cause them to rule over many, and shall divide the land for gain."

We are told in Revelation 13:2 "That the Dragon (Satan) will give him (The Anti-Christ) his power, and his seat (throne) and great authority." Using the power Satan gives him the Anti-

Christ will soon get control of the fortified cities of the ten federated Kingdoms which made up the original Roman Empire, he will supply them with men and munitions; he will tell them that this is necessary to keep peace and harmony in the world. He will flatter the people, winning their confidence and respect in this way; and since He is the Supreme ruler he will give honor, glory and authority to those who respect him,and for "graft" (gain) he will divide the land.

There is more I want to add at this point regarding the actions of the Anti-Christ. He will be the greatest spender the world has ever seen, he will do this in his effort to convince the people that he is their only home and Saviour. At the close of this verse 39 we are told that he will rule over many, then he will make the greatest mistake of his life for he will divide the land for gain.

The land mentioned is the land of Palestine. I have already told you that it is called "The Glorious Land", in verse 45 it is called "The Glorious Holy Mountain". Palestine is the geographical center of the world as far as Bible Prophecy is concerned. All distances mentioned are reckoned from Jerusalem.

Why did the Anti-Christ divide Palestime? No doubt he thought it would keep peace between himself and the Arab nations. But as soon as he did this the King of the South (that is these Arab nations) rose up in revolt against him for the Arab nations consider that all of Palestine belongs to them.

Before we continue on in our study I want to clear up any confusion you may have regarding the identity of "this willfull king" who he is and what he does. I have already told you in past chapters that the Roman Empire will be restored under a ten kingdom arrangement. We are now living in the space age, this union of ten kingdoms in Europe is already being formed under what is known as "the common market". This union of ten kingdoms will be completed when Jesus returns to earth and all we, who are born again believers, will be caught up TO BE WITH HIM.

"But I would not have you to be ignorant, brethren, concerning them which are asleep, that ye sorrow not, even as others which have no home.

For if we believe that Jesus died and rose again, even so them also which sleep in Jesus will God bring with him.

For this we say unto you by the world of the Lord, that we which are alive and remain unto the coming of the Lord shall not prevent (precede) them which are asleep.

For the Lord himself shall descend from Heaven with a

shout, with the voice of the archangel, and with the trump of God: and the dead in Christ shall rise first:

Then we which are alive and remain shall be caught up together with them in the clouds, to meet the Lord in the air: and so shall we ever be with the Lord.

Wherefore comfort one another with these words."

I Thessalonians 4:13-17.

When the Lord Jesus returns and we are caught up to meet Him in the air then an unusual experience takes place-THE BLESSED HOLY SPIRIT WILL BE TAKEN FROM THIS EARTH. Read the record given in God's Holy Word.

"For the mystery of iniquity doth already work: only he who now letteth (the Blessed Holy Spirit) will let, until he be taken out of the way."

II Thessalonians 2:7.

It is at this time that the Anti-Christ will be revealed. It is important that you know that he will not be revealed until AFTER our Lord Jesus returns. We will not be here when he arrives upon this world scene, we will be with the Lord. This Anti-Christ is "the wilful king" spoken of in this chapter XI. I have already shown you that he is motivated and controlled by Satan. I suggest you turn back and read once again what I have written in the explanation of verses 36-38, specially the seven things God's Holy Word says concerning him.

The Anti-Christ will rule for seven years. His first act will be to bring order out of chaos caused by the return of our Lord Jesus when all born again believers left this earth to be with our Blessed Lord. This will be no easy task for the entire social and economic system of the world has been disrupted and upset. He will make a covenant with the Jews, he will help them return to their own land, he will aid them in rebuilding of the Temple in Jerusalem. At the end of three and a half years, when the Temple has been completed and the sacrifices have been restored, the Anti-Christ will break the covenant he made with the Jews, he will personally enter the Holy of Holies in the Temple and demand that all the people worship him as God. He will demand that everyone accept his make, it is to be placed either in the forehead or in the palm of the hand. All who refuse to worship him as God, and who refuse to accept his make will be beheaded.

The Anti-Christ will have an assistant who is known in God's Holy Word as "the False Prophet". Now read what God's Holy Word says regarding him,-

"And I beheld another Beast coming up out of the earth; and he had two horns like a lamb, and he spake as a dragon.

And he exerciseth all the power of the first beast before him, and causeth the earth and them which dwell therein to worship the first beast, whose deadly wound was healed.

And he doeth great wonders, so that he maketh fire come down from Heaven on the earth in the sight of men.

And deceiveth them that dwell on the earth by the means of those miracles which he had power to do in the sight of the beast; saying to them that dwell on the earth, that they should make an image to the beast, which had the wound by a sword, and did live.

And he had power to give life unto the image of the beast, that the image of the beast should both speak, and cause that as many as would not worship the image of the beast should be killed.

And he causeth all, both small and great, rich and poor, free and bond, to receive a mark in their right hand, or in their foreheads:

And that no man might buy or sell, save he that had the mark, or the name of the beast, or the number of his name.

Here is wisdom. Let him that hath understanding count the number of the beast: for it is the number of a man; and his number is Six hundred three score and six."

Revelation 13:11-18.

Let us now continue with the explanation of the verses 40-42.

"And at the time of the end shall the King of the South push at him: and the King of the North shall come against him like a whirlwind, with chariots (tanks) and with horseman, and with many ships; and he shall enter into the countries, and shall overflow and pass over.

He shall enter also into the glorious land, and many countries shall be overthrown: but these shall escape out of his hand, even Edom, and Moab, and the chief of the children of Ammon.

He shall stretch forth his hand also upon the countries: and the land of Egypt shall not escape."

Daniel 11:40-42.

I want you to note that there are now two great powers upon the earth, they are the Anti-Christ with his armies and the King of the South and his armies. This King of the South is the head of all the Arab nations who live south of the land of Palestine. These Arabs are the descendants of Ishmael who was the son of Hagar, the Egyptian maid who was the servant of Sarah, the wife of Abraham. We are told that the King of the South shall push at him (the Anti-Christ). Why? Because he divided the land. I have already told you that the Arabs consider that all of Palestine belongs to them.

There is now a third power mentioned in this fortieth verse, this third power is called "The King of the North." We are told that this King shall come against the Anti-Christ like a whirlwind with chariots (tanks?) and horsemen. Who is this King of the North? God's Holy Word tells us that he is the head of the Northern Confederacy which is described in detail in the 38th and 39th chapters of the Book of Ezekiel.

I want to tell you more of this "King of the North" and the nation he represents. We are going to turn to the 38th and 39th chapters of the book of Ezekiel, I want to quote them and explain these verses as we continue with our study.

VERSE 1.

"And the word of the Lord came unto me, saying"-
I want you to note that the prophecy given in these two chapters is THE DEFINITE WORD OF THE LORD, it is God's message given to us for this space age and we need to give it serious consideration. We are now in that period of time known as "THE TIME OF THE END". So do not hurry through these pages for they are very important, they tell you what you need to know.

VERSE 2.

"Son of man, set thy face against God, the land of Magog, the chief prince of Meshech and Tubal, and prophesy against him,
In the study of these chapters I want, first of all, to make it clear to you who these nations are who compose this great Northern Confederacy. "GOG" is the prince or leader of this Confederacy, and "MAGOG" is his land. The entire prophecy given in these two chapters is against GOG and the nations associated with him.

Genesis chapter 10 verse 2 tells us that "MAGOG" was the second son of Japheth. The descendants of this son, according to the record of history moved northward to the southern territory of Russia. The two cities mentioned are Meshech and Tubal, Bible students have identified them as Moscow and Tobolsk. Moscow is the present capitol city of Russia, Tubolsk was the earliest province in Russia that was settled.

VERSE 3.

"And say, Thus saith the Lord God: Behold, I am against thee, O Gog, the chief prince of Meshech and Tubal:
I want you to notice that in the very beginning of this prophecy we are told that the Lord is definitely against Russia. Do you know why this is true? It is because Russia is the first nation in the world to become a nation definitely opposed to the worship of God. Do you know that it is now a criminal offense for

anyone to organize and teach a Bible class, or to own and distribute Bibles in Russia? No mother is allowed to teach her child a verse of Scripture or to tell her child a Bible story.

God alone knows how many hundreds of thousands ministers and professed Christians have been killed in Russia since 1918. I know that we are told by the press that there is now religious freedom in Russia this is a plain lie, it is but an attempt to deceive the people of the world. The leaders of Russia hate God, they say they will push Him off his throne. They are motivated by Satan and his demons, they are putting forth a supreme effort to convert the world to Communism which is Anti-God.

Since the Jews worship and sacrifice to God Russia has been outstanding in her persecution of the Jews, and of Israel. Russia has broken off relations with Israel, she has been aiding and working with the Arab nations furnishing them with munitions and helping them in every way she can.

Russia intends to conquer Israel, she plans to invade Palestine with a great army, who intends to wipe the name of God off the face of the earth. When will this great battle take place? You need not be alarmed if you are a born again believer for this battle will not take place until AFTER our Lord Jesus has returned and we have been caught up to be with Him. It will take place at the end of the seven year rule of the Anti-Christ.

VERSE 4.

"And I will turn thee back, and put hooks into thy jaws, and I will bring thee forth, and all thine army, horses and horsemen, all of them clothed with all sorts of armour, even a great company with bucklers and shields, all of them handling swords:

You can see from this verse that it is our heavenly Father who rules this world. While Russia and her allies may be able to amass a tremendous army, all Russia's efforts will avail her nothing, for it is prophecied that she will come to her end in Palestine.

VERSE 5-6.

"Persia, Ethiopia, and Libya with them; all of them with shield and helmet:

Gomer, and all his bands; the house of Togarmah of the north quarters, and all his bands: and many people with thee."

We are now told who the nations are who will be the allies of Russia, it is the union of all these nations who will compose this great Northern Confederacy, this great army which is led by GOG who is called "The King of the North". The first nation to be mentioned is Persia, the name of this nation was changed from Persia to Iran in 1935. The next nation mentioned is Ethiopia, the name is actually "Cush," this is not the Ethiopia of Africa, it is a land lying east of Babylon and north of Arabia, it is located not far from Iran.

Libya is now mentioned, this is also not the Libya of North Africa, it is a nation also located not far from Iran. The name comes from the word "PUT". Gomer is also a son of Japheth (See Genesis 10:2) Bible students tell us that Gomer and all his bands represents what is now Germany. We are not told who these bands are but they no doubt are Poland, Czechoslovakia, and Romania and etc. The nation called Togarmah is considered by Christian and Jewish Bible teachers to be Turkey.

VERSES 7-12.

"Be thou prepared, and prepare for thyself, thou, and all thy company that are assembled unto thee, and be thou a guard unto them.

After many days thou shalt be visited: in the latter years thou shalt come into the land that is brought back from the sword, and is gathered out of many people, against the mountains of Israel, which have been always waste: but it is brought forth out of the nations, and they shall dwell safely all of them.

Thou shalt ascend and come like a storm, thou shalt be like a cloud to cover the land, thou, and all thy bands, and many people with thee.

Thus saith the Lord God; It shall also come to pass, that at the same time shall things come into thy mind, and thou shalt think an evil thought:

And thou shalt say, I will go up to the land of unwalled villages; I will go to them that are at rest, that dwell safely, all of them dwelling without walls, and having neither bars nor gates,

To take a spoil, and to take a prey; to turn thine hand upon the desolate places that are now inhabited, and upon the people that are gathered out of the nations, which have gotten cattle and goods, that dwell in the midst of the land.

There are two oustanding reasons why Russia is massing this great army to march on Palestine. I have already told you the first reason, I repeat it, it is to completely do away with the name of God and everything that has to do with Christianity. Gog, the leader of this great Northern Confederacy, is opposed to Israel because Israel believes and worships the Living God.

Then there is a second reason why Gog and his allies are marching against Palestine, it is given in this verse 12 of this 38th chapter of the Book of Ezekiel, it is "to take a spoil". We are told that the land of Palestine is the most fertile of any nation in the world. All it needs is water and cultivation. In some areas it is possible to secure as many as five crops in a single year.

Russia knows that the minerals in the water of the Dead Sea

are worth literally billions of dollars, Russia wants to get possession of this wealth. Then Palestine has some of the most productive oil wells in the world, only God knows how much oil is available to those who will drill for it.

VERSE 13.

"Sheba, and Dedan, and the merchants of Tarshish, with all the young lions thereof, shall say unto thee, Art thou come to take a spoil? hast thou gathered thy company to take a prey? to carry away silver and gold, to take away cattle and goods, to take a great spoil?"

This verse tells us that Russia and her allies "known as "The King of the North", will march down from the north into Palestine, but when she arrives in Palestine she will find those who will definitely oppose her. There are those who are ready and willing to oppose this great of marching horsemen coming down from the north, who are these nations who will help Israel?

The nation of Sheba is mentioned in this verse 13, who is Sheba? Bible students tell us that Sheba is the name of a tribe of Arabs living in the south part of Arabia. While we know that "The King of the South" will unite with "The King of the North" yet we are told that there are certain Arabian tribes who will oppose this great "King of the North". Dedan is the name of a people in Arabia who are also opposed to this "KING of the NORTH".

Then this verse 13 tells us that "the merchants of Tarshish and the young lions thereof" will oppose this "King of the North". Who are these merchants of Tarshish and the young lions? Most of our Bible students believe that Tarshish refers to Great Britian and the young lions are Canada, Australia, New Zealand, the United States, and etc. If this is the true interpretation of this word "tarshish, and I believe it is, for we have, as a nation, been helping Israel furnishing munitions, we have been training their pilots, and etc.

While the King of the North was forming his great armies and his allies were working with him forming this Great Northern Confederacy the King of the South was also busy forming his federation of Arab states. Who the King of the South is not given to us, all we are told is that he is forming a federation of Arab nations living south of Palestine and he and his armies will fight the Anti-Christ. Why? Because he has divided the land.

Meanwhile the Anti-Christ, also known as "the wilful King" has come into possession of the fortified cities and fortresses of the ten federated Kingdoms which will quickly rise after the Anti-Christ has brought peace and quiet to a world that had been filled with chaos and unrest after the Rapture. The Old Roman Empire has once again been established. The Anti-Christ will now fill these Kingdoms with tens of thousands of soldiers. I have already

194

told you how he will help the Jews, he will help all those who want to return to Palestine, he will help them in the building of the Temple, they will accept him as their Messiah.

There are now three great armies moving into Palestine-
1. The armies of the King of the North. These are made up of Russia, and her allies who are Iran, Ethiopia, Libya, Germany, Turkey, Yugoslavia, Romania and etc.
2. The armies of the King of the South, they are composed of the Federated nations living south of Palestine.
3. The armies of the Anti-Christ. He has been busy mobilizing the nation and drawing from each nation the fighting force he needs to bring the entire world under his control.

VERSES 15-16.

"And thou shalt come from thy place out of the north parts, thou, and many people with thee, all of them riding upon horses, a great company, and a mighty army:

And thou shalt come up against my people of Israel, as a cloud to cover the land; it shall be in the latter days, and I will bring thee against my land, that the heathen may know me, when I shall be sanctified in thee, O Gog, before their eyes."

Ezekiel 38:15-16.

These verses tell us that Gog, this King of the North, shall enter Palestine with a tremendous army, all men riding upon horses, and all carrying swords. There is so many God-hating men in this army that they are like a cloud, covering the land.

This King of the North hates God with all the power of his being, and because the Jews worship God he hates the Jews, he is determined to destroy them all.

This King of the South hates the Jews because they claim God gave them all of Palestine, he hates the Anti-Christ because he divided the land.

This Anti-Christ hates the Jews because they give the worship he craves to the Living God instead of to him, and because he is empowered by Satan, whom he serves.

The armies of the King of the North and the King of the South now unite and together they attack the Anti-Christ. There will be a terrific battle on both land and the sea, many countries will be overthrown. God's Holy Word tells us that Edom, Moab, and the country of Ammon will be spared, however Egypt and Palestine (The Glorious Land) shall not escape.

"And at the time of the end shall the King of the South push at him, (the Anti-Christ), and the King of the North shall come against him like a whirlwind, with chariots, and with horsemen, and with many ships: and he shall enter into the countries, and shall overflow, and pass over.

He shall also enter into the glorious land, and many countries shall be overthrown; but these shall escape out of his hand, even Edom, and Moab, and the chief of the children of Ammon."

Daniel 11:40-41.

"He shall stretch forth his hand also upon the countries: and the land of Egypt shall not escape.

But he shall have power over the treasures of gold and of silver, and over all the precious things of Egypt: and the Libyans and the Ethiopians shall be at his steps.

But tidings out of the east and out of the north shall trouble him: therefor he shall go forth with great fury to destroy, and utterly to make away many.

And he shall plant the tabernacles of his palace between the seas (the Mediterranean and the Dead Sea) in the glorious holy mountain; yet he shall come to his end, and none shall help him."

Daniel 11:42-45.

It is at this time that the King of the North and the King of the South will begin a siege against Jerusalem, their large numbers and their power to destroy is vividly given to us in God's Holy Word.

"Behold I will make Jerusalem a cup of trembling unto all the people round about,when they shall be in the siege both against Judah and against Jerusalem.

I will gather all nations against Jerusalem to battle; and the city shall be taken, and the houses rifled, and the women ravished; and half of the city shall go forth into captivity, and the residue of the people shall not be cut off from the city.

Then shall the Lord go forth, and fight against those nations, as when He fought in the day of battle."

Zechariah 12:2; 14:2-3.

The Anti-Christ had brought his entire armies into Palestine when he completed his conquest of Egypt. He took all the gold, silver and precious stones they had, while he was still in Egypt he received bad news, it had come from the east, no doubt from Babylon his capitol city, and from the north, (possibly from spies). What was this bad news? I believe it was a report that the Kings of the East, with their millions of fighting men all mounted on horses were on the march, they were approaching Palestine. The "Time of the End" had come, God had dried up the river bed of the river Euphrates so these massive armies, all on horses, might march into Palestine, unhindered.

"And the sixth angel poured out his vial upon the great river Euphrates; and the water thereof was dried up, that the way of the Kings of the East might be prepared."

Revelation 16:12.

Who are these Kings of the East? God's Holy Word does not tell us, I believe they are massed armies of China, Japan and other countries. I hope you can visualize what the armies of these Kings of the East will be like. The time has now come for the Battle of Armageddon. There are now three great armies massed in Palestine; the armies of the King of the North; the armies of the King of the South; and the armies of the Kings of the East. They are all opposed to the Anti-Christ and his armies, he has the fourth great army now in Palestine.

I know you want to know more about this coming Battle of Armageddon, you want to know where it will be located, who will take part in it and how it will end. Let me say here and now that this coming Battle of Armageddon will bring an end to this present Gentile World System under which we live at the present time, and which is so imposing and powerful to-day. This Gentile world System is composed of five things, Force, Greed, Selfishness, Ambition and Pleasure. This Gentile world system is very imposing and powerful with armies and navies and all kinds of military equipment, it is outwardly religious, scientific and cultured; but it is seething with national and commercial rivalries and ambitions, it is upheld in any crisis only by armed force, and is dominated by Satan and his demons.

These great armies now massed in Palestine demonstrate these five things I have just mentioned. This Battle of Armageddon will be fought in Palestine, at a place called Megiddo, pronounced "Mageedo". This is at a junction of three continents, Africa, Asia and Europe. Many wars have already been fought here during the past centuries, its ground has been soaked with blood many times. When I was in Palestine I visited this place, I found Megiddo to-day to be but a small village located about fifty miles north of Jerusalem and ten miles south-west of Nazareth. It is at the south end of a great plain extending from Mount Gilboa to Haifa.

Before this great Battle of Armageddon begins there will appear a sign in Heaven, the sign of the Son of Man.

"And then shall appear the sign of the Son of Man: in heaven: and then shall all the tribes of the earth mourn, and they shall see the Son of Man coming in the clouds of heaven with power and great glory."

Matthew 24:30

When these great armies see this sign in heaven they will immediately stop their fighting with each other, they now unite their forces, the anti Christ and his helper the False Prophet assume the leadership in this battle against our Lord Jesus

197

Christ. The Apostle John says,-

"And I saw an angel standing in the sun; and he cried with a loud voice, saying to all the fowls that fly in the midst of Heaven, Come and gather yourselves together unto the supper of the great God;

That ye may eat the flesh of Kings, and the flesh of captains, and the flesh of mighty men, and the flesh of horses, and of them that sit on them, and the flesh of all men, both free and bond, both small and great.

And I saw the beast, and the kings of the earth, and their armies, gathered together to make war against him that sat on the horse, (our Lord Jesus) and against his army."

Revelation 19:17-19.

Let me try to describe the scene as it exists here upon the earth. Here are 200 million men, all mounted upon horses, all armed with swords, ready and waiting to kill our Lord Jesus as soon as His feet touch the earth. They are a cursing, God-hating mass of humanity determined to destroy God and take control of all of God's great Universe. This is a battle, not of man against man, or nation against nation, but of man against God!

Now let me try to tell you what is taking place in Heaven. No living man can truly describe this great event. I can only try to explain to you what God's Holy Word says about it. The time has now come for our Lord Jesus to return to this earth, this is the second aspect of our Lord's coming. He is now returning to earth WITH His true born again believers, not FOR them, this had already taken place seven years before. He is coming now to destroy these four great armies of 200 million men, all mounted on horseback and all led by the Anti-Christ. He is coming to the rescue of the oppressed and suffering Jews; to bring an end to this Gentile World System I told you about; and to set up His earthly Kingdom after He has brought an end to the four great armies, the Anti-Christ and the False Prophet, and after He has judged the nations. Then it is that He will begin His 1000 year reign of peace. What a picture our Heavenly Father has given us of these coming events!

Try if you can to visualize this tremendous scene-

"And I saw Heaven opened, and behold a white horse; and he that sat upon him was called Faithful and True, and in righteousness he doth judge and make war.

His eyes were as a flame of fire, and on his head were many crowns; and he had a name written, that no man knew, but he himself.

And he was clothed in a vesture dipped in blood: and his

name is called The Word of God.
And the armies which were in Heaven followed him upon
white horses, clothed in fine linen, white and clean.
And out of his mouth goeth a sharp sword, that with it be
should smite the nations; and he shall rule them with a rod of
iron; and he treadeth the winepress of the fierceness and wrath of
Almighty God.
And he hath on his vesture and on his thigh a name written,
KING OF KINGS, AND LORD OF LORDS."

Revelation 19:13-16.

And now everything is ready, a multitude, far greater than
the sands on all the combined sea shores of earth, are praising
God. Heaven rings with the joyful praises of this great multitude.
Angel choirs join in this chorus of praise. Everyone, the angels
and all the redeemed, is clothed in spotless white linen garments.
Their voices are like the sound of many waters, it is like the roar
of a million Niagaras all rolled into one. Dear reader, if you are a
true, born again believer you, too, will be there, you will be
clothed in white linen, you will be one of this number, you will join
in this chorus of praise! How wonderful this will be!

And now, everything is hushed, for our Lord Jesus Christ,
seated upon a white horse, appears. His eyes are like a flame of
fire. He has crowns upon His head, and He is clothed in a blood-
red garment upon which is written, "KING OF KINGS AND
LORD OF LORDS."

Then, suddenly, in a moment, the Heavens are rolled back as
a scroll. Then we, who are the redeemed, togehter with an unnumbered host of angels, led by our Lord Jesus, all of us mounted
upon white horses, return to earth. Not only will the massed
armies led by the Anti-Christ see our Lord Jesus come to earth,
EVERYONE UPON EARTH SHALL SEE HIM!

"And then shall they see the Son of man coming in the clouds
with great power and glory."

Mark 13:26.

"Behold, he cometh with clouds; AND EVERY EVE SHALL
SEE HIM, and they also pierced him: and all kindreds of the
earth wail because of him. Even so, Amen.

Revelation 1:7.

His first coming to earth was as a suffering servant. In His
second coming with all the redeemed and the host of Heaven He
comes as a conquering King. Before, He came to die to provide
salvation for us; now He comes to reign. Before He came as a
Lamb, now He comes as a Lion. Priase His Name! When you
became a born again believer you came under the banner of a

conquering Lord. He has never, no never, known defeat! Oh how wonderful it is to become a true born again believer! How can anyone go on rejecting our Lord Jesus when they know these things are true?

What a sight this will be! The man on horseback, dressed in red, with crowns upon His head is our Blessed Lord Jesus. His army is composed of the millions of Redeemed saints of God and the great unnumbered host of angels who have returned to this earth with Him. Against our Blessed Lord Jesus and His army will be the long battle line composed of 200 million cursing, blaspheming men, led by the Anti-Christ and the False Prophet.

This battle will be the supreme effort of Satan to achieve his plan which is to overthrow God and become the ruler of both Heaven and earth. All his plotting and planning from the time of the fall of Adam and Eve in the garden of Eden, throughout the centuries will then be centered in this one great battle to gain supremacy. IT IS NOW OR NEVER! THE CRISIS WILL HAVE COME!

Against the Anti-Christ and the False Prophet will be our victorious Lord Jesus who has never known defeat, mighty in His majesty, and with Him all the hosts of the Redeemed saints of God! What a contrast in the armies! What a difference in character! In the armies of the Anti-Christ and the False Prophet are wicked, blaspheming men, in the army of our Blessed Lord Jesus are we, the true born again believers, all clothed in white linen, shouting and singing the praises of our victorious Lord. Yes, dear reader, I say it again, I rejoice in the privilege I have in telling you, if you are a true born again believer YOU WILL BE IN THIS ARMY, YOU WILL WITNESS THIS WONDERFUL SCENE!

Not one of us need to lift a finger to destroy and kill in this mighty battle! Why? Because our victorious Lord Jesus has such power at His command that all He needs to do is to speak the command and His mighty power is released! I hope, dear reader, you know and realize the unlimited power possessed by our Lord Jesus. If unsaved men such as alcoholics, drug addicts and all sinners fully realized the power available to them, do you think they would go on rejecting Him? Do you think they would go on, living defeated, broken lives, conquered by the lusts of the flesh? Satan has men blinded, but thank God, they do not need to remain so! Victory through Christ is available to all!

When the feet of our Lord Jesus touch the Mount of Olives, a tremendous earthquake will shake the earth, the greatest earthquake this world has ever experienced. Every island will be covered with water, every mountain range will be leveled. Can you image the destruction and the loss of life that will take place? These are not idle words I am giving you, this earthquake will take place for God has said it will. Now read the record given in God's Holy Word as it has been revealed to us by the prophets,-

"In that day there shall be a great earthquake, a great shaking in the land of Israel;

So that the fishes of the sea, and the fowls of heaven, and the beasts of the field, and all creeping things that creep upon the earth, and all the men that are upon the face of the earth, shall shake at my presence, and the mountains shall be thrown down, and the steep places shall fall, and every wall shall fall to the ground."

Ezekiel 38:19-20.

"There were voices, and thunders, and lightnings; and there was a great earthquake, such as was not since men were upon the earth, so mighty an earthquake, and so great."

Revelation 16:18.

"The Mount of Olives shall cleave in the midst thereof toward the east and toward the west, and there shall be a very great valley; and half of the mountain shall remove toward the north, and half of it toward the south."

Zechariah 14:4.

Jerusalem will be divided into three parts, and all the cities of the world will be leveled to the ground. Try and imagine the destruction caused by this mighty earthquake! Think of it, Rome falls, Berlin falls, Paris falls, London falls, New York falls, Chicago falls, and etc. All the cities of the world are leveled to the ground no matter where they are located, so great is the power of this mighty earthquake.

THE END OF THE ANTI-CHRIST AND
THE FALSE PROPHET

The massed armies led by the Anti-Christ now see our victorious Lord Jesus with his great unnumbered host of angels and all the Redeemed. There will be no armistice declared in this battle, it is a fight to the death.

Our Lord Jesus speaks and God's power, like a mighty sword, is manifested. The Anti-Christ and the False Prophet are taken, they are completely helpless before our conquering, victorious Lord. They are immediately cast alive into God's Lake of Fire, burning with brimstone. This is the terrible end of these enemies of God.

"And the beast (the Anti-Christ) was taken, and with him the false prophet, that wrought miracles before him, with which he deceived them had received the mark of the beast, and them that worshipped his image. These both were cast alive into a lake of fire burning with brimstone."

Revelation 19:20.

The armies of the Anti-Christ, seeing the Anti-Christ and the False Prophet taken and cast alive into the Lake of Fire, and finding themselves surrounded by the great unnumbered army of God on every side, are at once in a great rout. They want to escape but there is no escape for them.

"In that day, saith the Lord, I will smite every horse with astonishment, and his rider with madness: and I will open mine eyes upon the house of Judah, and will smite every horse of the people with blindness."

Zechariah 12:4.

"And I will call for a sword against him throughout all my mountains, saith the Lord God: every man's sword shall be against his brother.

And I will plead against him with pestilence and with blood; and I will rain upon him, and upon his bands, and upon the many people who are with him, an overflowing rain, and great hailstones, fire and brimstone."

Ezekiel 28:21-22.

I am sure you get the picture of the destruction of this great army of over 200 million fighting men. With their horses smitten with blindness, and the men riding these horses all gone mad and killing each other, soon this great host of fighting men lie dead, bodies piled upon each other. Through the destructive earthquake and the terrible hail storm and fire and brimstone, so great will be the destruction of the armies of the Anti-Christ that ONLY ONE SIXTH will be left.

"Therefore, thou son of man, prophesy against Gog and say, Thus saith the Lord God; Behold, I am against thee, O Gog, the chief prince of Meshech and Tubal:

And I will turn thee back, AND LEAVE BUT THE SIXTH PART OF THEE, and will cause thee to come up from the north parts, and will bring thee upon the mountains of Israel:

And I will smite thy bow out of the left hand, and will cause thine arrows to fall out of thy right hand.

Thou shalt fall upon the mountains of Israel, thou, and all thy bands, and the people that is with thee: I will give thee unto the ravenous birds of every sort, and to the beasts of the field to be

devoured.
Thou shalt fall upon the open field: for I have spoken it, saith the Lord God."
Ezekiel 39:1-5.

As soon as the call was made by the angel the vultures and all manner of flesh eating birds and animals converged upon this battle field. But the larger number of the dead will lie unburied for months, God's Holy Word tells us that the stench of these unburied bodies will be so great it will stop the noses of all those who must travel through the land, and that it will take seven months to bury the dead.

"It shall come to pass in that day, that I will give unto Gog a place there of graves in Israel, the valley of the passengers on the east of the sea; and it shall stop the noses of the passengers: and there shall they bury Gog and all his multitude; and they shall call it The valley of Pamon-Gog.
And seven months shall the house of Israel be burying of them, that they may clenase the land."
Ezekiel 39:11-12.

Finally a calm descends upon a war torn world. Every enemy of God has been overthrown. Every opposing force has been permanently removed. Thus ends the Battle of Armageddon with a glorious victory for our Lord Jesus. God has vindicated His Son. Our Lord Jesus now takes His rightful place, ushering in the Dispensation of the Kingdom. The times of the Gentiles have ended.

There are many more details given in God's Holy Word, events that will take place in these closing days of the Times of the Gentiles. I have only given you the main events that are to take place. Now I hope you will complete the study for yourself.

There is one great outstanding fact I want to emphasize. If you are a born again believer, you and I will be there. We will be with this great army of our Lord Jesus when He returns to earth. How I hope and pray that you are a ture born again believer! If not, do nto delay, accept our Lord Jesus, NOW!

CHAPTER 12.
We come now to the closing chapter of this wonderful prophetic Book of Daniel. The final words of his prophecy and the conclusion of his vision is now before us. I want you to bear in mind that Daniel is still standing on the bank of the Tigris River

(Hiddekel), and that the last three chapters (10-12) are one vision. Daniel is now told to "shut up the words and seal the book" (Verse 4). I want you now to read Isaiah 29:10-12.

You can be sure that when the end time arrives the message that Daniel was told to seal will be made clear, and those living will understand (verse 10). See Revelation 22:10. I believe this time is very near, and I am sure you will agree with me in this. We now give thought to this closing chapter.

VERSE 1.

"And at that time shall Michael stand up, the great prince which standeth for the children of thy people: and there shall be a time of trouble, such as never was since there was a nation even to that same time: and at that time thy people shall be delivered, every one that shall be found written in the book."

You will notice as you read this verse that it begins with the words "And at that time..." This proves that this chapter 12 is a continuation of chapter 11. What do you think is meant by the phrase "at that time"? I think that it refers to the events which we studied in chapter 11. It is telling us what is going to happen in this period known as "the time of the end." We were told of the battles fought by the Anti-Christ, of the four great armies, of their meeting in Palestine at a place called "Megiddo", for this is the battle of Armageddon; of the return of our Lord Jesus with all the born-again believers and a great host of angels, and the final end of the Anti-Chirst and the False Prophet. This is the time when Michael shall come to the aid of the Jews.

WHO IS MICHAEL?

We have already seen in our past study that Michael was chosen by God to be the special guardian of the Jews. He is a great prince who stands for Daniel's people, the Jews. Where? Well, in Heaven. If that is not what this message given means, then what can it mean? He is not standdng there now. It is "at that time (that) Michael shall stand up." Who is standing there now? It is the one whom the Jews now reject and despise, the one who came unto His own but His own received Him not. It is our Blessed Lord Jesus. After He had entered the city on that Palm Sunday and the people had cast their clothing and palm branches on the street before Him, looking over the city He said, in agony of heart, the tears running down His cheecks, "O Jerusalem, Jerusalem, thou that killest the prophets, and stonest them who are sent unto thee, how often would I have gathered thy children together, even as a hen gathers her chickens under wings, and ye would not!

204

'Behold your house is left unto you desolate.
"For I say unto you, ye shall not see me henceforth, till ye
cometh in the name of the Lord!"
(Matthew 23:37-39)
The next time that Daniel's people, the Jews, as a nation are
going to see Him whom they crucified, is when they gladly cry
out, "Blessed is he that cometh in the name of the Lord!" The
Jews were not willing to do this when He came the first time.
They have not been willing to do it at any time since, and they are
not willing to do it even now! But the day is coming when they will
do so gladly. This is plainly indicated in what our Lord Jesus said
to them, "Ye shall not see me till ye shall say, 'Blessed is he that
cometh in the name of the Lord!'"
We are now considering who Michael is. Do you know that
Michael is mentioned three times in the Book of Daniel? The first
time is in Daniel 10:13:
*"The prince of the kingdom of Persia withstood me one and
twenty days; but, lo, Michael, one of the chief princes, came to
help me."*
And in Daniel 10:21:
*"There is none that holdeth with me in 'these things but
Michael, your prince."*
And in this first verse of chapter 12 Michael is called, "The
Great Prince." In the book of Jude, verse 9, he is called "The
Archangel". This passage in Jude tells of his contending with the
devil about the body of Moses. There is only one archangel
mentioned in all of God's Holy Word, and Michael is the one. In
Revelation 12:7 we are told that the Archangel Michael had
charge of the angels in Heaven when he fought with the devil.

THE COMING TIME OF TROUBLE

This first verse seems to be the culminating feature of
Daniel's entire visions. "And at that time shall Michael stand up,
the great prince which standeth for the children of thy people;
and there shall be a time of trouble, such as never was since there
was a nation even to that same time." (Verse 1)
This time of trouble spoken of in verse one begins when the
Anti-Christ enters the Holy of Holies in the Temple and demands
that everyone worship him as god, and all who refuse to worship
him are beheaded. This takes place at the beginning of the last
3½ years of the reign of the Anti-Christ. This is the time which
our Lord Jesus said was coming:
*"For then shall be great tribulation, such as was not since the
beginning of the world to this time, no, nor ever shall be.
"And except those days should be shortened, there should no*

flesh be saved; but for the elect's sake those days shall be shortened."

This terrible time of trouble will be followed by the darkening of the sun and the falling of the stars, then our Lord Jesus will return to this earth bringing the angels and we, who are redeemed, with Him:

"Immediately after the tribulation of those days shall the sun be darkened, and the moon shall not give its light, and the stars shall fall from heaven, and the powers of the heavens shall be shaken.

"And then shall appear the sign of the Son of Man in heaven; and then shall all the tribes of the earth mourn, and they shall see the Son of Man coming in the clouds of heaven with power and great glory."

Matthew 24:29-30

Did you say that you wonder if these things are actually going to happen? Indeed, they **will** happen! Now read what happened in the time of Moses:

"And the Lord said unto Moses, 'Stretch out thine hand toward heaven, that there may be darkness over the land of Egypt, even darkness which may be felt!'

And Moses stretched forth his hand toward heaven; and there was a thick darkness in all the land of Egypt three days.

They saw not one another, neither rose any from his place for three days; but all the children of Israel had light in their dwellings."

Exodus 10:21-23

This terrible time of trouble and suffering is described in both the Old and the New Testaments; it takes place here upon earth during the reign of the Anti-Christ and will be brought to an end when our Lord Jesus returns. The prophet Jeremiah calls it "the time of Jacob's trouble"; he compares the suffering of the Jews to the birth-pangs of a woman in travail:

"These are the words which the Lord spoke concerning Israel and Judah.

For thus saith the Lord, 'We have heard a voice of trembling, of fear, and not of peace.

Ask now, and see whether a man doth travail with child? Wherefore do I see every man with his hands on his loins, like a woman in travail, and all faces are turned into paleness?

Alas! for that day is great, so that none is like it; it is even the time of Jacob's trouble, but he shall be saved out of it."

Jeremiah 30:4-7

206

We now come to the last part of verse one, which tells us that "at that time thy people shall be delivered, every one that shall be found written in the book." I have already told you that God has a "Book of Life" in which are written the names of all true born-again believers. When you see yourself a sinner, and truly repent of your sin, and accept our Lord Jesus as your personal Saviour, then your name is written in this Book of Life. God's Holy Word says:

"Whosoever was not found written in the book of life was cast into the Lake of Fire."

Revelation 20:15.

I must stop here and ask you, "Is your name written in God's Book of Life?" You may be a baptized church member, you attend church and call yourself a believer, but if your name is not written in God's Book of Life **you will be cast into the Lake of Fire!**

Speaking of this time of trouble God's Holy Word says, "for the elect's sake, those days shall be shortened" (Matthew 24:22). The elect's are those whose names are written in the Book of Life. Those who will be delivered are those who are truly born-again believers. Our Heavenly Father does not write the names of unsaved people in His Book of Life. This is why I beg of you to make sure that your name name is written in God's Book of Life. This tells us very plainly that only those Jews who are true born-again believers are, at that time, going to be delivered and will enter into the glorious millennial kingdom of our Lord Jesus.

VERSE 2.

"And many of those who sleep in the dust of the earth shall awake, some to everlasting life, and some to shame and everlasting contempt."

This verse tells of one of the resurrections spoken of in God's Holy Word. Do you know that there are several resurrections spoken of in God's Holy Word? Some folks believe that there is to be but one general resurrection, a time when everyone will come out of the grave at the same time: the born-again believer and the sinner; and all will be judged at this resurrection. There is no such thing in God's Holy Word as a general re urrection. There is a 1000 years difference in time between the resurrection of the born again believer and the sinner. Now let me tell you of these resurrections.

1. **There is the resurrection of the born-again believer.** It is your dead body that is placed in the grave, to sleep until our Lord returns. Your spirit does not die; it will live forever and ever. All that death can mean for the born-again believer is "moving

day". When this moving day (death) comes, the Blessed Holy Spirit goes with you, and in a moment--in the twinkling of an eye-- you are with the Lord. You will see our Lord Jesus and your loved ones face to face. II Corinthians 5:8 tells us that "to be absent from the body is to be present with the Lord." The Apostle Paul in Philippians 1:23 says, "I am in a strait betwixt two, having a desire to depart and be with Christ, which is far better." All that goes into the grave is your dead body. All that can come out of the grave is your body. At the Second Coming of Christ (see I Thessalonians 4:13-17) for His saints, all true born-again believers will receive their glorified bodies, while the wicked dead will not be raised until the white throne judgement which takes place **after** the 1000 year reign of our Lord Jesus here upon this earth. (See Revelation 20:5)

"And I saw a great white throne, and him that sat on it from whose face the earth and the heaven fled away, and there was found no place for them.

"And I saw the dead, small and great, stand before God, and the books were opened, and another book was opened, which is the book of life. And the dead were judged out of those things which were written in the books, according to their works.

"And whosoever was not found written in the book of life was cast into the lake of fire." (Revelation 20:11-12, 15.)

So we see that the first resurrection is the raising of the body of the born-again believer. Is it clear to you now that there is a 1000 year's difference in time between the raising of the born-again believer to everlasting life, and the raising of the wicked to face shame and everlasting contempt? (Verse2) The righteous shall rise to the "resurrection of life" before the 1000 year reign of our Blessed Lord Jesus, and the wicked to the "resurrection of damnation" at the close of our Lord's reign.

"Marvel not at this; for the hour is coming, in which all that are in the graves shall hear his voice,

"And shall come forth, they that have done good, unto the resurrection of life; and they that have done evil, unto the resurrection of damnation." (John 5:28-29)

I have tried to explain to you the coming physical resurrections. There is so much more I could give you; I hope you will continue this study of the resurrections, for it is greatly worth-while and will bring you many blessings. But I must tell you that this twelfth chapter of Daniel deals entirely with the Jews.

2. **This verse 2 speaks of a Jewish resurrection.** When I first read this verse I naturally inferred that it told of the physical resurrection of the body, which we know will take place in God's

own time; but when we study these chapters it seems to refer to a Jewish resurrection, for Israel is now raised and revived, and is now recognized as one of the nations of the earth. For years Israel was nationally dead, buried in the graveyard of the nations of the earth and the islands of the sea. The Jews have been scattered throughout the world for over 2500 years, but now they are fast returning to their own land. This was prophesied hundreds of years ago by the prophet Jeremiah who said-

"Therefore, behold, the days come, saith the Lord, that it shall no more be said, The Lord liveth, that brought up the children of Israel out of Egypt;

But, the Lord liveth that brought up the children of Israel from the land of the north, and from all the lands whither He had driven them: and I will bring them again into their land that I gave unto their fathers." (Jeremiah 16:14-15)

Note also what the apostle Paul has told us-

"All Israel shall be saved; as it is written, "There shall come out of Zion a Deliverer, and shall turn away ungodliness from Jacob;

"For this is my covenant unto them, when I shall take away their sins." (Romans 11:26-27)

Have you wondered why the Jews have been scattered throughout the nations of the world? It was because of their sinful lives. God had warned them over and over again that if they continued to disobey His laws, which were given to them for their happiness and well-being, they would be carried into captivity. On more than one occasion, they were scattered throughout the nations of the world, but they have always retained their identity; a Jew is a Jew no matter in what nation he may be living. I do not know of a nation that does not have Jews living in it.

Yes, the Jews are fast returning to their own land. Israel now has a seat in the United Nations, it has its own government, its own coinage, and pure Hebrew is being taught and spoken, as well as other languages.

Do you realize that all this tells us that we are now living in the end time; that is, the closing days of the "Times of the Gentiles"? Have you given thought to this: that it is one of the clearest signs that the return of our Lord Jesus is near? The question is, "Are you ready for His return?" If He should come today, would you be left behind? Are your loved ones ready? Believe me when I tell you that all signs before us tell me that His coming may be very near. When will He come? No one knows -- not even the angels who are in Heaven. We are told to watch and be ready.

"But of that day and hour knoweth no man, no, not the angels of Heaven, but my Father only."

"Watch, therefore, for ye know now what hour your Lord doth come."

"Therefore, be ye also ready; for in such an hour as ye think not, the Son of man cometh." (Matthew 24:36, 42, 44)

Verse 3

"And they that be wise shall shine as the brightness of the firmament; and they that turn many to righteousness, as the stars forever and ever."

I have a few questions to ask you. Who are the wise? What does God's Holy Word say about them? What wonderful promise is given to soul winners?

Real wisdom consists in putting our Lord Jesus **first** in your life; in giving the Blessed Holy Spirit, who lives in your body, complete control of your life. We turn now to I Corinthians chapter one, where the apostle Paul shows us that there is a great difference between the wisdom of this world and the wisdom of God. He tells us that the wisdom of this world is foolishness with God and the foolishness of God is wiser than the wisdom of this world.

"The foolishness of God is wiser than men, but God hath chosen the foolish things of the world to confound the wise; and God hath chosen the weak things of the world to confound the things which are mighty;

And base things of the world, and things which are despised, hath God chosen, yea, and things which are not, to bring to nothing things that are,

That no flesh should glory in his presence." (I Corinthians 1: 25, 27-29)

How to Become Wise

Do you know want to become wise? If so, consider carefully what I tell you.

1. I've already shown you there is a decided difference between the wisdom we learn from men and the wisdom we learn from God. True wisdom is a gift given by the Holy Spirit to those who give Him complete control of their lives. I mention once again Romans 12:1-2. Consider these verses God's command especially to you, for this is true, they **are** especially for you. Do what they say and God's wisdom will be given to you!

2. We learn from God's Holy Word that the fear of the Lord is the beginning of knowledge (Proverbs 1:7), and that "he that winneth souls is wise" (Proverbs 11:30), and in this third verse of the 12th chapter of Daniel we are told that, "The wise shall shine as the brightness of the firmament."

The margin in your Bible reads "teachers" in place of the word "wise", so we quote this verse like this, "They that be teachers shall shine as the brightness of the firmament." In this verse Daniel is speaking particularly of the teachers of Israel. Jesus made it clear to us that one of the oustanding signs of the end of this Gentile age in which we are living will be false prophets and false teachers, preaching a false gospel and wrongly dividing and presenting God's Word, thus leading the people astray. (Matthew 24).

How do we, who are born-again believers, become true teachers? First, by a daily study of God's Holy Word; by living a life so transparent that the world can see the Holy Spirit is living in our bodies. Then, by our positive actions; our heart desire to see loved ones, friends and unsaved become Christians. You, dear reader, can become a wonderful teacher; truly you can! The "shining" spoken of may refer to the power radiated by a surrendered life. What a striking illustration this is, to be told that we shall shine as the brightness of the firmament!

Now note the last half of this third verse. What a privilege is given to us to be a soul-winner! I repeat what I have told you: real wisdom consists in putting our Lord Jesus first in your life, and seeking to win the lost to accept Him as Saviour and Lord. This is a vital fact you should learn. Be a soul winner! The demons about us will do all they can to hinder you, but in the strength and power of the indwelling Holy Spirit, go forward to win others to Christ!

Note the reward God will give you. Think of what a wonderful promise this is! Who of us can realize, even in a small way, the magnitude of the stellar worlds of God's universe!

God's Last Message to Daniel
Verse 4

"But thou, O Daniel, shut up the words, and seal the book, even to the time of the end; many shall run to and fro, and knowledge shall be increased."

Daniel is now told that the prophecy which has been revealed to him telling of the things that are to come, which extend to the end of the "Times of the Gentiles", is complete. All the information our Heavenly Father wants the world to know has been given. Daniel is now to close the book and seal it, for no more prophecy is to be given to him.

This verse tells us that "Many shall run to and fro." How clearly we see this prophecy fulfilled today! This is indeed a day of travel and speed. Have you ever stopped to consider the progress man has made in a single lifetime? I am sure grandpa and grandma remember the horse and buggy days. Those were the days when ox teams were occasionally seen upon our streets.

Automobiles and airplanes and fast ships were unknown. I remember well the coming of the automobile. My sister and I were thinning sugar beets on my father's farm when I was a small boy; we had been told that a horseless carriage had been invented, and now we heard one chug-chugging down the road! We heard it when it was a good half-mile away, so we ran from the field where we were working and watched it when it passed, and thought "How wonderful it would be to own one!"

Today automobiles are manufactured by the millions, and airplanes circle the earth continually. You have been in a large city airport and seen the throngs of people traveling and seen the planes taking off--several every minute in some airports.

As to automobiles--it is now getting very difficult to find a parking place in some cities. Do you know that God's Holy Word contains a prophecy describing the modern automobile two thousand years before an auto appeared on our streets? Read the prophecy: "The chariots shall rage in the streets, they shall jostle one against another in the broad ways; they shall seem like torches, they shall run like lightnings." (Nahum 2:4)

Now let me put this prophecy into modern English so you can understand it: "The autos shall race in the streets, they shall jostle one against another in the freeways; their head lights are like torches, they shall run a hundred miles and more per hour."

Do you think this is a good paraphrase of this verse?

Yes, this is indeed the age of travel and speed that Daniel told us was coming in the last days. Today airplanes travel at a speed faster than sound. A plane longer than a football field and several stories in height, that travels at a speed over 1500 miles per hour, is now in service in Europe, and I expect it will be here in the United States soon. And only last week Congress authorized the construction of four space shuttles that will take off into space and will land safely upon thier return and be usable for continued flight.

Now let us consider the last part of this verse, "Knowledge shall be increased." Never, in the history of the world, has there been such an increase of knowledge in every field, in literature, in science, in medicine, in inventions of all kinds. I am thinking now of radio. I began radio broadcasting the gospel back in the 1920's; then came television--first in black and white, and then in color as we have it today.

Then God permitted man, by the knowledge He has given him, to tap the secret of the universe. We know now what matter is composed of, for we have been able to separate it into its component parts, and release the power of the atom. Scientists tell us that the discovery of atomic energy, and the making of the atomic bomb is the greatest invention man has ever made or will make. Daniel predicted all this over two thousand years ago when he said, "Knowledge shall be increased."

I want to add another word here before we go on to the next verse. As we consider this fourth verse we see that Daniel is telling us that his book will be a sealed book, not understood by the people living throughout the hundreds of years until the time of the end, when the age will reveal many running to and fro and knowledge being increased.

We are now living in this travel age, the age of increased knowledge. Do you realize what this means? It means that the return of our Lord Jesus is near. He could come today!

VERSE 5.

"Then I, Daniel, looked and, behold, there stood two others, the one on this side of the bank of the river, and the other on that side of the bank of the river."

Keep in mind that from chapter 10 to the end of this book Daniel is standing on the bank of the river Heddekel (the Tigris). All I am giving you is part of Daniel's last vision. Daniel now sees two other angelic persons, one on each side of the river.

VERSE 6.

"And one said to the man clothed in linen who was upon the waters of the river, 'How long shall it be to the end of these wonders?' "

This man clothed in linen is the same man mentioned in chapter 10, verses 5 and 6, where a detailed description is given of his person. Daniel's description is the same as that given of our Lord Jesus by the apostle John in Revelation 1:9-18. Please turn to this passage and read it. This man clothed in linen was none other than our Lord Jesus.

Now note the question that one of the men standing on the bank of the river asked the man clothed in linen; "How long shall it be to the end of these wonders?"

VERSE 7.

"And I heard the man clothed in linen, who was upon the waters of the river, when he held up his right hand and his left hand unto heaven and swore by him who liveth forever, that it shall be for a time, times, and an half; and when he shall have accomplished the breaking up of the power of the holy people, all these things shall be finished."

When this question was asked of the man clothed in linen he raised up both arms high and sware by the Almighty God that it should be for a "Time, times, and a half," or three and a half years, for the word "time" refers to one year, "times" to two years, and a "half" to a half year.

There are two things in this answer, "the oath" and the "length of time". As to the oath, we are told that the man clothed in linen sware by Him "that liveth forever" (he could swear by no one higher). As to the length of time, we turn to the Book of Revelation, chapter 10, verses 1-6. The book of Revelation should always be studied with the book of Daniel. Why? Because the book of Revelation helps in the interpretation of the book of Daniel, and the only way to understand God's Holy Word is to compare Scripture with Scripture. This is the method you should always follow. Now we consider Revelation 10:1-6:

"And I saw another mighty angel come down from Heaven, clothed with a cloud; and a rainbow was upon his head, and his face was as though it were the sun, and his feet like pillars of fire.

And he had in his hand a little book open; and he set his right foot upon the sea, and his left foot on the earth,

And cried with a loud voice, as when a lion roareth; and when he had cried, seven thunders uttered their voices.

And when the seven thunders had uttered their voices, I was about to write; and I heard a voice from Heaven saying unto me, Seal up those things which the seven thunders uttered, and write them not.

And the angel whom I saw standing upon the sea and upon the earth lifted up his hand to heaven.

And sware by him that liveth forever and ever, who created Heaven, and the things that are in it, and the sea and the things which are in it, that there should be time no longer."

These verses you have just read throw much light on the closing words given us in this 12th chapter. This mighty angel, says John, stood with one foot on the land and the other on the sea. The things he did, the way he was dressed, and what he said, leads us to believe that this mighty angel and the man clothed in linen is not a created being. This person was our Lord Jesus Christ; you can believe this for it is true.

In the Old Testament the angel who spoke to Moses from the midst of the burning bush was called "The Angel of the Lord" (Exodus 3:2-18). This person was none other than our Lord Jesus.

This mighty angel, like the man clothed in linen, swears by the Almighty God, that there shall be **time no longer**. And as this mighty angel uttered these words in the **middle** of Daniel's seventeenth week, there was only three and a half years to run, or forty-two months(Revelation 13:5), which is the exact time given by the "Man clothed in linen", for forty-two months is the same as Daniel's "time, times, and a half" (verse 7). Thus we see that Daniel and Revelation agree as to the length of the "time of the end", and that it is given by the same person, the Lord Jesus

Christic.

Verses 8-9.

"And I heard, but I understood not. Then said I, O, my Lord, what shall be the end of these things?

And he said, Go thy way, Daniel; for the words are closed up and sealed till the time of the end."

While Daniel heard the message he did not understand its meaning, so he repeated the question. All this was a mystery to him. How much better we are for we have the completed Holy Word of God; and we have the Holy Spirit living in our bodies, Who has promised to show us "the things to come." (John 16:13)

The man in linen did not repeat what had already been given to Daniel. All he said was, "Go thy way, Daniel!" For the words are closed up and sealed until the time of the end." "Daniel, the message has been given to you, you have recorded it, now close the book and seal it, for what has been told to you is for those who will be living at the time of the end."

Verse 10.

"Many shall be purified and made white, and tried, (tested) but the wicked shall do wickedly; and none of the wicked shall understand, but the wise shall understand."

This tenth verse applies to the **time of the end** and not to our time at all. Two classes of people will then exist, as seen before, among Daniel's people, the Jews. Many, who believe, will be purified, made white, and tried. They will live separated lives. They will be called upon to face severe persecution (II Timothy 3:12). These separated believers will understand in these dreadful days. The great unbelieving mass of people who are blinded will do wickedly; they are blinded by the god of this age and do not understand. They do not know God's plans or program, they do not know what God is doing, they do not believe that the end is near, they believe that everything is going to come out all right and man will bring in a millennium of peace.

The last part of this tenth verse says, "The wise shall understand."

I am sure you will agree with me when I say that there has never been an age in history when the truths of God's Holy Word have been so widely made known. From the pulpit, through literature, radio, and television, the message of the true gospel goes forth. The wise know that our Lord Jesus is coming just as He promised. Those who are born-again believers see the end of this age drawing near, but those living worldly lives are not in the least concerned or alarmed. They live day by day as pleases themselves; they have no time for God and no desire whatever to meet Him. Modern conditions today are much as they were just before the flood. Note what God's Holy Word says:

"God saw that the wickedness of man was great in the earth, and that every imagination of the thoughts of his heart was only evil continually.

The earth also was corrupt before God, and the earth was filled with violence.

And God said unto Noah, The end of all flesh is come before me; for the earth is filled with violence through them, and behold, I will estroy them with the earth." (Genesis 6:5,11,13.)

There you have the record before you, now consider conditions today. Before the flood people were eating and drinking, marrying and buying and selling -- and conditions in the hearts of men were just like they are today! Truly the wicked do not understand but the wise shall understand.

Are you one of the wise? Are you ready if our Lord should come today? Are your loved ones ready? These are questions you should honestly answer.

VERSES 11-12.

"And from the time that the daily sacrifice shall be taken away, and the abomination that maketh desolate be set up, there shall be a thousand, two hundred, and ninety days.

Belessed is he that waiteth, and cometh to the thousand three hundred and five and thirty days."

There are two other time prophesies given to us, which completes the book of Daniel. We know from other passages that the time of the tribulation period begins when the daily sacrifice offered in the temple is taken away and the "abomination that maketh desolate"is set up, as fortold in verse 11. This tribulation period, also known as "the time of Jacob's trouble", is to last for a **time, times, and a half,** or three and a half years, or 1260 days. This eleventh verse tells us that from the beginning of this tribulation period, there shall be a thousand two hundred and ninety days. The extra thirty days will, most likely, be given over to cleansing of the kingdom of all things that offend and need to be done away. Our Lord Jesus will suddenly appear, to deliver the remnant and to bring an end to the rule of the Anti-christ and the false prophet. This will take place at the end of the 1260 days.

In verse 12 we are told of a still longer period, 1335 days in length. Some think that this would carry on the time to the celebration of the first millennial feast of tabernacles, as in the 14th chapter of Zechariah. At any rate, it clearly points us on to the full establishment of the kingdom in power and glory.

Thus we see that we have three measures of time given in this book of Daniel, all dating from the middle of Daniel's seventieth week.

1. The 2300 days of Daniel 8:13-14, extending 1040 days